Behold the Man

Re-reading Gospels,
Re-humanizing Jesus

Behold
the Man

*Re-reading Gospels,
Re-humanizing Jesus*

Scott McCormick, Jr.

CONTINUUM · NEW YORK

1994

The Continuum Publishing Company
370 Lexington Avenue, New York, NY 10017

Printed in the United States of America

Library of Congress Cataloging-in-Publication Data

McCormick, Scott.
    Behold the man : re-reading Gospels, re-humanizing Jesus / Scott
McCormick, Jr.
      p.   cm.
    Includes bibliographical references and index.
    ISBN 0-8264-0680-7 (hard : alk. paper)
    1. Jesus Christ—Humanity.   2. Jesus Christ—Historicity.
3. Bible. N.T. Gospels—Criticism, interpretation, etc.
I. Title.
BT218.M33   1994
232'.8–dc20   94–21308
                                                     CIP

To
Mary Helen

Contents

PREFACE 9

INTRODUCTION 13

What Is a Genuine Sense of Jesus the Man?
And How Are We to Arrive at It?   15

Jesus of Nazareth: Human or Divine?   18

Critical Knowledge of Jesus and Christian Faith   21

Chapter 1
CONCEIVED OF A VIRGIN? 25

Was the Virginal Conception a Basic Belief?   27

Did the Virginal Conception Happen?   29

The Meaning of Matthew's Narratives   41

The Immanuel Prophecy   43

Two Final Questions   46

Chapter 2
ALL-KNOWING? 51

Preliminary Considerations   52

Jesus' Eschatological Predictions   58

Other Predictions Attributed to Jesus   63

Self-Awareness as Messiah/Suffering Servant?   69

The Mystery of Messiahship in Mark   80

Conclusion   92

Chapter 3
WITHOUT SENSE OF BEING A SINNER? . . . . ·93

God Alone Is Judge   95

The Evidence   97

Jesus' Sense of Being a Sinner "Explained"   100

The Historical Jesus and Traditions of His Righteousness   109

Jesus' Baptism Re-viewed in Mark   115

Conclusion   123

Chapter 4
ABLE TO DO MIRACLES AT WILL? 125

Apologetics Running in Circles   126

The Miracle-Tradition: Rooted in Fact   130

The Miracle-Tradition: Subsequently Embellished   139

Conclusion   155

Chapter 5
IMMORTAL? 157

The Perspective of Faith   158

The Fullness of Jesus' Death   162

The Fullness of Jesus' Resurrection for Christian Faith   175

POSTSCRIPT 183

NOTES 185

BIBLIOGRAPHY 205

INDEX OF PASSAGES 210

Preface

A book about the humanity of Jesus might not seem to need much apology nowadays. But this one may. Intended for general readers, it sets Jesus' verifiable humanity against popular notions of his divinity. Yet not from a doctrinal or philosophical basis. Rather, the approach here is in view of knowledge now available through historical and literary scholarship. As a matter of fact, critical studies now help one to answer rather firmly the leading questions that this book addresses; however, the particulars of scholarly research are still slow in reaching the public. Opinions of the "Jesus Seminar," for instance, often make the news, but not the evidence and arguments in support of those opinions. More importantly, sentimental ideas about Jesus have hardly vacated church premises, not to mention the homes of most Christians. And sentimental ideas positively detract from the exceptional man that he was.

The actual humanity of Jesus is essential to Christian faith and to Gospel reports of his significance as the Christ. The Gospels themselves are loaded with riches for both historical investigation and Christian understanding, but a way must be cleared for nonexperts to get at them. Hence this book's format. While raising questions that may first seem irreverent if not flatly heretical, it is not meant to be insensitive or shocking. It is meant instead to call attention to aspects of Jesus' human experience and to Gospel materials about him that are often slighted or taken amiss in popular Jesus-talk. My hope is that this book will promote discussion where it seems most needed — among laypersons and parish clergy alike. If as a result of such discussion there ensues a keener appreciation of the Gospels and of Jesus the man, I shall be more than gratified.

In writing for general readers, I have assumed their willingness to consider various details and reasoning that scholars themselves must employ in dealing with questions about Jesus. It would have been easier merely to cite critical opinions regarding this or that important item, take a position, and then hurry on to another. But that would have been to indoctrinate readers (which is hard enough to avoid anyway) rather than to engage them in conversation. Besides, a discussion of controversial matters is sure to meet resistance, so that readers need to be convinced. For that to happen, attention to pertinent facts, sometimes in fine detail, is a must. Still, I have tried to present materials in a manner that is clear and interesting to non-experts. Terms and tools of scholarship that may need explanation (e.g., form criticism) are therefore defined at those places where notice of them seems most helpful for grasping the matters at hand. Also, in the interest of a freer-flowing text, biblical and other references, as well as additional observations for ambitious readers, are often relegated to endnotes.

The primary sources for a study of Jesus the man are largely limited to the first three Gospels: Matthew, Mark, and Luke, commonly called the Synoptic Gospels because of their close correspondence. The Gospel of John, on the other hand, is so different in its view of Jesus, in fact so totally colored by advanced christological reflection, that its historical value for information about him is extremely difficult to assess. By "christological" reflection is meant *Christian* thinking about Jesus: post-Easter statements of faith concerning his significance as the Christ, the promised Messiah. The Synoptic Gospels are also christological, as we will abundantly see; but their underlying traditions, by comparison, are vastly superior to John's narration regarding Jesus' actual words and deeds. Whereas the Johannine materials mirror Christian faith through and through, Synoptic traditions often seem to open the door to historically based facts emanating from Jesus' own ministry. So we will concentrate on the Synoptic witness. When carefully examined, it yields an image of Jesus that is both far more reliable and far more human than the Fourth Gospel's presentation of him.

Current New Testament studies reflect the "knowledge explosion" common to academe. This is especially so in the use of "new" or redefined tools for doing the complementary chores of literary, historical, cultural, and social analysis.[1] The fortunate news is that we are learning new things pertinent to early transmissions of the Jesus-tradition. The frustrating news, at least when writing for general readers, is that often little consensus exists regarding *what* we have learned or how to apply it. Problematic for all "histories" of the Jesus-tradition, all explanations of how it developed, is the fact that little is known about the early groups of Christians who produced it: exactly what they believed and when they believed it. Consequently, for example, diverse opinions circulate regarding the date, content, and character of important noncanonical Christian texts, both actual and hypothetical, and their relation to Gospel materials. Reconstructions of the historical Jesus and the effects that he had on his followers are thus increasingly varied, more so now than in many a decade.[2] It is too early to say how pioneering New Testament studies will affect conventional approaches to the Jesus-tradition; and it would be less realistic than ever to suggest that any one reconstruction of Jesus will likely win the day.

Unlike a holistic view of the historical Jesus, the scope of this book spares several critical problems and complications. The former would require, for instance, attention to particular realities of Jesus' social and political world and what he evidently sought to accomplish in that particular world. But this view of Jesus' experience that makes him actually "one like us" allows attention to focus, for the most part, on Gospel materials themselves. And customary use of critical tools remains an adequate method for determining the probable authenticity of many Gospel items. At very least, it seems adequate for introducing readers to a critical view of Jesus' humanity, particularly concerning the leading questions posed in this book.

When speaking of the origins and growth of traditions about Jesus, I have assumed that the so-called "Easter experience" was a vital factor in that development. According to an early confessional formula reported by Paul (1 Cor. 15:3-5), it was a temporal experience. After the crucifixion Jesus "was seen" by some of his own followers. He "appeared" to them — whether "on the third day" or in what form matters not — and from that experience they (and others) came to believe that God had raised him from the dead. This is not necessarily to say that _all_ of Jesus' followers so believed, not even all of those who carried on under his influence. Nor must one suppose that no believers in Jesus' resurrection ever had second thoughts about it and, perhaps, became associated with a different Jesus-movement. Palestinian and other Jews were not unanimous concerning resurrection and life after death, or what constituted "the good life" in their world, or what was imminently or finally in store for their world. Given that fact, plus the fact that the Jesus-tradition has a variety of characteristics and apparent concerns, a plurality of early Jesus-movements is not difficult to imagine — and a diversity among early _Christian_ groups regarding Jesus' significance now seems evidentially clear. In any event, the position I have taken has long been a conventional view among scholars and, though not unopposed, is still critically viable. To wit, temporal appearances of

Jesus to some of his own followers issued in the belief that he was raised from the dead: hence the origin and subsequent development of that version of Christian faith that won out in the first century and has prevailed ever since.

In this book the position I have just identified provides, so to speak, a place (but surely not the only place) where New Testament criticism and regularly confessed faith in Jesus Christ can meet for discussion of his humanity. My readers, who have heard much faithful yet ill-advised talk about what Jesus did and experienced, needn't be told to start all over regarding Christian origins or to exclude from the Church's *earliest* confessions belief in Jesus' resurrection. Such a tack, I suspect, would hardly succeed among most of the readers I have in mind, much less play well on Sunday. In other words, conversation requires common ground. And while this book is a critical offering for general readers, it is also in effect a conversation with traditional Christian faith.

A word now about nouns and pronouns. I have tried to avoid sexist language, especially when expressing what I in particular have to say. However, when presenting ancient expressed views about, say, God and "his" purpose for "man," I have often let such terms stand pat for sake of smooth constructions.

It is fitting to acknowledge one's debts. Besides thanks due scholars beyond my naming here, I owe much to two friends and former students of mine: John Harrington and Philip "Mac" Martin, who read portions of the manuscript in its early stages and encouraged my work on it. I am similarly indebted to another friend and former student, Gordon Watley, a budding scholar himself. Jack Dean Kingsbury, Professor of Biblical Theology at Union Theological Seminary in Virginia, read a completed version of the manuscript and offered helpful suggestions for its improvement. People familiar with Kingsbury's excellence as a New Testament scholar will agree that whatever shortcomings remain of this book belong to me alone. My own study was assisted by a sabbatical leave from Hastings College during the spring term of 1987, and throughout by the former and the present Director of Libraries at Hastings College, Charles Gardner and Robert Nedderman, both of whom were ever gracious and prompt in securing materials that I needed to consider. Not least of all are the thanks due my wife, for whose company and many kindnesses the dedication of this book is poor payment indeed.

Scott McCormick, Jr.
Hastings, Nebraska

Introduction

Was Jesus of Nazareth really human? "Yes, but...," and then comes some word about his being *more* than human.

The Church, in the main and ecumenically at least, has been speaking of Jesus that way since A.D. 325. Briefly put, Jesus was human, yes, but he was also truly divine. Consider terms from the Church's great creeds — the Creed of Nicaea, the "Nicene" Creed, and the Chalcedon Definition (of Christ's two natures): "one Lord Jesus Christ"; "begotten of the Father"; "begotten not made"; "true God of true God"; "of one substance with the Father"; "came down from the heavens"; "was made flesh"; "became man"; "suffered"; "was buried"; "rose on the third day"; "at once complete in Godhead and complete in manhood, truly God and truly man"; "two [distinct] natures...coming together to form one person...not...separated into two persons"; and so on. Consider those terms indeed, but do not feel inadequate if you cannot make sense of them. They have baffled the ablest of Christian theologians, none of whom has definitively explained — and very few theologians now try to explain — how a man could be fully human and at the same time fully divine.

Small wonder that Jesus' humanity, when discussed in popular circles today, regularly provokes controversy and almost always involves confusion. Influenced by creedal confessions, traditionally held to be true, and by New Testament depictions of Jesus that often present him as one of a kind, many devout layfolk do not picture Jesus of Nazareth as a man like all other men. Countless religious professionals share the difficulty as well. Again to put it briefly, popular notions of Jesus' divinity keep getting in the way of his being recognized as thoroughly human. So runs a common argument: "Jesus was human, to be sure, but he was not saddled with customary human frailties. Having a divine origin and nature, he was imbued with divine abilities. Read the Gospels and see for yourself." Then someone else in the circle asks, "Does 'human' not actually mean being limited as a man? Does not the term 'complete in manhood' entail a real human experience like ours?" So the fight is on, with neither side wanting to budge, lest faith seem weak or intellect silly. Whether creeds or Gospel items are appealed to – and often both are brought into the fray – heat may be generated but seldom much light.

Is there, for serious-minded people today, any escape from such confusion regarding the man Jesus? A way out that sacrifices neither Christian faith nor one's own intelligence? There is indeed, though the journey is not apt to be trouble-free. Laypersons generally, as well as most clergy, need to face questions about Jesus' humanity/divinity which may seem, at first sight, like an open can of worms. At issue here are popular interpretations of Jesus' divinity that minimize his real humanity. That divinity is commonly associated with five debatable ideas about Jesus that remove him from the rest of humankind: (1) he was conceived and born of a virgin; (2) he had special, suprahuman knowledge; (3) he thought of himself as sinless; (4) he was able to perform miracles at will; and (5) he was, like God, immortal.

Any one of those ideas makes Jesus of Nazareth something of a stranger to us. Taken together, they make him an alien figure whose humanity resembles that of a ghost – a man so spiritual and full of power that he could not have known, firsthand, the fundamental conditions of our existence: doubt, anxiety, guilt, frustration, what the Bible frankly calls "the weakness of the flesh."

Many good people do not want to think Jesus experienced any or all of that. He was above it, they say. But to start and stop with that contention not only discredits Jesus' humanity, it pays no mind to several early traditions about him. Rather, if popular discussion is to get beyond mere pulpit pounding, attention must turn to critically discernible evidence concerning Jesus of Nazareth. Notions of his divinity that customarily isolate him from what we ourselves experience must be examined for their validity. Was he, in fact, conceived of a virgin? In fact, all-knowing or nearly so? In fact, guiltless in his own mind? In fact, able for any miracle? In fact, inherently immortal? This book will devote a chapter to each one of these questions. In each case, our primary focus will be on what answer, if any, is best suggested by the pertinent evidence. It seems an appropriate way to uncover a genuine sense of Jesus the man for the vast majority of people nowadays who like to talk about him.

What Is a Genuine Sense of Jesus the Man?
And How Are We to Arrive at It?

Some readers may object that this book is prejudiced from the very start. Treasured beliefs about Jesus are being questioned here – an enterprise which may seem to smack of unbridled liberalism, perhaps even heresy that ought to be outright condemned. Any number of churchgoers might well ask, "Will the enemies of Christian tradition stop at nothing? And who is the person to say that *our* sense of Jesus isn't genuine? It is genuine to us," many loyal Christians forthrightly maintain, "because we believe what we read in the Bible."

In truth, I should immediately note that the most conservative of Christians are correct in their basic regard for the Scriptures. They want to take the Bible seriously. And primarily through it alone, the first three Gospels especially, can we hope to achieve any genuine sense of the man Jesus – any understanding of his humanity, any knowledge of his experience – that is rooted in historical facts. Let those who simply define what manhood means and then use their imaginations to make Jesus conform to the model – let them learn from the most conservative Christians that the Gospels are the place to begin. Whatever facts may be known about him, that is where they start coming to light.

With that said, however, we have only begun to answer the questions, What is a genuine sense of Jesus the man? and How are we to arrive at it? True enough is the answer already suggested: an understanding of Jesus rooted in historical facts which may be known by way of the Gospels. But letting it go at that would lead to *mis*understanding. There is widespread confusion about what the Gospels are, what kinds of facts they contain, and how to approach them both for historical knowledge and for their intended meanings. The layperson, whose head may be crammed with Gospel details, is often unaware of the need to make any distinctions between them. He/she ordinarily assumes instead that most Gospel words about Jesus, whether believable or not, were at least meant to be taken as part of a factual, objective report, like the minutes of a committee meeting. Many preachers seem to preach that way. Without critical information at hand, how could anyone know better?

The Gospels and the historical Jesus. We shall, repeatedly, return to the singular fact that *the Gospels present Jesus of Nazareth from the* *standpoint of Christian faith.* Many of the traditions on which they mainly rely were formulated as a result of the "Easter experience" – an occurrence, or series of occurrences, that brought Christian faith as we know it into being. It was a new faith for Jesus' followers. It issued in beliefs about him, and beliefs about themselves as well, that they had not previously owned. Accordingly, with Christian faith born and growing, numerous traditions were developed or reworked concerning Jesus, yet not to preserve precise, historical data. Rather, such Jesus-traditions were formulated to express "post-Easter" understandings – beliefs about Jesus' significance, beliefs about his followers' relationship to him, and various encouragements regarding the daily practice of Christian faith. Although specifics in that development will receive our attention often, at this juncture we may speak of the process in the broadest of terms. Here follows the rationale for it.

During his lifetime, no doubt, "traditions" circulated about Jesus, much as hearsay generally makes the rounds about a commanding public figure. But hearsay was not destined to travel alone. Rather, after his crucifixion and burial, some of Jesus' followers experienced his presence among them. He "appeared" to them, according to the earliest written formula we have of primitive Christian beliefs (1 Cor. 15:3b–5). Assuming that Paul's report of that confessional formula is essentially trustworthy,[1] it was upon those appearances of Jesus that some of his followers began to view him in a new and different light. He is the Christ, they said, meaning the Anointed One, the Messiah, the ideal king who had long been promised to save God's people and to seal the victory of God's purpose on earth. Jesus was raised from the dead, his followers believed and announced from their own experience. The resurrection struck a revolutionary note which, they also came to believe, signified God's victory over sin and death for the world. But that is not all those early Christians believed. Of utmost importance here, the risen Christ was with them still. The same Jesus of Nazareth who had lived and died was ever present as Savior and Lord. It was he, they believed, who was leading them into new truth while sustaining them as his people. Hence the development of numerous Jesus-traditions that lay beneath the Gospels. Though often recalling how Jesus had behaved and taught, the earliest formulators of those traditions were not to be bound by simple recall. On the contrary, Christian faith dictated that his ministry be reviewed, that it be seen and reported through Christian eyes, lest Jesus himself be misunderstood in his ongoing significance for both the Church and the world. Strictly historical recollections would not fit the agenda. Needed instead were depictions of Jesus in what he meant and continues to mean for people, all of it comprehended in the Gospels from this side of Easter. As such, the Jesus-traditions were transmitted by faith *for* faith, not for historians who want to recover what actually transpired on this or that occasion.

Much remains to be said about the role of the Gospel writers in their presentations of Jesus, particularly how they used and influenced existing traditions concerning him. We shall get to that often. The point here is that the Gospels offer essentially two kinds of facts. (1) There are facts to be discerned about the historical Jesus himself: who he was and what he was like, what he said, did, and experienced, how his fellows regarded him. And (2) there are facts to be discerned in the Gospels about the early Church's life and faith: what Jesus' followers came to believe about him after Easter, what they considered to be their role and destiny as Christians, how they applied all of that to the various situations in which they found themselves. Since both these kinds of Gospel facts appear together, the key term here is "discern." Insofar as possible, one must distinguish between the facts — between facts about Jesus as he actually was and facts about the Church's subsequent understanding of him. Which facts are which? Which Gospel items emanate from Jesus' own ministry (and therefore reveal things about *him*) and which ones come, instead, from later days and Christian faith? Unless that distinction is made, a genuine sense of Jesus the man — a knowledge of his humanity that rests on solid ground — cannot be achieved.

The promise and limits of literary-historical study. The big question in all of this is How? If one must identify those Gospel items that provide authentic information about Jesus, how are they to be distinguished from other Gospel items that express later, Christian points of view? Better still, since all the Jesus-traditions available to us are in effect post-Easter formulations, how are we to tell which aspects of them reflect things as they were with him? To use a biblical metaphor, it is like separating wheat from chaff — and at this late date, how can we get back to the wheat?

The question is in fact so big that I am not going to give a detailed answer just now. To do so would exceed the proprieties of this introduction. The answer entails principles of literary and historical analysis, generally called literary-historical criticism. The relevance of its principles in reading the Gospels, however, can be appreciated only as they are applied to specific issues and materials. Suffice to say here that critical use of such principles often pays off, at times quite handsomely. Developed and tested through scholarly use, yet within a layperson's ability to grasp, they afford us the possibility of some reasonably sure knowledge of Jesus – hard knowledge, so to speak, though not so hard as cast in stone; rather, knowledge gained from what appears to be reliable evidence. Admittedly, the early Jesus-traditions impose limits on that. Neither their character nor their special concerns allow us to know as much about him as we would like to know, or nearly as much as once was supposed. Questions for which discernible facts are either absent or insufficient cannot beg a solid answer. Curiosity raises a host of them. And scholars continue to debate findings about Jesus that once seemed fairly secure. In this regard, as is generally the case, the historian's work is never finished. Even so, literary-historical study enables us to know far more about Jesus of Nazareth than many people might imagine.

Further to the point, the particular questions that *we* are asking about Jesus can be answered with reasonable certainty. To repeat: Was he conceived of a virgin? Did he have suprahuman knowledge? Was he without any sense of guilt? Could he perform miracles when-ever he wished? Was he by nature immortal? Pertinent to the first four of those questions there seems to be trustworthy evidence. In each case, ascertainable facts suggest a rather clear (though per-haps surprising) answer. And while the fifth question is unavoidably a matter of faith – faith about Jesus' nature or even human nature in general – we can discern whether his earliest followers likely believed him to be immortal. Regarding these particular questions, therefore, we are better off than before. Thanks to literary-historical study, which began among biblical scholars only two hundred some years ago and which has grown and been refined ever since, we can know *more* about Jesus' humanity than did the best informed of our Christian "fathers" after the first century A.D.

To arrive at such knowledge, however, requires that we "distance" ourselves from the fathers. Their ways of "knowing" cannot be ours, nor can be their "sureties" of Jesus' divinity. That fact must now be emphasized.

Jesus of Nazareth: Human or Divine?

The question posed here is ambiguous. It is asked, not to imply an either/or answer, but to question what kind of knowledge can be had about Jesus and what that knowledge demands of Christian faith. This book's position on that may be stated succinctly. *We can know only of Jesus' humanity, not of his divinity; and Christian faith, even when speaking of Jesus Christ most devoutly, must not disregard whatever facts are to be known about him.*

Although aspects of Jesus' humanity can be factually verified, his traditionally affirmed divinity cannot. Any talk about divinity, whether in terms of a Creator or ascribed to Jesus of Nazareth, is faithful talk. While related to facts, it goes way beyond them. Wanting to "make sense" of facts, it interprets them in line with beliefs about God — and there is the rub. Because of its essence, divinity transcends empirical verification. We can test the law of gravitation but not the existence of God who "makes gravitation work." Were the latter within our means to demonstrate, atheists and agnostics would be laughingstocks, like a gathering of flat-earthers railing against "theories" of this planet's roundness.

None of this means that all talk of Jesus' divinity should cease. Only that it should not be confused with fact or, worse, fly in the face of facts. Rather, belief in Jesus' divinity must be scrutinized in full view of his humanity. Otherwise, as the so-called Antioch school of theology feared as early as the fourth century A.D., Christian faith courts the danger of forsaking its historical roots. Whenever faith says anything about Jesus Christ, it is speaking of a particular man about whom some things can be ascertained. His divinity must therefore be qualified by what we can know of his manhood. In that regard, the Church's great creeds, for all their ecumenical worth, should not be taken to limit the boundaries of current discussion or to control the content of it. Formulated in the fourth and fifth centuries, those creeds could not justly be expected to offer standards for contemporary knowledge of the man Jesus, much less infallible guidance for affirmations of his divinity. Faithful talk of that divinity these days should be in terms of God's revelation in and through Jesus, not in absolute terms that make Jesus' real humanity perplexing.

The creeds established at Nicaea (A.D. 325), Constantinople (A.D. 381), and Chalcedon (A.D. 451), and respected to this day in the Church's worship, own importance beyond measure in the growth of post–New Testament christology (i.e., talk about Christ). Born of controversy and adopted by majority vote of the bishops in attendance, those creeds were designed to refute popular heresies about the person of Jesus Christ: Arianism, Apollinarianism, and Nestorianism. These heresies were promoted by church officials, yet they conflicted with the Church's major understanding then of New Testament materials. One shudders to think where christology would have gone had the bishops not voted "correctly." Had Arianism prevailed, for example, Jesus would have been seen, who knows for how long, as neither human nor divine, but as a demigod of sorts.

At the same time, the traditional doctrines expressed in the creeds were destined to move with "reverse english," like a billiard ball with backspin. Initially derived from interpretation of the New Testament, they have largely spun back upon it. For most Christians over the years, those doctrines have prescribed what is to be "learned" from the New Testament, what one may expect to find in it. Because of doctrinal interest in Jesus' divinity, the Gospels have often been read for confirmation of that. (Eisegesis, we call it, as opposed to exegesis: reading a meaning *into* something, instead of reading the meaning *from* it.) The tendency began long before Nicaea. With commonly believed attributes of God at hand — ideas like those we will test in their being associated with Jesus — supposed confirmations of his divinity were found throughout the Gospels. Not surprisingly, Gospel contradictions and difficulties were either smoothed over or deemed fairly unimportant, hardly worth the notice. Tradition, after all, is tradition.

Such was the case, generally, prior to the advent of literary-historical study. Not even the sixteenth-century Protestant Reformers, who posited the sole authority of the Scriptures in determining Christian truth, objected to the terminology and interpretive influence of the Church's great creeds. Understandably, Luther and the others held in effect that those creeds aptly reflect New Testament teaching paired with sound reason — a position, by the way, not unlike the Roman Catholic view of authority against which the Reformers vigorously protested. Tradition was tradition, indeed.

That was then, now is now. No longer may proper discussion of the man Jesus simply line up with traditional church teaching, however long and well such teaching has served the Church. Nor may a doctrine of authority rightly take over — either that of the Church's authority or that of the Bible's authority, still less a nebulous doctrine of the authority of Christian tradition (as if Christian tradition were a static, singular thing, not a composite of many, sometimes conflicting traditions that need to be looked at critically). Newly gained knowledge is not for nothing: it cannot go home in reverse. Rather, questions about Jesus the man are historical questions. They are to be addressed historically, from knowable facts available *now*. This means that popular, time-honored interpretations of Jesus' divinity, particularly those that put a dimmer on his real humanity, must be reconsidered accordingly. That is the thrust of this book – and with no less gratitude for the good faith of our Christian ancestors.

(Their faithfulness, it could be argued by the way, shines more brightly than ours. So we meet still another question here.)

Critical Knowledge of Jesus and Christian Faith

Observations above notwithstanding, or maybe because of them, Christian readers of these pages may yet well ask whether this journey is necessary. Or, perhaps, even helpful. Christian faith and critical knowledge of Jesus are not, after all, long-standing companions – and at times they have seemed to be at loggerheads. Thus, apart from the barest facts that Jesus lived among men and died on a cross, does verifiable information about him matter much to Christian faith? Or should it? The quest for the historical Jesus – Who was he? What was he like? – is difficult enough for scholars who have made it their professional business. Should its findings also engage the attention of nonexpert churchgoers? Certainly, with the passing of Jesus' own followers, *verifiable* knowledge of his words and deeds and humanity was not within the Church's reach; yet Christian faith got along rather well. And for the most part, so it has ever since. Why then bother with questions about Jesus the man that are the special province of scholars? And, in this case, *controversial* questions.

The answer, in part, is that the conventional wisdom to "let sleeping dogs lie" may put the congregation to bed as well. Ours is a critical age. Curiosity and skepticism occupy church pews every Sunday. Uncritical Jesus-talk these days, failing to verify information about him, risks becoming a yawner, if not indeed bordering on fiction. Even more basic is the fact that traditional Christian faith does not purport to function *without* reliable knowledge of the historical Jesus. Before pursuing this matter, however, we must qualify it by returning momentarily to the fundamental perspective of Christian faith.

Whatever his importance might seem to be, the historical Jesus himself has never been the object of traditional Christian belief. That object has rather been the earthly Jesus who was crucified and was raised by God from the dead. To repeat, Christian faith as we know it resulted from the Church's "Easter experience" of Jesus' presence. It did not arise simply from his own effects. On this there has been wholesale agreement among New Testament critics. More-

over, as I will argue later,[2] the historical significance of the historical
Jesus himself adds up historically to zero. Whatever that significance
might have been, had it been allowed to stand on its own, was pre-
empted by *post-Easter* understandings of his importance. In other
words, only from the eyes of early Christian believers, who saw Jesus
as raised from the dead, do we know or could we begin to know anything about him. Christian confessions, likewise, are confessions of
a faith traditionally controlled by resurrection-belief. No word in this
study of Jesus the man presumes to offset that faithful perspective.

Nonetheless, the quest for the historical Jesus, though disquiet-
ing at times, cannot be ushered out of the house like some unruly
guest. The guest won't leave — and shouldn't. Christian faith has
never divorced itself from knowledge of Jesus the man. The search
for such knowledge may, to be sure, depart from Christian faith,
or at least put it on hold; but the converse isn't so. For various of
the Church's confessions, not to mention exhortations to "be like
Christ," have regularly assumed "known" facts of Jesus' life and ministry: facts concerning his birth, his understanding of God's will,
his faithfulness, his authoritative justice and mercy in dealing with
people around him, and so on. Only nowadays, to whatever extent
is possible, critical verification seems called for. Does Christian faith
know anything of what it has traditionally claimed to know? Or is
"knowledge" about Jesus of Nazareth merely a collection of pipe
dreams? Since current disciplines of historical and literary analysis
offer some reliable information about Jesus, traditional confessions
of what he was like may often be considered critically, in light of
pertinent evidence. Given that possibility, were communication of
the gospel to turn willfully away from positive findings of Jesus-
research, it would seem to make ignorance a virtue. Worse yet, it
would invite the view that Christian faith, while heralding God's
redemptive action in Jesus' own history, has nothing historical to
commend it. In such a case, we might imagine, better that the
audience doze off early.

Benefits of reliable information about the historical Jesus will appear at numerous points in this study — sometimes in understanding
early Christian confessions, sometimes in support of them, other
times in view of loyal Christian believers who nonetheless want
some facts to assuage their unbelief. At this point, however, one
basic confession will highlight the need today of critical knowledge
of Jesus the man. It concerns his goodness as a man.

The early Church's belief that Jesus atoned "for our sins" through
his *death* (1 Cor. 15:3b) was expanded to incorporate his life and his

person as well. According to Paul and other New Testament writers, that atonement for sins entailed Jesus' thoroughgoing righteousness in both his being and his behavior.[3] Without any sin of his own, he was tempted as we are, yet remained faithfully obedient to God. Indeed, he was one of a kind among men, one whose actual, unique righteousness has made other people righteous in him. While Jesus' atoning goodness is an item of faith that goes beyond verification, confessions of it either derived in part from solid information of what he was like or else fall into the category of breezy myths. Either he was known to be a good man or else confessions of his redemptive righteousness have no historical warrant and thus fly apart at the seams. This poses two questions for Christian faith nowadays. (1) Although absolute goodness cannot be confirmed, is there reasonably sound evidence to indicate that Jesus' post-Easter reputation of being unusually good was probably grounded in his own behavior? Notwithstanding the fact that "good" is a culturally conditioned and subjective term, we will see from apparently authentic Jesus-traditions that it was an apt description of him.[4] But in any case, if only for honesty's sake, Christian faith today is obliged to look into the matter.

(2) The other question here regarding Jesus' goodness returns us to the main focus of this study. Namely, was it the goodness of _a man_ and not of some superman who could never realistically be identified with us? Confessions that he was tempted as we are but did not sin, was faithful to God and trusted in him, fulfilled God's demand for everyone's righteousness — such confessions, to make any sense at all, require a genuinely human experience for Jesus: an experience including doubt, anxiety, and failure, frustrations common to the weakness of the flesh. Terms like "faithful obedience" and "trust in God" presume human limitations. On the other hand, divine knowledge and abilities, so often credited to Jesus in popular thought, _dis_credit the reality of his atoning goodness. They remove (or at least lessen) the possibility of authentic faith and trust in God. Hence, once again, the focus of this study on verifiable aspects of Jesus' full humanity. That is, a discernible humanity like ours.

At first glance, the leading questions raised in this book (Was Jesus conceived of a virgin? etc.) may seem hostile to Christian faith. As a matter of fact, none of them is. We shall see that early Christian faith depended not in the least on an affirmative answer to any one of them.

Nor is this book concerned merely with answering those leading questions. It also seeks to explain why the Gospels read as they do. For example, if Jesus was not actually conceived of a virgin, what meaning did Matthew intend to convey in his story of the virginal conception? Why did he "publish" the story in the first place, and what are we to derive from it? To let such secondary questions go unanswered would leave general readers in the lurch, some more confused than ever and perhaps none too thrilled with critical answers to the leading questions. Gospel words about Jesus of Nazareth deserve better treatment than that.

Throughout our discussion we will be focusing on the historical Jesus as the Gospels present him — that is, as the Lord Jesus Christ who lived and died and was believed to be raised from the dead. Each chapter below will not only deal with some aspect of Jesus' humanity; it will also necessarily consider depictions and confessions of his redemptive significance, particularly with regard to the biblical materials under review. If anything, laypersons and parish clergy not already well versed in the critical concerns of this book should come away with a deeper appreciation of Gospel items. That is because literary-historical study enhances both authentic knowledge of the man Jesus *and* understanding of the Gospels' riches.

If our discussion upsets some popular ideas about Jesus of Nazareth, as it certainly will, that is as it must be. Making shocking statements for the fun of it is, to be sure, a poor form of indoor sport. But education is unsettling, no less in biblical/theological inquiries than, say, in questions of physics. For analogy, were Sir Isaac Newton to hear what has newly come from the Copenhagen school of theoretical physics (Einstein, Heisenberg, Bohr, et al.), the great man would roll over in Westminster Abbey. Special relativity alone would spin him, and the principle of nondeterminism make him look for ear-plugs. Nevertheless, critical scholarship, however upsetting, exists in the long run not as an enemy of Christian faith but as one of its very best friends. Among sundry benefits, it keeps faith in touch with its historical roots, and it opens eyes ever wider to what splendid, stimulating productions the Gospels truly are. I encourage you to read on and to make your own discoveries in that happy regard.

Chapter 1

Conceived of a Virgin?

Was Jesus of Nazareth conceived and born of a virgin? Church tradition answers affirmatively, but can we? Pertinent evidence will need our attention — evidence that strongly suggests a negative answer.

Jesus probably was *not* conceived of a virgin? If that be so, two major results would rush in upon us. First, a long-standing interpretation of his divinity would need to be put aside. From the second century at least, Christian thought has tended to associate the divinity of Jesus with his "being born of a virgin." Note that I say associate, not identify, as though one depended on the other. No reputable theologian or biblical critic today would rest a doctrine of Jesus' divinity on the mode of his conception.

Still, the so-called Virgin Birth has largely been seen as a manifestation of Jesus' divinity, a sign that confirms it to Christian faith. And many laypersons nowadays take the matter much farther. For numerous reasons — their upbringing, what they might still hear "in church," bold assurances of popular evangelists — the uniqueness of Jesus' birth is, to them, proof of his divinity. A negative answer to this chapter's leading question would dismiss all of that as groundless romanticism, historically inaccurate and actually misleading. It might not be a deplorable loss, for appreciation of Jesus' humanity would thereby be enhanced.

The other major result of a negative answer to our leading question here would be no less important for popular understanding. If the virginal conception did not occur, the birth and infancy narratives of Matthew and Luke would need a radically different reading than custom has given. Instead of displaying the reality of Jesus' divine nature, much less offering proof of it, they should then be read as dramatizations of kerygmatic beliefs — beliefs long found in the "kerygma," a technical term for what the early Christians preached about Jesus. In that case, call those narratives creative art. But do not take that description as a put-down. If Jesus was not conceived of a virgin, the birth and infancy narratives would be inspired inventions of faith that still deserve the Church's grateful attention — simply because they express, with dramatic power, the ultimacy of God's saving action in Jesus.

During the last two centuries New Testament scholarship has been moving toward the conclusion that the birth and infancy narratives are best seen as creations after the fact: stories composed in the service of early Christian faith. Although the term "myth" does not well fit them — since their concern is the redemptive significance of a real, historical figure — they have nevertheless been increasingly seen as "made-up" stories. Interestingly, that is similar to a position held by some second-century Jewish Christians (called Ebionites) who taught that Jesus, while being the Messiah or Christ, was conceived and born naturally. This trend in New Testament studies has marched from a somewhat laughable business to a quite serious one. Starting largely from eighteenth-century rationalizations, *a priori* assumptions about what can and cannot happen, it has gained substantial weight through refinements in literary-historical research. The tools of study are better now, and their use more mature than before, so that Jesus' being actually conceived of a virgin has steadily lost ground.

Understandably, Roman Catholic scholars, along with their extremely conservative Protestant counterparts, have generally resisted this "skeptical" view. It cuts across church teaching. However, no less a Catholic expert than Raymond E. Brown has recognized that the authenticity of Jesus' virginal conception is fraught with difficulties. In his masterful commentary on the Matthean and Lucan narratives,[1] data once thought to uphold the historicity of those stories are often shown to be no evidence at all or only tenuous evidence at best. While reaffirming his belief that the virginal conception is historically based, he does so, not because the evidence itself is compelling, but because he finds church tradition even more compelling. Brown admits as much himself. Noting that the Church's teaching "from A.D. 200 to 1800" was virtually unanimous in support of the virginal conception's authenticity, he writes: "For many of us this is an extremely important, even deciding factor."[2] That appended word echoes Brown's previous admission that, for him as a Roman Catholic, the "problem" of Jesus' virginal conception cannot be resolved apart from the authority of "a teaching church," meaning the Roman magisterium.[3] Such honesty warrants applause. But it reflects a commitment that seems spiritually at odds with independent study and the attempt to arrive at conclusions objectively. Although no scholar can justly lay claim to pure objectivity, in questions of historical criticism evidence alone is what matters. Not dogma, not unanimity of tradition, however long such things last, but discernible facts and what appears to be the most probable accounting of them. (One is reminded of a wag's graffito: "The earth is flat.–Class of 1491.") Nonetheless, with current New Testament scholars galore, I am indebted to Father Brown's erudition; and I recommend his commentary on the birth and infancy narratives as a work of unparalleled excellence.

Was the Virginal Conception a Basic Belief?

To free the spirit for critical evaluation of the virginal conception, we should ask whether belief in it was fundamental to apostolic faith. That in time it became fundamental, inherently a part of the Church's growing christology and creedal confessions, is a fact of history. But was it a basic belief in the New Testament period itself? Not just a belief obtained by a privileged few, rather a significant item in the Church's life?

The only possible answer is a thousand times No. To begin with, reports of the Church's first preaching are silent regarding the matter. For instance, according to the "conservative" view, Acts 10:36–43 reflects an early expression of the kerygma (beliefs preached and taught). It is thought to have come from a liturgical formula which, as reproduced by Luke (the author of Acts), encapsulated the Church's beliefs about Christ. But it contains no word of the virginal conception. The same holds for a form of the kerygma quoted in bits and pieces by Paul (e.g., Rom. 1:2–5; 1 Cor. 15:3b–5). Such formulas were probably used in baptismal rites, whereby newly converted Christians confessed their faith in Jesus as the Christ, the promised Messiah of God. Yet the manner of his conception, apparently, was of no import. It lacked significance for acceptable Christian belief.

Equally telling is the fact that, of all New Testament writers, only Matthew and Luke speak of the virginal conception – and, as we shall see, some critics would eliminate Luke in this. Usually dated around A.D. 85 (though Luke may be nearer A.D. 110), their Gospels appeared rather late. Probably written after Matthew were the Fourth Gospel (c. A.D. 90?) and Revelation (c. A.D. 95). The authors of these latter two books, while referring to Jesus' birth,[4] do not even clearly hint at extraordinary circumstances surrounding it — a noteworthy absence, given their concern with his uniqueness and, in the Fourth Gospel's case, the author's interest in Jesus' pre-existence.[5]

Nor does belief in the virginal conception get a hint from any other New Testament writer. Paul, for one, seems to have been ignorant of it. Writing to the Philippians of Christ's pre-existence and exemplary humility, he takes off with a Christian hymn and, for a moment, soars into regions unknown:

> ... Christ Jesus, who, though he was in the form [Gr. *morphē*, essential nature] of God, did not count equality with God a thing to be grasped, but emptied himself, taking the form [*morphē*] of a servant, being born in the likeness of men. And being found in human form [*morphē*] he humbled himself and became obedient unto death, even death on a cross. (Phil. 2:5b–8)

But, once again, no clue whatever, here or elsewhere in Paul, to Jesus' being born of a virgin.[6] To this giant of early Christian thinkers, the idea was either not known or unimportant.

Accompanying the silence of the rest of the New Testament, belief in Jesus' virginal conception *itself* is not even fundamental in the Gospels of Matthew and Luke. One could cut the virginal conception out of them with a pair of scissors and not disturb another word (except for a questionable, parenthetical allusion to it in Lk. 3:23).[7] Necessarily gone would be only Matthew 1:18–25 and perhaps Luke 1:34–35. Or one could cut out the birth and infancy narratives completely, with the same result. In each case the author's understanding of Jesus and of God's accomplishments through him would remain unchanged. But not so were scissors taken to a kerygmatic belief — say, the meaning of Jesus' death and resurrection or the confession that he is the Christ. In that case, those two books would be in shreds.

From every angle, therefore, it is clear that Jesus' virginal conception was not fundamental to first-century Christian faith. Indeed, it was not even close to being a basic belief, if in fact its historical authenticity had any importance at all. Moreover, as we have noted, New Testament writers implied (or let us infer?) the divinity of Jesus Christ, vis-à-vis his pre-existence, without the slightest reference to Mary's virginity. So we need not be fearful of compromising apostolic faith of the New Testament era by asking whether the virginal conception really occurred and then letting the evidence speak.

Did the Virginal Conception Happen?

This question, it seems, must also be answered negatively. But *not* because a virginal conception couldn't have happened. And not because its real occurrence must mean that Jesus, for genetic reasons, would have been less than completely human. Such objections are biased regarding theology and, from a biblical view, pitifully so. Assuming the existence of One who is said to be Creator and to have raised Jesus Christ from the dead, surely *God* could have brought it off — and without a hitch in Jesus' fully human nature.

Rather, the pertinent evidence simply suggests, lopsidedly in fact, that the virginal conception did not occur. Otherwise, certain traditions about Jesus would in all probability be different than they are. Further, the birth and infancy narratives do not seem intended for historical information. They were meant to be read in another, far richer way — as "inspired" declarations of who Jesus is and what he signifies as the Christ. Besides being editors of Jesus-traditions, the authors of those narratives were artists. Each of them, following his own special genius, put "the truth" in a new form. It was a form that had stirred him and that he hoped would stir his audience as well: a form appealing not merely to their minds but, more importantly, to the deeper levels of their being. We shall see that for ourselves, particularly when looking at the meaning of Matthew's narration. But first, the question before us here: Did the virginal conception happen?

The likely reality of the virginal conception is progressively diminished by three factual observations. (1) It lacks solid, identifiable support in pre-Gospel traditions. (2) The Gospel narratives thought to support it, when taken as historical reporting, have major difficulties of their own. And (3) it goes markedly against other Gospel items which, most surely, are basically reliable in providing knowledge about Jesus. Any one of those observations, I think, is enough to negate the virginal conception's historical genuineness; together they appear to settle the issue beyond critical dispute. That is my judgment — but see what you think about them (and a Bible nearby may be useful).

1. The problem of early tradition. All critical scholars agree that the birth and infancy narratives express Christian beliefs extant at the time of their composition: more precisely, beliefs that had developed since Jesus' followers came to regard him as one raised from the dead. But some critics nonetheless maintain that Matthew and Luke, whatever they may have put into those narratives on their own, considered the virginal conception to be factual. Arguments for that position usually assign excessive value to the parenthetical remark that Jesus "was the son (as was supposed) of Joseph" (Lk. 3:23) – so awkward an allusion in Luke's genealogy of Jesus that its originality is frequently questioned. Be that as it may, the position teems with problematic, often extremely improbable assumptions. It assumes, among other things, that a pre-Gospel tradition of the virginal conception existed, that it was somehow historically authentic, and that Matthew and Luke reported it as such with the expectation of being believed.

Well then, was there a pre-Gospel tradition of Jesus' birth? If so, what was in it? And how did it originate? Answers to these questions have been numerous and varied, to say the least. While many commentators think Matthew and Luke relied on one or more traditions of an angelic annunciation foretelling Jesus' birth as Messiah, it is not clear that a tradition of his virginal conception also predated their Gospels. To illustrate, some have argued that a virginal conception is not suggested in Luke's account: this on the grounds that (1) Mary is not said therein to have abstained from sexual relations after moving in with Joseph as his "betrothed" (i.e., his wife, according to Jewish marital custom), and (2) Luke doesn't indicate that the birth was earlier than should have been expected for a married couple.[8] In other words, there was time enough for Joseph to sire Jesus. Luke's annunciation story says merely that Mary's child will be the Son of God (= the promised Messiah, expected by Jews to be born naturally, as we shall see) through the power of the Holy Spirit (1:35). Granted, Mary hears that from the angel while she is still a virgin (1:27, 34); but Gabriel does not say she will be one when the child is conceived.[9] And two scenes later for Mary, before Jesus is born, she is shown to have been living with Joseph (2:1–5). Accordingly, no pre-Gospel tradition of the virginal conception need be posited, word of it being confined to Matthew and therefore explainable as his own creation. It is a nice solution to a knotty problem, and maybe someday the only one that will make much sense.[10] But the major opinion is still the traditional view that Luke, however his narration was originally meant to be read, intended to identify Mary as a virgin at Jesus' conception. Which means that here, too, Matthew and Luke, writing independently of each other, perhaps relied on an earlier tradition. By no means, however, does that solve the problem of authenticity; it makes it only more perplexing.[11]

Supposing a pre-Gospel tradition of the virginal conception existed, scholarship that sides with its reliability has been at a loss to explain satisfactorily when and where it came from. To be authentic, and not simply a later creation, it would have had to originate with Mary (and Joseph?), who must have passed the word to someone who, in turn, passed it to someone else, and so on. And it did not surface for about ninety years? That seems hardly probable.

Nor is it probable that a tradition of Jesus' virginal conception existed very long before Matthew and Luke wrote their Gospels. No such word about a notable person is easily kept from the public. To the contrary, admirers spread the word with joy, while detractors belittle it as best they can. Significantly in this regard, Jewish polemic accusations that Jesus was born illegitimately are not reflected in extrabiblical materials until far into the second century, nearly a hundred years after the Gospel word of his miraculous conception was first "published." Further, aside from Matthew's narrative (at 1:25), nothing in the New Testament itself clearly or even likely indicates that Jesus' birth was early or that the Jewish charge of illegitimacy had yet appeared to refute his virginal conception. But scholars have certainly tried to find something of the sort.[12]

Mark 6:3 and John 8:41, often taken to reflect an accusation that Jesus was illegitimate, lack force in the matter. The context of Mark 6:3, where his countrymen snidely remark that he is "the carpenter, the son of Mary," indicates a complaint of his being a commoner who has no right to lecture them, not a rumor that he was born out of wedlock. Similarly, the prideful saying of Jewish leaders in John 8:41, "We were not born of fornication," is in response to Jesus' word that Abraham is not their father. Their boast is within the context of a theological debate about who are God's genuine children by reason of faith and behavior (8:31–47); *natural* descent is beside the point. Indeed, had a charge of illegitimacy been circulating from Jesus' opponents, whose other alleged accusations are stated forthrightly, why would any Gospel writer make only the most veiled allusion to this one and thereby shield Jesus' detractors from still another display of bad faith? Such was not the evangelists' habit, nor was it how Jesus-traditions developed to counter Jewish unbelief. The tendency was to *enlarge* the supposed faults of Jesus' opponents, which we will see on occasion in chapters below.

Consider now one more item: Matthew's word that Joseph did not "know" Mary until she had borne Jesus (1:25). Critics who see this item as a *defense* against the illegitimacy charge seem to have the cart before the horse, since the only clear evidence of that charge appears so very much later — to repeat, nearly a century after Matthew wrote. Instead, the early birth in Matthew serves another, I think quite obvious, purpose. It is there to make the story of a virginal conception *work*. In this respect, Matthew's narration is considerably superior to Luke's. For as we have noted, absence of an early birth makes the virginal conception less emphatic in Luke, perhaps even doubtful as part of the story.

This is all to say that an authentic pre-Gospel tradition of Jesus' virginal conception, a tradition supposedly rooted in historical fact, creates more problems than it seeks to solve. The apparent silence of those who would most surely have witnessed to it, either affirmatively or in opposition, is deafening. Add to that the problems yet to be discussed of the virginal conception, and a negative answer to this chapter's leading question seems well nigh unavoidable.

2. The nonhistorical character and intent of the narratives. In the last analysis an author's intent must be understood not merely from traditions he may have inherited but from how he used them and what he wrote. The evidence then suggests that the birth and infancy narratives of Matthew and Luke, besides lacking historical character, were not meant to be taken historically. When such is the case, generally, an author may be expected to "tip his hand" — to write in a way that would not mislead knowledgeable readers.[13] And that, especially, is what these stories provide: difficulties so outstanding as to advise against viewing them as historical. In other words, Matthew and Luke put the reader on guard. So fanciful are their narratives, and so furnished with incongruities for people "in the know," that one is intentionally discouraged from taking them historically.[14]

ABNORMALCY IN ABUNDANCE. In the first place, the birth and infancy narratives do not *sound* like historical narration. True, as illustrated at some length in our next chapter, nothing in the Gospels is strict history writing by modern standards. Unconcerned to report history for history's sake, Gospel writers, or the traditions they employ, often embellish an event. The event *and* its meaning for Christian faith are interwoven in a single narrative. Still, the description of the event is not so thoroughly fantastic, so utterly filled with extraordinary details, as to make the event itself seem questionable. In the stories at hand, however, extraordinary items abound from beginning to end, creating a wholesale sense of abnormalcy.

The Lucan narration (1:5–2:40) is marked throughout by direct, heavenly inspiration offered and received in patently unusual circumstances. Angels are all around: (1) giving precise information to old, childless Zechariah, John the Baptist's father-to-be, and striking him dumb (1:8–23); (2) imparting even more information to the virgin Mary about herself and her kinswoman Elizabeth, who in her old age is now bearing John the Baptist (1:26–38); (3) appearing to the shepherds outside at night and directing them toward the Christ-child lying in a manger (2:8–12); and (4) in the shepherds' presence, a multitude of angels breaking forth in poetic praise (2:13–14). In addition to these angelic revelations, Simeon and the aged prophetess Anna recognize baby Jesus as the Messiah upon unmediated inspiration of God (2:25–38). So too had Elizabeth realized that Mary was bearing the Christ, when the babe in her own womb leaped as Mary greeted her (1:39–45). Indeed, on even a casual reading of Luke's narration, there is precious little that is not out of the ordinary — only 16 of 116 verses[15] — and those scattered verses tell no meaningful story at all. Hence, despite ancient credulity regarding angels and the like (which wasn't universal anyway), a first-time reader might well have asked, "Am I reading about something that really happened?"

Similarly, the extraordinary holds sway throughout Matthew's narration. His birth narrative (1:18–25), excepting a marvelous reference to Isaiah 7:14 (itself a cautionary insert, as we will see), revolves entirely around an angelic annunciation to Joseph. Likewise, in Matthew's infancy narrative (2:1–23), angels direct the holy family's flight to Egypt (2:13–15) and their subsequent return to Judea (2:19–21), after which Joseph is warned in a dream to withdraw to Galilee (2:22). So also the wise men, upon their visit to worship baby Jesus, had been warned in a dream not to return to the conniving King Herod (2:12), whose fear of the child is shared by all the Jewish officials in Jerusalem (2:3–5)! Sandwiched between these angelic and dream directives are items so odd that, when viewed together, only an uncautious reader could accept them. To start where Matthew does, wise men from the East see a star and thereby know the Messiah has been born (2:1–2), which, by the way, *was* very wise, since the Messiah's birth had not been connected with such a sign. They follow the star and, sure enough, it leads them to the Bethlehem house (not a manger, as Luke writes) where the child is readily found (2:9–11). Meanwhile, Herod, who has been told of the star by the wise men (and of the town of birth by the Jewish officials) and who feels he must destroy the child (2:3ff.), hasn't the presence of mind to follow either the star *or* the wise men. In fact, he cannot even hire reliable informers of the babe's whereabouts — and never mind that Bethlehem is no large place, just five miles down the road. Clearly, as this story has it, King Herod, though depicted as a man to be feared, is incredibly inept and borders on being deficient.

So, on surface, Matthew's narration sounds no more historical than Luke's. Had either of these writers intended to promote the genuineness of any item in view, the virginal conception included, would he have locked it into such a larger, questionable narration? Would he have surrounded that item with extraordinary particulars which, from start to finish, make abnormalcy the routine, thus requiring extreme credulity of the audience? The nonhistorical character of the literary forms employed by Matthew and Luke is all the more significant since, as we have seen, an underlying tradition of Jesus' virginal conception was neither basic to Christian faith nor likely extant very long, if at all, before they wrote their Gospels. Therefore, an effort to foster belief in Jesus' being conceived of a virgin would have dictated a considerably different literary approach.

GENERALLY KNOWN INCONGRUITIES. That Matthew and Luke did not intend their birth and infancy stories to be read as historical reporting is also suggested by the fact that their narrations involve glaring incongruities with what was known at the time. (And this says nothing about Jesus' alleged birth in Bethlehem, for which there is no supporting evidence whatever — only the prophecy of Mic. 5:2, said in Mt. 2:6 to be fulfilled.) In other words, as is evident from extra–New Testament sources, the birth and infancy narratives contain clear-cut contradictions of original readers' own knowledge.

Though relatively small in importance to us but still worth noting, Luke's focus on Jesus' birth itself (2:1-7) offers two curious and related difficulties, neither of which the most reverent scholarship has been able to remove. First, the census under "Quirinius," as Luke describes it, conflicts with what is known of Roman practice in census-taking. And, second, the Lucan chronology in 2:2 agrees neither with the best of extra–New Testament data nor with the additional chronological information supplied in 1:5 and 3:1, 23.[16] Luke seems to have contradicted not only popular knowledge but himself as well. Despite the ingenious efforts of some critics to minimize these patent incongruities, my own inclination is that Luke arranged them on purpose — to discourage readers from taking his early narration historically and thus missing the point. How easier to explain such close inconsistencies from the hand of one who, it is generally conceded, was a rather careful and a very clever writer? But that is a guess at best, and mine alone.[17]

It is Matthew's narration, however, that I think first readers would have questioned most. So vastly irreconcilable with extra–New Testament data, it defies historical authenticity. Scholars generally agree that Matthew's audience included Christians with a Jewish background, people who knew the Old Testament Scriptures *and* the tribulations of their fellow Jews in Palestine. On both of those counts he posts unmistakable roadblocks to historical credibility: a blatant "abuse" of Isaiah 7:14 (to "authenticate" Jesus' having been conceived of a virgin), followed by a story that no Jew in the world could accept as factual. Surely, therefore, it was no accident that second-century Jewish Christians rejected the idea of Jesus' virginal conception: apparently they thought they knew better. Nor is it mere coincidence, in my judgment, that incongruities loom even larger in Matthew's narratives than in Luke's. Giving a decidedly clearer word of the virginal conception, Matthew "validates" and follows it with more obvious cautions against taking his narration historically, lest its meaning be lost on the reader.

In saying that Matthew "abuses" Isaiah 7:14, the well-known Immanuel prophecy, I do not imply that his reference to it (at 1:22–23) is haphazard or without theological justification. As we will note below in a special section of this chapter, it was a stroke of genius, sharply in line with early Christian faith. Also to be noted, it may well explain the inspired origin of Matthew's birth narrative. Nonetheless, the point here is that the reference is too far-fetched, scripturally, to convince a Jewish reader that Jesus as the Christ was actually conceived of a virgin. Indeed, Matthew's declaration, "All this took place to fulfill what the Lord had spoken by the prophet," would have had the opposite effect for someone in the know. Why? Because Isaiah's prophecy itself bore no relation whatever to the kind of story Matthew tells of Jesus' birth. Never had the Jews taken that prophecy to signify a virginal conception, which is not at all surprising. In Isaiah 7:10–17 the unborn child to be named Immanuel, whose mode of conception is neither virginal nor of any consequence, functions as a sign of God's impending doom on Judah. According to Isaiah, the nation will suffer a severe calamity soon after Immanuel is born; and when the disaster occurs, its only valid explanation will be in this child's name. A form of prophetic symbolism — an enacted parable of God's word — the naming of a child was a device that Isaiah used on other occasions as well.[18] In this instance he relates "Immanuel," meaning in Hebrew "God-with-us," to the arrival of devastating destruction. Before the child is old enough to know right from wrong, he will be eating curds and honey — famine fare. For God is about to visit his people; not in joyful redemption, coming in the form, say, of the Messiah or some other savior. But in judgment, in the crushing form of the king of Assyria! And *that* prophecy, Matthew informs his readers, was fulfilled in Jesus' virginal conception and birth? Surely, unless Matthew was a charlatan or just inept, his story of Jesus' birth must be concerned with something *other* than Jesus' birth. Thus, his readers are put on guard immediately.

On the heels of Matthew's birth narrative comes a completely impossible story. The tale of Herod's opposition to the infant Jesus and his God-thwarted efforts to kill him places a capstone on the nonhistorical intent of Matthew's narration. Here again the knowledgeable Jewish reader encounters a barrier of difficulties insurmountable for realistic belief. Consider the following facts that are plainly discernible from extra–New Testament sources: (1) Herod, while of quasi-Jewish lineage, believed not in the coming of a Messiah but in the mighty power of Rome; (2) he had at his disposal, in leading towns and cities, at least one centurion in command there of fifty or one hundred Roman soldiers; and (3) Herod, who had political enemies aplenty, was subject to Roman law and justice, meaning he could not have effected a senseless, wholesale slaughter of innocent children without incurring Roman judgments against him. Regarding each of these facts, Matthew's infancy narrative is historically absurd: (1) Herod is scared witless by a fantastic word that the Messiah has been born; (2) advised (by Jewish officials who hate him!) that Bethlehem is to be the Messiah's birthplace, and with occupational troops to spare, Herod is at a total loss to locate the child, in fact doesn't even half try; and (3) as a last resort he kills all the male children in the region two years old and younger, as if he could get away with it. Though that deed of "furious rage" (Mt. 2:16) could not have been covered up, no word of it appears in any Roman records. Also to be considered here is the pervasive silence of the Jews themselves, who often complained about annoying aspects of Roman rule: the ever-present army, burdensome taxes inequitably assigned, and so on. But mere child's play, those things, alongside Herod's so-called Slaughter of the Innocents. Yet there exists no Jewish tradition to substantiate the slaughter — and traditions like that do not vanish. So we must conclude that it did not occur. And for the same reason, the Jewish Christians in Matthew's audience knew it didn't occur: they had not heard of it from their Jewish ancestors. Nor would Gentile members of the audience have been kept in the dark about that (see note 13 for this chapter).

Given the movement of Matthew's narration and what he could

expect of his readers, I cannot imagine how he might have "tipped his hand" to them more skillfully. Of course, he could have explicitly directed that they not read it as historical narrative. But in addition to insulting their intelligence and corrupting an art form, such a pedestrian placard would have ruined the recreative force of his stories. It would have disallowed readers the deep, inner excitement of seeing the truth for themselves – the redemptive significance of Jesus as Matthew dramatized it anew. To that meaning we shall presently turn, after considering one other problem of the virginal conception.

3. The tension between Jesus and his family members. Most important of all observations regarding the virginal conception is that its supposed reality fails to mesh with historically reliable items that lead to some knowledge about Jesus. By "historically reliable" I mean, in this case, items which were embarrassing to the Church and which, therefore, would not have been manufactured out of the blue. Incidentally, Gospel writers did not try to conceal all such embarrassments. Coming from traditions that had circulated orally, embarrassments could not be brushed away. Nor were they initially a minus for Christian faith itself – a hindrance in communicating the good news of the gospel – else, they would not have been transmitted, either orally or in writing. They appear plainly concerning several matters. The embarrassment in bright lights for us to see here is a tension between Jesus and his family.

Had Jesus been conceived of a virgin, certainly his mother would have recognized the situation: namely, Jesus has come straight from God; he is God's own son, no one else's. Joseph might have harbored suspicious doubts, but not Mary, according to Matthew's story. Therein she remains a virgin until Jesus has been born (1:23–25). Which is to say, in line with the story, Mary has unquestionable knowledge of Jesus' God-effected uniqueness. By the time Jesus begins his public ministry, Joseph has disappeared, leaving only Mary to testify that Jesus' miraculous conception makes him someone special. However, Mary proves to be just about the worst witness imaginable. Apparently, she does not consider Jesus a person of inherent authority; nor has she taught her other children to respect and follow him. And yet, if she knew he had arrived as God's son, not Joseph's, and if she cared about her family's religious commitments, would not she have behaved and guided them differently?

To speak thus of Mary may seem unkind or even wicked. In

fact, however, only one Gospel story shows her to be sympathetic (more or less) with Jesus' chosen ministry. "Do whatever he tells you," Mary says to the servants at the Cana marriage feast when the wine is all gone (Jn. 2:5). While that advice may be spiritualized no end, John's story of the Cana wedding celebration (2:1–11) has less credibility than the guests had drink. So laden with post-Easter understanding and Christian symbolism – "an embarrassment of riches," in Father Brown's nice description – it must be critically regarded as a Christian creation, not a historically based story from Jesus' own ministry.[19] (Recall the distinction between different kinds of "Gospel facts" noted in our introduction.) Aside from Mark 3:21 (a grave problem for Mariology, we will see), Mary's only other speaking role in the Gospels after Jesus' birth is part of another Christian invention, Luke's story of the boy Jesus in Jerusalem with his parents (2:41–51). And that story has Mary and Joseph not merely astonished to find him conversing incisively with rabbis in the Temple: they do not understand his word to them that he must be in his "Father's house." (It is a strange portrayal, is it not, if Luke at 1:34–35 meant to depict Mary as a virgin when Jesus was conceived?)

Turning now to items that seem to be basically reliable, nothing in the Gospels explicitly says that Mary neither deemed Jesus a person of authority nor taught her other children to honor and follow him. But several items clearly imply it. Chief among them is the comment that Jesus is "beside himself" – out of his mind. Reported by Mark, it is part of an incident described in 3:19b–21 and, following a twofold Marcan interruption (vss. 22–26 and 27–30), most likely continued in 3:31–35. Although we cannot reconstruct the exact order of events in Jesus' ministry, Mark's preceding materials seem to reflect that ministry generally and well enough to offer a plausible milieu for the comment. Jesus has been eating with outcasts, breaking sabbath regulations with abandon, speaking with an authority that seems blasphemous to many, arguing with Pharisees about matters in which they are supposed to be experts. All in all, he has been making a nuisance of himself and, what is more, incurring the displeasure of no few religious elite. To intimates who considered him but an ordinary man, a person without authority of his own to justify all that, such behavior would seem presumptuous at best, at worst downright dangerous, if not in fact out of control. Hence the incident of Mark 3:19b–21. Jesus goes into "a house," reads the Greek (3:19b); a crowd gathers (3:20); then "his own," presumably in concern for his safety, "went out to seize him, for they [not 'people,' as in some translations] said, 'He is beside himself' " (3:21). Who are these intimates of Jesus? Not his friends, as in some translations, but his family members, as 3:31 indicates: "And his mother and his brothers came; and standing outside they sent to him and called him."

While commentators agree that Mary's thinking Jesus to be mad is irreconcilable with his virginal conception, some seek a way out of this difficulty by suggesting that Mark 3:19b–21 and 3:31–35 represent two independent traditions. Thus would they dissociate Jesus' mother and brothers mentioned in 3:31 from "his own" in 3:21 who say he is beside himself. This attempt at dissociation, however, seems to be grasping at straws. First of all, it is clear from the wording of 3:31–35 that something originally preceded it. A tradition would not commence with "And his mother and his brothers came, and standing outside they sent . . . " Standing outside *what?* Further, it is by no means certain that more than one basic tradition is involved here. Whereas 3:31–35 is pre-Marcan in form, 3:19b–21 is lucidly Marcan in vocabulary and style. This shows that Mark, unless totally inventive, reworked a formal tradition underlying 3:19b–21 to make it fit in with the allied materials following in 3:22–30. That the incident described in 3:19b–21 was previously joined with 3:31–35 is at least possible. I think it is highly probable in view of the relation of "house" and "outside" (noted again below). Moreover, even if they were not so joined, the embarrassment of Mark 3:21 remains. The reference therein to Jesus' intimates who think him mad is, by itself, ambiguous. Their identity then depends on the context that Mark himself supplies. Writing freely, he calls them simply *hoi par autou* (literally, "the ones alongside him"). This term is a Greek idiom that could signify any one of several groups such as a man's envoys or his neighbors, friends, or relatives. At 3:31 the ambiguity is resolved: Jesus' intimates are his mother and brothers. There they stand outside (i.e., outside the house that Jesus is said in 3:19b to have entered), and there they call for him. *They* are "his own" who, thinking him mad, went to lay hold of him. To interpret *hoi par autou* otherwise in Mark 3:21 is to suggest that Mark did not understand the obvious drift of his own narration.

Admittedly, it is possible that Mark, at 3:21, for reasons of his own made Mary and Jesus' brothers appear less respectful of him than they actually were. But, in that case, why did he not explicitly identify them then and there? If anything, his use of an ambiguous term at that point takes the edge off their disrespect. The likelihood of a pure (and daring!) Marcan invention at 3:21 seems even more remote by the fact that Mark 3:21 stands anywhere but alone in this matter. Jesus' sharp words about his *true* mother and brothers who do the will of God, a pre-Gospel tradition recorded first by Mark (3:31–35) and followed by Matthew (12:46–50) and Luke (8:19–21), betray a tension between Jesus and his family members – at the very least, their lack of sympathy with what he was doing. The same kind of tension is strikingly evident in the pre-Gospel tradition of Luke 11:27–28.[20] Surprisingly, in response to a woman's enthusiastic blessing of the womb that bore him and the breasts that fed him, Jesus counters, "Blessed rather are those who hear the word of God and keep it!"[21] John 7:5 bears further witness to Jesus' being at odds with his family. There, as a passing fact in widespread opposition to Jesus, it is said that "even his brothers did not believe in him." And in Mark 6:4 (followed in Mt. 13:57), concerning the disbelief and surliness that his countrymen have shown him, Jesus says of himself, "A prophet is not without honor, except in his own country, and among his own kin, and in his own house" – another pre-Gospel tradition.

The implication of those traditions is clear: Jesus' closest relatives knew nothing of his divine origins. Instead, the traditions report, his mother and brothers apparently viewed his maverick activities not as within his right but as symptomatic of emotional instability; his brothers failed to believe in him; his household, like his jaded countrymen, did not honor him; and he uttered harsh words about his kinsfolk, his mother included. Such traditions do not convey that Mary and her other children held Jesus to be someone made special by God. They convey just the opposite.

And it also seems clear that those traditions are basically reliable in reflecting tension between Jesus and his family. The early Church would not have invented from scratch items that needlessly slandered any one of its members, much less the mother of its Lord. Nor would first-century Christians, who wanted to promote Christian faith, have concocted items suggesting that those who had known Jesus the longest time did not regard him as an authoritative person to be believed in and followed. Best we acknowledge, therefore, that Jesus' siblings were unaware of his virginal conception and that Mary does not appear to have been aware of it either.

Conclusion. Thus, sifting the evidence from every relevant quarter, we are compelled to conclude that the Virgin Birth did not occur. We must also conclude that Jesus' virginal conception was not originally meant to be taken as historical. When dogma and doctrinaire exegesis are set aside, the discernible facts considered as a whole appear to be overwhelming.

Within the boundaries of this conclusion otherwise insoluble problems are laid to rest. The New Testament's silence about the virginal conception apart from Matthew (and Luke?), the lack of a solid pre-Gospel tradition to substantiate that conception, the unhistorical literary character of the birth and infancy narratives themselves, their glaring incongruities with original readers' own knowledge, the disbelieving behavior of Mary and others of Jesus' family: every one of these problems vanishes. It is, to be sure, an easy conclusion — so very easy, in fact, that it seems to me irrefutable.[22]

The Meaning of Matthew's Narratives

This chapter began with the suggestion that the divinity of Jesus may not rightly be associated with his having been conceived of a virgin. Yet, as we noted, that association was made at least by the second century and continued with mounting success. In fact, though not unopposed, it commenced quite early, apparently no later than A.D. 110.[23] This would tell, from the conclusion just reached, that relatively soon after Matthew and Luke wrote their Gospels something must have begun to go haywire in the way the birth and infancy narratives were interpreted. And so it did, for a number of reasons. Indeed, the interrelation of such factors virtually assured that misinterpretation would not take too long to develop.

That development started up naively and progressed with the growth of church doctrine. To appreciate it, one must first consider the intended meaning of the birth and infancy narratives. We will confine discussion to Matthew's stories since it was his narration that eventually was most apt to be misunderstood. Whereas Luke wrote only for Gentiles, Matthew's efforts to inspire a community that included Jewish as well as Gentile Christians put a greater cultural/interpretive distance between initial and later readers. In short order the readership of his Gospel became all but totally Gentile in makeup. Also, in clearly depicting a virginal conception and relating it to the "God-with-us" prophecy of Isaiah 7:14, Matthew's narration was especially susceptible to the kind of later misinterpretation that we have in mind — namely, a reading which took that conception as historically real *and* as indicative of Jesus' divinity in accord with post–New Testament christology.

Matthew's birth and infancy narratives contain many nuances in meaning. But, for our purposes, we need concentrate only on the major thrust of each story and then, in a separate section, note the significance of the Immanuel prophecy as it bears on both stories.

The birth narrative. The predominant factor in Matthew's story of Jesus' conception and birth is that God, not Joseph, is Jesus' father, which in turn makes Jesus God's unique son. In other words, Jesus is the long hoped-for Messiah, Israel's ideal king who would reign in righteousness and whose eternal rule would extend to the ends of the earth.[24]

In the Old Testament, "son of God," though occasionally referring to God's chosen people,[25] is also applied to Israel's king of Davidic descent. As such, the term connotes the king's special relationship with God.[26] Of particular interest here is its appearance in Psalm 2:7, part of a royal psalm to be sung as God's word at a new king's enthronement: "You are my son, today I have begotten you." God's son, begotten by God! Not, of course, that the psalmist contemplated virginal conceptions. Like David, who was sired by Jesse, all heirs to the throne had human fathers, as would the Messiah in Jewish belief.[27] Even so, the similarity of Matthew's story with the terminology of Psalm 2:7 is much too striking to be merely coincidental. Furthermore, in Psalm 89:26–27 the royal Davidic heir, as God's son, is designated "the first-born." Thus, Matthew's description of Jesus' unique conception — begotten by God and a first-born — declares that Jesus is Israel's king as no one else ever could be or, henceforth, ever can be. He, and he alone, is the royal Messiah, the Son of God *par excellence.*

In this vein, the item of miraculous birth — an invasion from above — implies a mighty word of eschatological triumph. God has broken through the old, the routine, of this world and ushered in the new, so that nothing will stay as it was before. That was to say dramatically, as the kerygma said straightly, God's victorious rule has arrived in the Messiah whose name is Jesus. And his other name, Matthew tells us, is "Immanuel" — so parenthetical and awesome a name that we must hold it in abeyance for awhile.

The infancy narrative. Matthew's infancy narrative, following that of Jesus' birth by barely a breath, points up the nature of the messiahship just announced. Another dramatic word of kerygmatic import, it likens Jesus' significance as Messiah to what was accomplished through Moses. Most Christians today, unless directed to Exodus

1:8–2:10, miss the comparison by miles. To readers like Matthew's Jewish Christians, however, Moses was the foremost of Old Testament heroes. They knew his life story as if it were their own — and in their religious heritage, which incorporated them with all Israel of old, it was indeed their own story. So, in a tale focusing on Jesus' infancy, Matthew writes about a time when a wicked, pagan king, dominating the people of God and gripped by inane fear, committed brutal infanticide against them, yet with one special child providentially spared (in Egypt, no less). Hence dawns the light: baby Jesus is just like baby Moses! What a thrill that realization must have been to first-time readers, unspoiled by the sentimentality that regularly inundates Christmas.

The ultimate focus of the story, however, is not a baby — instead, a man. As we have seen, original readers could not have taken it historically short of discarding knowledge and believing the impossible about Herod. With this in mind, we come to understand that the story drives home the word that Jesus, the Messiah, is to be regarded in light of Moses' particular significance, only more so. Then who was Moses? The one through whom God delivered his chosen people from Egyptian bondage and, according to tradition, gave the Law. And who is Jesus, according to early Christian faith? The one in whom people are delivered from bondage — only not the bondage of Egypt or even of Rome, rather the infinitely greater bondage of sin and death. Also, like Moses as "Law giver," Jesus is the one to be obeyed. All of which means: Jesus Christ is Savior and Lord. In other words, Rejoice — and while you're at it, pay attention to him.

"Rejoice and pay attention." Which brings us into the sobering presence of him who is called "Immanuel."

The Immanuel Prophecy

As explained above, Matthew's reference to Isaiah 7:14 guards readers from taking the birth narrative historically. But its significance far exceeds that. On the one hand, it provides the best clue we have for uncovering the origin of Matthew's story of Jesus' conception and birth. And, on the other, the reference purposely functions as a word of judgment with respect to Jesus' messiahship.

The stimulus underlying Matthew's birth narrative. In the Hebrew text of Isaiah 7:14, it is said that an *almah* will conceive and bear a son. Although *almah* usually means "young woman," the word could also designate a woman about to be married – a "pledged" woman or one whose marriage might be soon.[28] When the Old Testament was translated into Greek – the so-called Septuagint translation, begun in the third century B.C. – no single Greek noun was available to render this special connotation of *almah.* The closest Greek noun was *parthenos,* meaning "virgin," since a Jewish woman about to be married, presumably for the first time, would normally have been a virgin. Which likely explains the Septuagint's translation in this case. In any event, the Septuagint at Isaiah 7:14 reads *parthenos:* "A virgin shall conceive and bear a son. . . . "

Here, then, is what probably happened. Matthew (or someone before him who devised Jesus' virginal conception?) was reading Isaiah 7:14 in the Greek. A son born of a *virgin,* he imagined to himself, would be a son of God. Jesus had long been called "the Son of God" in reference to his being the Christ (e.g., Rom. 1:3–4). So Matthew, more likely than anyone else,[29] came up with the ingenious idea of expressing Jesus' messiahship dramatically in terms of Mary's being a virgin when he was conceived and born. In composing his story Matthew probably built on an earlier narrative in which Joseph was the central figure;[30] yet he reworked that narrative to include a virginal conception as its new and dominant factor.

An explanation of the origin of Matthew 1:18–25 along such lines is appealing enough on the surface, and I find no compelling evidence to make it seem improbable. Granted, it is only conjecture, as must be any attempt to uncover the beginnings of the virginal conception in Christian thought. Numerous scholars argue against the suggestion, especially those who see Luke teaching a virginal conception independently of Matthew and obviously without reference to Isaiah 7:14. However, as we have noted, Jesus' virginal conception is at least questionable in Luke's narration; and one may only wonder why Luke wasn't clearer about it if that is what he meant to depict. Further, for reasons unrelated to the virginal conception, several critics date Luke's Gospel twenty-five years or so after Matthew's; and in that case a Lucan identification of Mary as a virgin at Jesus' conception could be the result of *indirect* Matthean influence. (Recall that word of the virginal conception was circulating within twenty-five years of Matthew's writing – i.e., c. A.D. 110.) But in no case need one agree with the contention that Matthew (or whoever first told of the virginal conception) could scarcely have been influenced by Isaiah 7:14. That is argued on the grounds that the Immanuel prophecy, in both the Hebrew and the Greek, is not concerned with the manner of the child's conception, much less with a *virginal* conception, nor had Hellenistic Jews read the Septuagint as though it were. Carefully advanced by Brown,[31] that argument, while correct in its observations, unreasonably limits the potential for human inspiration. As if one like Matthew could not have been moved by his faith in Jesus Christ, the unique Son of God, to see and use Isaiah 7:14 in a new yet also responsible way. That Matthew did so himself is evident in his joining Isaiah's prophecy with Jesus' messiahship.

A word of judgment. Whatever the stimulus behind Matthew's birth narrative, his reference to the Immanuel prophecy strongly implies a word of unequivocal judgment. That prophecy, we have seen, originally announced onrushing doom at the hands of the king of Assyria, whose wreckage of Judah was to be understood as the name Immanuel, "God-with-us." Not that the Assyrian king was divine, but that through Assyria's destruction of the land God would be present among his chosen. He would be with them in effecting his judgment upon them. It was a distinctive Yahwist motif: the Lord, Yahweh, is present as he acts in history. And in this impending event, the Assyrians would arrive at his own whistle (Isa. 7:18). Even so, to the prophet's mind "God-with-us" went beyond mere tragedy. His Immanuel prophecy stood alongside another daring word. According to Isaiah, the coming judgment was to be redemptive as well as disastrous, for a chastened remnant of Israel would then repent (10:20–23). That too is a Yahwist motif: judgment and redemption appear in tandem. Such is the fact for Matthew's narration. In naming Jesus "Immanuel," Matthew suggests that his appearance as the Christ is likewise judgmental. That means God's historical judgment in person — "God-with-us," no less. For in Jesus Christ, God has acted decisively, revealing the truth which saves and which, at the same time, exposes hideous error as doomed.

Isaiah's Immanuel prophecy thus gets a "new" fulfillment in Matthew's usage. Elsewhere as well — most notably for us, in his infancy narrative — Matthew gives new but not totally dissimilar meaning to Old Testament words.[32]

But it remains for us to ask about the object of judgment implied in Matthew's citation of Isaiah 7:14. Exactly what error(s) did he mean to condemn? Although the possibilities are many in Matthew's Gospel, the citation's immediate context suggests concern with the messianic role itself. Inserted near the end of the birth narrative, whose meaning is qualified by the infancy narrative that immediately follows, the reference seems most apropos for both of them taken together. While the story of Jesus' birth dramatizes his being the Davidic Messiah, and the infancy story his being the one who delivers "Israel" from bondage, the fact is that "his own people received him not" (Jn. 1:11), either before *or* after Easter. That is not hard to fathom. For the most part, first-century Jews who entertained messianic hopes were anticipating a different kind of Messiah: one whose victorious rule would be largely nationalistic, restoring Israel to its former glory under Kings David and Solomon. They thought not of a royal Messiah who would die for their sins, as Matthew's birth narrative at 1:21 implies — the idea was unheard-of and appalling! Instead, the hoped-for Messiah would prevail over their enemies, free them from the bondage of Rome. Nor could they well believe that Jesus as the Christ had been resurrected, thus breaking the bondage of death. In the general Jewish view, Jesus had been a false teacher, one who broke the Law and perhaps even blasphemed — not the kind of person whom God would ever vindicate. This is all to say that the kerygma, on which Matthew's Gospel is ultimately based and which his birth and infancy stories dramatically express, ran afoul of Jewish messianic expectations.

So we have Matthew's felicitous use of Isaiah 7:14. Not to substantiate, by fast exegetical footwork, that Jesus was conceived of a virgin, but to say that his messiahship stands in judgment on all messianic notions to the contrary. And not to declare that Jesus himself was divine, but to announce that in him God is with us, speaking his active word which redeems and, simultaneously, condemns. Thus, in Jesus of Nazareth, and only in him, God's promises to Israel are surprisingly fulfilled, whether Israel likes it or not. . . . Immanuel!

Two Final Questions

As we bring this chapter to a close, two questions call for additional remarks. First, if it is really so clear that the birth and infancy narratives were not meant to be taken historically, how did the Church come to read them that way? And second, what positive bearing does Jesus' *not* being conceived of a virgin have on his humanity?

Later misunderstanding of the narratives. The answer to the first of these questions lies in widespread ignorance of the crucial items we have been discussing. That ignorance came to the fore in the second Christian century and was compounded by the passing of time and by developments within the Church's confession. In a word, the personnel of the Church underwent a radical change.

Thanks to missionary successes, the Church experienced a transformation in makeup as early as New Testament times. Initially a group of Palestinian Jews who confessed Jesus to be the Christ, the Church became increasingly Gentile in membership. The significance of this for the apostolic period itself has often been overstated, especially since early Gentile converts, apparently, were instructed rather carefully in Old Testament concepts underlying the Church's kerygma. For instance, Paul's letters, addressed to Gentile congregations, frequently take for granted familiarity with the Scriptures and Semitic ways of thinking. Nevertheless, a predominantly Gentile Church, whose percentage of Jewish members was steadily on the decline, would surely have trouble understanding the birth and infancy narratives – and all the more so because of their ingenuity and late appearance. Secondary readers, scattered around the Roman Empire and without interpretive help at hand, lacked the particular knowledge that Matthew and Luke assumed of their readers. For example, glaring incongruities, originally giving the reader pause, would eventually go unnoticed, much the same as they do for general readers today.

By A.D. 135 the Jewish wing of the Church had all but vanished. This left New Testament interpretation in the hands of Gentiles who, culturally and chronologically, were more and more removed from the historical and theological milieu of the birth and infancy narratives. Significantly, older traditions about Jesus fared much better. They had gained a foothold that ensured against essential and widespread misunderstanding – as is evident, for example, in the Church's successful struggle against heresies denying Christ's humanity, real death, and resurrection. Not so, however, the birth and infancy narratives. Though fictitious to the bone and wanting traditional support, they appeared too late for extensive misreading of them to be adequately corrected. By the time these creative stories began to circulate with the First and Third Gospels, only a handful of Christians had the wherewithal for interpreting them aright – and their Jewish influence, alas, was as good as dead. Thus, superficial reading became the order of the day.

Coupled with the crucial ignorance of later readers was their intellectual proclivity for systemization. Indeed, apart from the Hellenistic mind-set of Gentile converts to the Christian faith, history could not explain the heresies that soon arose and the Church's creedal responses to them. Whether heretical or orthodox, the Hellenistic "mind of Christ" wanted things neatly arranged. Accordingly, as christology progressed beyond the New Testament and under Gentile control, the birth and infancy narratives were read in association with developing beliefs about the person of Jesus Christ. Had that association not been made, the modern student of historical theology would be dumbfounded by its absence. For the Church was moving inexorably toward Nicaea and Constantinople and Chalcedon, where the Trinity and Christ's human and divine natures would be written in stone.

So the Gospel stories of Jesus' birth and infancy could hardly have escaped being taken amiss soon after they started to circulate. Secondary readers were confused by Old Testament terms, were far afield from the Palestine of Jesus' birth, and were packing intellectual baggage tagged for Nicaea and points beyond. They read those stories as best they could: Jesus was God's son, not Joseph's; Herod slaughtered the innocent children, just as Matthew says he did; and Isaiah predicted that the Christ would be born of a virgin and would be truly divine, with Mary to be hailed in due time as "Mother of God."[33] To be sure, Matthew and Luke had tipped their hands rather generously, encouraging a different approach to their rich and stimulating narratives. But by the middle of the second century, for all practical purposes, the clues had disappeared and pressing christological concerns were rushing in to take their place.

Small wonder, therefore, the Church's long-standing teaching of an actual virginal conception. Virtually unanimous from A.D. 200 until fairly recently – and still very much alive in the established confessions of mainline churches – it has been tied with other traditions which, like good wines, are supposed to improve with age. And in this particular matter, we acknowledge that tradition does not easily die.

The meaning for Jesus' humanity. The other question closing this chapter prefaces, in kind, the remainder of our study. Namely, what significant bearing does Jesus' *not* having been conceived of a virgin have on his humanity? Early on we rejected the argument that a virginal conception would have kept him from being completely human. We did so on the thinkable grounds that God, say with a mind to, could have created a fully human nature in Jesus without Joseph's cooperation.

The importance of Jesus' conception for his humanity must rather be viewed "existentially" – that is, in regard to what he realized himself as a man. From the standpoint of historical interest, the question is not whether his *nature* was fully human but whether his *experience* was.[34]

If Jesus had been virginally conceived, surely Mary, unless terribly confused, would have informed him of it. And he, presumably, would have believed her. This means that Jesus, armed with that belief, would have felt less need for faith than human beings normally do. For the rest of us faith is a risk, but for him it would have been more like a charade. Thinking his own origin to be unquestionably divine, and "sure" of his being special before God, Jesus could have had little room within himself for genuine doubt, hence that much less room for genuine faith and trust in God. He would have "known" too much for that.

There are adults, of course, who habitually think that they *know* good things about God and themselves which can only be *believed.* We call them naive or dull or sick. Whatever the cause, their thinking is out of touch with the realities of the human condition. And so is their experience. Supposing they have a desired relationship with God that is beyond any question, they simply do not question it. It is a fool's tautology, beginning with and repeating bad faith — faith that denies the existence of faith and even a need of it. People so sure of themselves fail to realize what human finiteness itself entails: not merely eating, drinking, and getting on with life, but uncertainty, anxiety, and a sense of meaninglessness as well. These troublesome realities may be coped with through faith, but not removed by knowledge that isn't suprahuman. One who does not experience them as native within his or her existence must be deemed abnormal, in the poorest sense of the term.

Hence, had Jesus been conceived of a virgin and been told of the fact by Mary, had he believed her report and therefore felt utterly sure of his uniqueness within God's purpose, he would have been like no competent person we know. A man for whom personal uncertainty and doubt would have seemed fairly absurd. A man who could speak perceptively about anxiety but not know much of its pain. Indeed, a man of relatively little faith, except for great faith in his mother, because he needed little else. Such a person, with so impoverished a human experience, resembles none of us.

Happily for his humanity, the picture just given does not resemble Jesus of Nazareth either. In view of discernible facts to be discussed next, it fails even as a caricature.

Chapter 2

All-Knowing?

We don't know where we are, or who we are.
We don't know one another; don't know You;
Don't know what time it is. We don't know, don't we?

—Job, according to Frost

Was Jesus of Nazareth omniscient? Or nearly so? Or at least for all practical intents? Suppose he was not. If that could be demonstrated to public satisfaction, popular understanding would take a huge step toward linking his experience with ours. Customary perceptions of Jesus' humanity would be relieved of keeping company with what is perhaps the most debilitating notion of his divinity — suprahuman knowledge.

Omniscience, especially in Western thought, has been a favorite theological attribute. Along with two other large O's, omnipotence and omnipresence, it sets God off from man. Personally in control of his purpose, as Jewish and Christian traditions have rightly understood their Scriptures to teach, the Almighty is not in for surprises. Rather, he knows all, including why the innocent suffer and who wrote the book of Hebrews, not to mention the beginnings of *Beowulf* and untold other mysteries.

Accomplished persons of letters as well as comedians have had their fun with omniscience — sometimes with important results. For one, Robert Frost's "A Masque of Reason," while presenting a delightfully irreverent contrast between God's all-knowingness and man's inviolate ignorance, may be the most incisive commentary ever published on the book of Job. And in the world at large, as one might expect, jokes about omniscience are legion (to which God responds, e.g., "I didn't know that"). Who but a nervous pietist would not be tickled by Stanley Elkin's one-liner, in his fantasy *The Living End,* when God, seeking sympathy in the strangest of places, complains to the people of hell that omniscience gives him eyestrain!

In the last analysis, omniscience is no mere laughing matter, least of all concerning christology. Popular interpretations of Christ's divinity to the contrary, critical New Testament scholarship in the main has located the historical Jesus as a man of quite limited knowledge. I will put the matter concisely. *Whatever may seem to be true regarding the divinity of Jesus Christ, nothing near omniscience played a part in his earthly career. To the contrary, so finite was his knowledge that he had to risk being wrong about items of the greatest import — namely, God's redemptive purpose and his own special role in it.*

Preliminary Considerations

The reader who takes offense at the italicized statement just above is hardly alone in the Church. Countless Christians, many of them clergy, cringe at the suggestion that Jesus' understanding of God's purpose could have been anything less than perfect. Years of church school classes and Sunday sermons, sometimes seminary instruction as well, have guaranteed their reaction: "Jesus knew what was going on, all the time and with everyone." What's more, the Gospels themselves depict Jesus as fully aware of who he was and of what God had in store for him: the suffering Christ who would die on a cross and on the third day be raised, thus atoning for the sins of all and conquering death in their behalf. Look through Mark, for example, the earliest of the Gospels. There you will find a running mixture of heavenly revelations, clear-cut messianic activities on Jesus' part, and, from his lips, predictions that come true with astounding success. Little wonder that Jesus has commonly been viewed by the Christian faithful as endowed with special knowledge — indeed, suprahuman knowledge which, for all practical intents, bordered on omniscience.

But if that is how the Gospels read, that is not how they are to be understood. Whether looking for their message or trying to ascertain what Jesus was like, we must approach the Gospels in light of their special character. When that character is disregarded, the Gospels are an unsolved puzzle, a mystery that can only mislead.

The postresurrection vantage point. First, recall the fact (from our introduction) that the Gospels are written from the vantage point of postresurrection faith. Long recognized by critical scholarship, that fact bears repeating here. The Gospels are Christian literature of a peculiar sort. While focusing on the historical Jesus, they are not precise recordings of historical data. They were not meant to be. Rather, each of the Gospel writers was primarily concerned with Jesus' redemptive significance and whatever that seemed to imply (i.e., according to the writer's understanding and the situation at hand). So-called pure history, or history recorded for history's sake, held no moment for any of them. Instead, the evangelists' great interest was the *euangelion,* the good news of God's accomplishments in Christ as seen from this side of Easter. They wrote about Jesus of Nazareth, yes, and they relied on earlier traditions, many of which emanated from eyewitnesses. But those traditions had been formulated or later reworked to express postresurrection faith — faith about Jesus that began to develop *after* the Easter experience. The Gospel writers, like the early Christians who preceded them, were looking at Jesus anew, through eyes of faith. They were concerned not simply with what he said or did, or exactly what occurred on a given occasion, but also with what *God* was doing and saying through him. Thus, they felt quite free, indeed felt obligated, to tell the "story" of Jesus of Nazareth from a later point of view.

In other words, and now more sharply, the Gospels transport Christian faith backward to where it necessarily belongs — back to Jesus' own life and death, yet a life and death which, from the evangelists' standpoint, make no sense apart from God's intent.

Historical-interpretive literature. The special character of the Gospels is also to be seen in the fact that they are, to a large extent, historical-interpretive literature.

"Historical-interpretive" denotes a kind of writing common in the Bible. An event, on the one hand, and faith's interpretation of it, on the other, are combined in a single narrative. Accordingly, historical details have often been altered to depict what was believed to be the deepest meaning of real events. In the widest sense, the Gospels focus on but one event, the so-called Christ-event — Jesus' life and death and resurrection: what that meant and means for Christian faith. Even so, that one event is composed of many parts. There were specific occurrences, planted in history, and they too are important. Without them there would be no Christ-event. But their importance in the Gospels is never self-contained, never isolated from the whole. On the contrary, single occurrences are described and arranged in a manner to express the Church's kerygma or basic beliefs. Better to say, the Gospels abound with dramatic expressions of kerygmatic beliefs — occurrences which, in the telling, dramatize Jesus' significance as that eventually came to be understood.

In applying "historical-interpretive" to Gospel materials, I would exclude from this genre stories like the birth and infancy narratives. As we have seen, they also are dramatic expressions of kerygmatic beliefs, but they apparently lack historical roots. They seem to be imaginative inventions completely. Moreover, they are not actually concerned with what they describe. While telling of a birth and infancy, their interest is neither Jesus' birth nor his early years but, instead, something else — his significance as a man. The Gospels generally, however, are not so indirect as they zero in on Jesus' ministry. Although legendary items show up at places, and though events are often embellished, the concern nonetheless is the meaning of that ministry itself. It was a real ministry, historically based, structured in events that were open to public view. But — and this is distinctive of historical-interpretive materials — actual events *and* their meaning for faith are so tightly interwoven in a single fabric that precisely what happened on a given occasion is simply impossible to reconstruct.

THE CHALLENGE TO SCHOLARSHIP. Before turning to a case in point, we may note that, in scholarship's quest for the historical Jesus, the Gospels' special character poses a challenge both more complex and yet less discouraging than most people are apt to think. To complicate matters, historically based and other traditions that circulated regarding Jesus went through a process of development and revision even during oral transmission. Theological and situational factors were much at work in the process and issued in a variety of adaptable forms or types of traditions. Then, when the Gospel writers used such traditions, the same kinds of factors were again at work. Each of the evangelists selected, edited, modified, and arranged traditions in line with his own theological and practical concerns. The difficulties that all of this presents in a search for the historical Jesus can scarcely be exaggerated, particularly since none of the traditions now available was designed to aid such a quest. And strictly biographical questions — for example, What human factors during childhood and later years influenced Jesus? — are not even raised obliquely, much less given the slightest hint. Clearly, a "Life of Jesus" would be a dilettante's enterprise nowadays.

However, we need not throw up our hands. For all the difficulties inherent in the search for Jesus as he actually was, such as identifying the contexts of pre-Gospel traditions, distinguishing between oral and written traditions, uncovering somewhat the historical development of the Jesus-tradition in general — for all of these difficulties and more, we can know some things about Jesus with reasonable certainty. As we saw in chapter 1, there are items regarding him that would have been too embarrassing for the early Church to fabricate. And as we will observe hereafter, there are items to be deemed authentic for still other reasons. Unconcerned with writing history for its own sake, and therefore giving us less information than we would like, the Gospel authors gave us, incidentally, more information about Jesus of Nazareth than detractors of the Gospels often suppose.

MARK 15:38, A CASE IN POINT. To substantiate the Gospels' historical-interpretive character, Mark 15:38 is a vivid case in point. (We shall return to it before completing this chapter; hence my using it as an example here.) It is Mark's statement that, when Jesus finally died, "the curtain of the temple was torn in two, from top to bottom." Precisely speaking, such a rending of the curtain did not happen. And to appreciate Mark's meaning it is best to know that. Otherwise, one might take the verse simply as describing a curious incident: marvelous indication, perhaps, that back in biblical times the Almighty had ways of getting people's attention. At least, according to the next verse, the centurion standing by lost no time in making a Christian confession! But faithfully speaking, from a postresurrection viewpoint, the curtain's tearing in two symbolizes *exactly* what happened in Jesus' death.

Mark's crucifixion narrative (15:16–39) undoubtedly rests on historical fact. The crucifixion itself (1) is mentioned by the Jewish turncoat and historian Josephus (governor of Galilee once war broke out between the Jews and the Romans in A.D. 66), (2) is noted in some detail by the Roman writer Tacitus early in the second century, and (3) is taken for granted in polemical rabbinic traditions from the first two centuries.[1] Since it lay at the heart of earliest Christian preaching in and around Jerusalem, the crucifixion, had it not occurred, would surely have been refuted. It wasn't. Finally here, the Church would not have created Pilate's sentencing Jesus to death as "King of the Jews." Highlighted in all four Gospels, that charge suggests that Jesus was officially perceived as a real or would-be insurrectionist.

So, no question about it, Jesus' crucifixion under Pontius Pilate happened. But how? What were its immediate details? Mark's Gospel supplies plenty, with the details mostly arranged in striking parallel to the resentful part of Psalm 22. The arrangement so neatly fits the "God-forsaken" psalmist's several complaints, it seems made to order. At points, in fact, the patterned design is implausible.[2] One can hardly but notice that Mark's narrative through 15:34 is indeed contrived. Then, as the story moves to its climax in the centurion's confession, comes this amazing declaration to settle forever the historical-interpretive character of Mark's crucifixion account: When Jesus "breathed his last...the curtain of the temple was torn in two, from top to bottom" (15:37b–38).

The curtain most probably in mind here was the royally colored veil of rich linen that closed off the Temple's inner sanctum.[3] That curtain was a monument of extreme importance in Jewish religious practice. Nothing comparable to its numinous significance can be found in Western structures. A massive veil of blue and scarlet and purple embroidery, it guarded the way to the Holy of Holies. From the days of Israel's portable tabernacle, that inner room connoted God's dwelling in the midst of his people. Therein had sat the ark of the covenant, with its mercy seat a kind of throne symbolizing God's presence and rule. By Jesus' day the ark had long been lost; still, the Holy of Holies retained its awesome air, and the curtain its significance. That veil hung there as a splendid yet terrible Yahwist reminder that sin separates God and humanity. No one was permitted behind the barricade, save Israel's high priest – and he could enter the room but once a year, to offer atoning sacrifices for the people's sins, his own included. Indeed, a person dared not get too near the curtain. To touch it even accidentally was a crime punishable by death. No ordinary curtain, that.

Now, had that Temple curtain been torn in two when Jesus died, the occurrence would have been traumatic for every God-fearing Jew within earshot. The word would have spread like wildfire, and all the more since it was Passover season, when Jerusalem was awash with pilgrims from near and far to celebrate Israel's greatest feast. But of that alleged occurrence no reliable evidence exists. There is simply no Jewish word to substantiate it. Therefore, it did not happen. Otherwise, one might just as well assume that the Washington Monument could suddenly collapse, yet without news of the disaster ever reaching the wilds of Baltimore.

The intent of Mark 15:38, at least on the surface, is not difficult to grasp. It is saying, with dramatic force, something about the *meaning* of Jesus' death – something about the barrier between God and humanity as wrecked by God in the cross of Christ. We shall return to this at another level. Here we need only note that the meaning came not as a wholly new word. A pre-Pauline form of the kerygma had declared something of the same: "Christ died for our sins."[4] Years before the Gospels appeared Paul himself stressed such a word; for example, "God was in Christ reconciling the world to himself" (2 Cor. 5:19). So too the anonymous author of Hebrews, whose book may also antedate the Gospels.[5] Mark's narrative, with a similar understanding of Jesus' redemptive significance, puts the matter uniquely: when Jesus breathed his last, the Temple veil was rent in twain and, at that, from above. It is, somewhat, "the old, old story," but told in a way to pierce one's bones.

All right, then. If Mark felt free to work a post-Easter confession into his story of the crucifixion, what was to keep him from doing that sort of thing elsewhere? What was to keep him, say, from putting Christian beliefs back into Jesus' own mouth and experience? The answer is, of course, "Nothing." As a matter of fact, he had little choice in the matter. Writing around A.D. 70, Mark necessarily relied on oral traditions which, for the vast part, had been circulating independently (i.e., not joined with one another).[6] Those traditions, however, had already been christianized. The historical-interpretive process had long been under way. Mark's special contribution was not just that he preserved extant traditions and thus helped authenticate the essential reality of Jesus' ministry. In reviewing that ministry from a postresurrection vantage point, Mark structured his Gospel to stress that Christian faith alone can comprehend the meaning of the historical Jesus. All other attempts to understand his significance are headed down a blind alley, where the secret of who Jesus was and is remains an inscrutable mystery.

The irrelevance of omniscience. To these preliminary remarks may now be added one more, particularly to "liberate" readers who might otherwise be defensive. When considering the essence of Christian faith, the possibility of Jesus' having been omniscient or nearly so, indeed of his having any suprahuman knowledge at all, is a thoroughly irrelevant matter. Historically, the early Church's kerygma depended on the Easter experience and not on any assumption that God had endowed Jesus with "heavenly" understanding. This is not to say (1) that Jesus had no more insight than anyone else. As we will observe in our next chapter, his "knowledge" of the kind of righteousness that God demands set him radically apart from other teachers. Yet — and this is just to the point — he chided the experts of his day for not seeing that righteousness as he did (Mk. 7:1–23). To Jesus' mind, their understanding of genuine righteousness could and should have matched his own understanding of it. Nor is any of this to say (2) that the notion of Jesus' being endowed with suprahuman knowledge was irrelevant in later, mostly post–New Testament christological speculations. If for no other reason, the idea was sure to gain currency as the special, post-Easter character of Gospel materials failed to be recognized. At the outset, however, it was belief in the resurrection, irrespective of Jesus' having a direct wire to God, that empowered the Church to life and enabled its faith to prosper.

Significantly in this regard, the first two Synoptic Gospels (Matthew and Mark), far from depicting Jesus as a man who could not be wrong, make little or no attempt to cover up the fact of his limited knowledge. Even while pushing postresurrection faith back into his public ministry and private experience, those Gospels openly suggest that he was, at times, mistaken about matters pertaining to the success of God's purpose.

To that fact we now must turn without questioning the basic validity of Christian faith. From the kerygma's vantage point, the Easter word matters, as does belief in Jesus as God's Messiah, the world's surprising Savior and Lord, but not what he knew about himself as such or that he was able to predict the future.

✤

In discussing what the Gospels indicate about Jesus' limited knowledge, we shall consider the following matters: (1) Jesus' eschatological predictions; (2) other predictions attributed to him; and (3) his alleged self-awareness as Messiah/Suffering Servant. Then, in view of all that, I shall offer a positive word regarding Jesus' mysterious messiahship as Mark relates it to Christian faith. All of this may seem somewhat arbitrary, particularly since questions of modern historical criticism are, in each case, an invasion of the Gospel writer's logic. But there is in this approach much to be learned about Jesus' humanity and about early Christian understanding of him.

Jesus' Eschatological Predictions

The most "obvious" (though ultimately least important) evidence of Jesus' limited knowledge is found in his eschatological predictions. He seems to have taught that the Eschaton, or the End of this age as we know it, was imminent.[7]

The background in Yahwist theology. Expressing a utopian hope of sorts and not uncommon among Jews and Christians of the first century, such talk of eschatological imminence today is beyond serious credence for all but a tiny fraction of people. Especially since predictions of the Eschaton's nearness have proved, without fail, to be somewhat ahead of schedule. Eschatological hope began with Israel's prophets and arose as a logical outgrowth of long established Yahwist thought. God acts in history and controls it, meaning that his purpose is sure to succeed. Hence, in the worst of times, when all seemed lost or nearly so, the prophets envisioned a time when all would be perfectly right – in fact, a new creation. Sin would cease, prosperity abound, righteousness and peace overtake the earth. That hope assumed several forms: land and food aplenty, a faithful and victorious Messiah, a new covenant, a self-effacing Servant to suffer and die for the world's redemption. Whatever the form, it was ancient Yahwist belief that bred and fed it, keeping the hope alive when it met immediate disappointment. By Jesus' day there had been no shortage of quickened but disappointed eschatological expectations. More were still to come for both Jewish and Christian believers. Even so, the logic went, God's historical purpose is bound to succeed, and succeed completely: _he_ will see to that.

Early Christian expectations. New Testament writers as different as Paul and John of Patmos shared belief in a soon-to-be-realized Eschaton. Poles apart in temperament and outlook, and removed in their writings by about four decades, these authors nonetheless agreed on the nearness of the End and counseled their readers to behave accordingly. For example, it is best not to marry, wrote Paul around A.D. 55; the time for attending to the Lord's affairs is short, demanding a single-minded effort that marriage would only frustrate.[8] On the other hand, to paraphrase John the Seer's esoteric and repeated advice: do not succumb to Domitian's insistence on emperor worship; Rome's power to persecute is limited since the days are now few when Christ will return victoriously for the faithful and when his enemies will receive their just deserts.[9] Similarly, the early Jerusalem church, influenced by belief in Jesus' resurrection as a brand-new act of God, was a community in waiting. Expecting Christ's return soon, its members, along with Christians living elsewhere, developed apocalyptic assurances that the End was near. So they thought. And why not? Their Lord apparently had thought so himself (though scholars disagree on this).[10]

Jesus' expectations and post-Easter hopes connected. The comment of Jesus as reported in Mark 13:30 is particularly indicative of a connection that was made between his own eschatological expectations and subsequent, Christian hopes that the Eschaton would soon arrive: "Truly, I say to you, this generation will not pass away before all these things take place." (Pause for a moment and read Mk. 13.)

Frequently called the "Little Apocalypse," the thirteenth chapter of Mark is composed of several sayings from various strata of oral and, perhaps, written tradition with Marcan modifications here and there. In the form of a lengthy discourse, it has Jesus telling some of his disciples about identifiable historical occurrences such as the destruction of the Jerusalem Temple that will shortly precede the Eschaton. Mark 13 is the first extended piece we have of Christian apocalyptic literature (the Revelation of John being the most famous but, because of its strangely symbolic and secretive character, a thousand times more difficult for the untrained reader to comprehend). Apocalypse or "revelation" was a late, prophetic development in Yahwist eschatology. It used events of the near past and present to assure the faithful that "the End" was imminent, *as if* those events had long ago been prophesied through a marvelous unveiling of "the final things" of God's purpose. Events already well known or certainly about to take place were pushed backward into the allegedly visionary mind of some authoritative figure of the past. That person's purportedly fulfilled prophecies were then to be current signs of the speedily approaching Day of Yahweh. While such an enterprise today would smack of a hoodwink, the apocalyptist believed his message to be God-inspired and wished to hearten people of his time whose faith was in trouble. Threatened with persecution from men opposed to their beliefs, or discouraged for other reasons, the faithful were then tempted to throw in the towel. Hence the apocalyptist's word to them: "Keep the faith, for the End is at hand – see what things are happening!"

In the composite of Mark 13, a similar apocalyptic purpose seems evident: suffering Christians needed encouragement to endure (vss. 9–13). Although some of the sayings, in one form or another, may have originated with Jesus, scholars widely agree that the material was undoubtedly affected by Christian indoctrination and adapted to later situations. Allusions to the Holy Spirit (vs. 11) and to Jesus' being the *true* Christ (vss. 6, 21–22) and named "the Son" (vs. 32) seem to reflect post-Easter doctrinal developments and not Jesus' historical teaching.[11] Moreover, words about the Temple's destruction (vss. 1–2), which in fact did not occur until A.D. 70, and about "*the* desolating sacrilege" (vs. 14), which the reader (not Jesus' own listeners!) is enjoined to understand, assume that these events have recently happened. This was to say, apocalyptically, that the Eschaton is drawing near (though perhaps, Mark allows in vss. 7b and 32–35, not as quickly as some may think).

It was thus within the framework of contemporary apocalypticism that Mark set Jesus' own teaching of an imminent Eschaton. Coming from *the* authoritative figure for Christians, that teaching served a double function: to support the Church's similar view of the Eschaton and, particularly in this case, to justify apocalyptic assurance of its nearness — "this generation will not pass away before all these things take place." Although we cannot recover Jesus' words underlying Mark 13:30, let alone reconstruct their original setting, I do not much doubt the saying's reliability as a *reflection* of his thinking. A proclamation that the End would materialize before his own generation had passed, the prediction was, strictly speaking, already wrong by the time Mark put it in writing (c. A.D. 70). Surely, neither Mark nor his Christian predecessors would have manufactured a word that incorrectly depicted Jesus as mistaken about any aspect of God's purpose.[12] On the other hand, if such was indeed Jesus' teaching, its oral circulation would not let it disappear. Best then, Mark evidently thought, to use it as he did — as an updated guarantee of the Church's eschatological hopes, however those hopes had been disappointed.

An objection and a response. Some people have been known to object that Jesus was not really wrong about the Eschaton's proximity — on the grounds that "generation" in Mark 13:30 is to be taken spiritually or generically, not chronologically. To that objection several things can be said, although three comments here should suffice. (1) Of its twenty-nine appearances in the New Testament (counting parallels), all but four of which are attributed to Jesus, concerning no other matter does "generation" in the singular (Gr. *genea*) have any such nonchronological meaning.[13] Rather, "generation" customarily signifies the people or a period of about twenty-five years. (2) There are two additional sayings, at least one of them basically authentic in the same sense as Mark 13:30, which also indicate that Jesus expected the Eschaton to arrive within the lifetime of his hearers. Though it may be Mark's own composition, at 9:1 he has Jesus promising, "There are some standing here who will not taste death before they see the kingdom of God come with power." The other saying is part of Matthew's version of Jesus' sending out the twelve to preach the coming kingdom of God (10:5–23), a story indelibly stamped with eschatological urgency. The disciples are to pursue their mission in haste, for, says Jesus to them, "You will not have gone through all the towns of Israel before the Son of man comes" (10:23b). The "son of man," often an apocalyptic figure that developed from Daniel 7:13 (written c. 165 B.C.), is referred to here in the third person as one yet to arrive. Thus it may not rightly be construed as a self-allusion by Jesus. Nor will good sense permit some extended meaning for "all the towns of Israel," as if Israel were another name, say, for the world in general. Such whimsical exegesis of candid language distrusts words and plays sport with Jesus-traditions. What then of Matthew 10:23b and Mark 13:30? While neither of them must be taken as a precise saying of Jesus, their existence in early church tradition strongly suggests a mistaken eschatology on his part. Moreover, their continued use by the Church after such predictions had failed to materialize indicates, at very least, a willingness to acknowledge that Jesus was capable of misunderstanding.

This brings us to observe (3) that Mark seems to take for granted the fact of Jesus' having been wrong regarding the Eschaton's nearness. Following the sayings in 13:29–30 — about the coming Son of man being near and about "last things" taking place before the existing generation passes away — Mark adds two other sayings which, *in this context,* strike an apologetic note. The first of them, "Heaven and earth will pass away, but my words will not pass away" (vs. 31), is implicitly in contrast to the generation that *has* passed away, the generation Jesus addressed. Although the saying may well be genuine,[14] one detects an apology in Mark's own use of it. Namely, so what if that generation's passing indicates Jesus was mistaken about the *time* of the Eschaton? Heaven and earth will pass away, yes (itself an eschatological word), but *not* the fundamental truth of Jesus' eschatological promises! Mark edited like a faithful Yahwist.

An apologetic note figures even more prominently in the next saying: "But of that day or that hour no one knows, not even the angels in heaven, nor the Son, but only the Father" (vs. 32). Were Mark 13 to be taken wholly as Jesus' own teaching, this saying would turn it all into a wonderfully preposterous speech. Here then would be a man claiming to speak with authority and making the most daring of detailed predictions, only to confess that he doesn't really know what he is talking about. That is a psychological *non sequitur.* Some critics, in a justifiable concern to authenticate as many Gospel items as possible, have defended the genuineness of this saying. However, it does seem a later invention, especially in its doctrinal mention of "the Son" along with "the Father." Granted, the saying bears an offensive word—that is, Jesus did not know precisely when the Eschaton would arrive. But the argument that its offensiveness guarantees its authenticity[15] fails to give full weight to the situation that prevailed in the Church. Eschatological predictions, both of Jesus and of his followers after Easter, had already encountered disappointment. So the saying here, rather than creating anything offensive, simply acknowledged an offense that was undeniably extant. No one *had* known when the Eschaton would arrive—not Jesus and not members of the Church. Except for God, the saying stresses, no one knows that now. With the insertion of this saying into the discourse, Mark not only cautions against a frenzy of apocalyptic confidence which, if the End fails to come at once, might cause Christians to lose heart and result in diminishing faithfulness. Also, in linking Jesus here with all other humans, he deftly apologizes for Jesus' having been wrong about the Eschaton's nearness: as a man, indeed even as the Christ, his knowledge was, of course, limited....Of course!

Other Predictions Attributed to Jesus

If Gospel reports of Jesus' eschatological predictions are to be judged authentic, particularly in view of their having been wrong, just the opposite holds for his other so-called predictions that "proved" to be astonishingly right. Were the latter authentic, their correctness would, to be sure, require of him suprahuman knowledge—exactly what this chapter contends he did not have. But, let me emphasize, my position is not that such knowledge would have been impossible for him—an *argumentum in circulum,* which begins with its conclusion and simply circles back to it. Rather, the question continues to be one of reasonably ascertainable facts and of how best to explain them. In that approach to the Gospels, the authenticity of Jesus' marvelously correct predictions fails to be confirmed. Instead, what apparent facts can be gleaned relative to those predictions measure heavily *against* their genuineness. In mind here are predictions attributed to Jesus concerning the immediate future of himself and others—details of his death, his resurrection, Peter's threefold denial of him, and so on — all of which are reported to have materialized in extremely neat and short order.

Germs of historicity? At the root of such predictions, one may often detect, or at least surmise, a germ of historicity. For example, Jesus' telling in advance of Peter's denial (Mk. 14:30). This denial prophecy, like Mark's narrative of the denial itself (14:66–72), makes Peter look bad. While critics have not agreed on the authenticity of either of these items, it is highly unlikely that both are mere fabrications. If one is wholly legendary (as the denial prophecy may be), the other most probably is not. Otherwise, however these traditions originated, they would have been particularly anti-Petrine for no necessary reason. One might assume that they simply reflect an anti–Jerusalem church attitude within pre-Gospel Christendom; but the genesis of the denial narrative would then require a schism far more vicious in early Christianity than the evidence indicates – though schism was a fact, even within the Jerusalem church (Acts 6:1).[16] Further, it is unthinkable that the tradition of Peter's denial was concocted by the Jerusalem church itself. That community was not given to naming one of its leaders for especially unfair chastisement. But now, for sake of discussion, let us assume that *both* traditions are historically rooted: namely, that Peter denied Jesus and that Jesus, one way or another, had suggested he would – perhaps some word, later recalled, about being disloyal or losing courage. Such a general prediction on Jesus' part need not entail suprahuman knowledge. It could issue merely from firsthand observation of the kind of impulsive yet self-deceptively weak person that these traditions show Peter to have been before Easter. However, this would not mean that the prediction and what actually occurred meshed precisely with each other as reported – that is, in a threefold denial trumpeted by two crows of a cock.

Much the same sort of notice can be made of Jesus' reportedly foretelling his death at the hands of his enemies (e.g., Mk. 8:31), maybe even his death in Jerusalem (Mk. 10:33). Unless the Gospels and earliest tradition bear no resemblance whatever to historical fact – an impossible premise – it is certain that the Jewish authorities were unalterably opposed to Jesus and wanted him out of the way. (No doubt sincere and striving to serve the greatest good, they apparently regarded him not only as a false teacher, but as a potentially dangerous figure – one whose popular appeal and words about the coming kingdom of God might prove to be disruptive, so much so at Passover time in crowded Jerusalem that severe Roman reprisals would ensue for many people.) Had that opposition to Jesus not been the fact, the Church's tradition of it, arising as it did in Jerusalem, would have fallen flat on its public face. The point then is that, given the intensity of such negative feelings concerning him, Jesus needed no special knowledge to realize that his days were probably numbered. Indeed, he willingly contributed to it all, like a canoeist who must battle the wind or else lose control of the boat. Whereas maverick teachers can often be conveniently dismissed through administrative maneuvers or pressured into conformity, no such unobtrusive options were open to Jesus' opponents. Everything reported of him reveals an integrity beyond question: so radical a commitment to teaching what he believed of God's kingdom and demand for righteousness that death alone could silence him. Evidently, his opponents came to know that much about him. He would have been dull not to realize that they knew it. Although they scarcely decided "to destroy him" as early as Mark suggests (3:6, an editorial composition), their intent must have been clear to him soon after he arrived in Jerusalem, where his last days were to be spent. That Jesus and his disciples discussed the possibility of his approaching death, if they ever discussed any personal thing, is thus to be expected. Furthermore, we may well suppose that he initiated the discussion. On the one hand, he was surely more aware than they of his own willingness to endure suffering and death rather than back away from his mission. And, on the other, Jesus' bringing up the matter before his disciples themselves recognized the possibility would account for the tradition portraying the heated argument that he and Peter had about it (Mk. 8:32–33) – another Petrine embarrassment, not likely pure invention. Again, however, a prediction of his suffering and death in fine detail, as offered in the Gospels, will not withstand critical examination (as we shall see).

A germ of historicity, perhaps, may even be found for Gospel reports that Jesus predicted his resurrection. However, apart from Easter and the Church's ensuing faith, no kind of microscope could enable one to see it. That germ is Jesus' alleged word that God would finally vindicate him. Recorded independently by Mark (14:25) and Luke (22:15–16) from liturgical traditions, that word, at least in essence, probably issued from Jesus himself. Consumed with a sense of mission and of God's favorable presence, beset by intense opposition from Jewish authorities, and believing the success of God's purpose would soon be manifest in the Eschaton's arrival, Jesus expected vindication, certainly. That he said so to his disciples should not seem remote, not even to the most cautious of critics. But that is one thing; Jesus' predicting God's vindication of him through his approaching death and resurrection is something else.

Jesus' anxiety and the disciples' behavior. Those predictions assigned to Jesus that would have required special knowledge on his part are loaded with difficulties, many of them quite technical and beyond our need to argue here. Suffice to say, the probability of their genuineness is often decreased by evidence of (1) later developments in Jesus-traditions underlying the Gospels and (2) editorial initiatives in the Gospels' use of such traditions. Of more interest and help to general readers, particularly concerning prescience of the resurrection, is Jesus' reported anxiety shortly before his arrest and in the face of virtually certain death:

> And they went to a place which was called Gethsemane; and he said to his disciples, "Sit here, while I pray." And he took with him Peter and James and John, and began to be greatly distressed and troubled. And he said to them, "My soul is very sorrowful, even to death; remain here, and watch." And going a little farther, he fell on the ground and prayed that, if it were possible, the hour might pass from him. And he said, "Abba, Father, all things are possible to thee; remove this cup from me; yet not what I will, but what thou wilt." And he came and found them sleeping, and he said to Peter, "Simon, are you asleep? Could you not watch one hour? Watch and pray that you may not enter into temptation...." And again he went away and prayed, saying the same words. And again he came and found them sleeping.... And he came the third time.... (Mk. 14:32–41)

That scene does not reflect a person who knew or even believed that God would raise him from death in a matter of days. Admittedly, the Gethsemane narrative, publishing words of private prayer and mentioning the "cup" in apparent allusion to the atoning significance of the death to come,[17] bears legendary marks of subsequent christology. Likewise, the advisory motif about guarding against temptation seems more appropriate to some later matter of concern to the Church than it does to sleepiness. But the story, casting Peter, James, and John in an unfavorable light and stressing so acutely Jesus' anxiety as his own death neared, most assuredly rests on historically sound tradition. Thus it counters the notion that Jesus knew of, or expected, his coming resurrection. Death troubled him.

Even stronger to the point with regard to the alleged and amazingly accurate predictions of Jesus is the disciples' behavior as those predictions reportedly came true. In a word, it seems his disciples remembered virtually nothing of what he supposedly had said to them — a remarkable impotence of memory that a psychologist would be hard pressed to explain of people in the environs of normalcy.

Although formally exaggerated, the behavior of the disciples within Gethsemane itself, if Jesus actually shared special knowledge with them, betrays an attitude inexplicably casual. Only moments before, as Mark has it (14:27–31), he told the twelve (or eleven?) they would all fall away prior to his resurrection. After Peter's objection that he, for one, would not (which allegedly evoked the prediction of a threefold denial "this very night"), they all followed Peter's strenuous lead in promising Jesus loyalty to the death if need be. But then in the garden, with Jesus' confided anxiety still ringing in their ears, the privileged three fell asleep. Well now, could slumber be so easy on the heels of Jesus' predictions about himself and them? Would they have had nothing to prove or nothing to be concerned about that terrible night?

In a similar vein, Jesus' reported prediction of Peter's denial, supposedly fulfilled to the letter, could have gone *un*fulfilled for all the effect it had. At the cock's second crow, we are told, Peter "broke down and wept" (Mk. 14:72). One would think, however, that a man in such a circumstance would be moved to something more — something like expectancy or hope that Jesus' happier predictions would also come true. Would Jesus, after all, be raised from the dead? But neither Peter nor his colleagues looked for that. This, in spite of precise rejection, death, and resurrection predictions which, if authentic, would have engendered hope in the most disheartened of followers.

Consider, for instance, the eighth chapter of Mark, which highlights special information purportedly given to the disciples well before "Passion Week" (and most of it repeatedly so, according to Mk. 9:9, 12, 31; 10:33–34). In line with Peter's Great Confession on behalf of the twelve (vss. 27–29), Jesus acknowledges himself to be the Christ (vs. 30). He then goes on to spell out exactly what that will entail: "The Son of man [eventually a Christian title with messianic import] must suffer many things, and be rejected by the elders and the chief priests and the scribes, and be killed, and after three days rise again" (vs. 31). Taking offense at that, Peter rebukes Jesus, only to be told in effect to curb his tongue, it being a tool of the devil (vss. 32–33). Not the kind of information and exchange likely to be forgotten! Moreover, next comes the well-known saying about (Christian) discipleship in terms of denying self, taking up one's *cross,* and following Jesus (vs. 34). Addressed to "the multitude" as well as to "his disciples," the saying, in its Marcan context, plainly suggests an open-air notice from Jesus that his death would be by crucifixion. No mean prediction, that – even from one cognizant of his opponents' intent, since presumably he could have been killed some other way (by stoning, for one, if convicted of blasphemy).

This is all to say that Jesus' disciples, given such information in advance of his arrest and death, had reason enough and more to anticipate his resurrection. With predictions rushing one after another into reality before their very eyes and ears, every fulfilled word disclosing specific knowledge that could have come to Jesus only from God – well, the disciples might at least have hoped a *little.* The arrest, the so-called trials, Peter's denial, the rejection and condemnation, the scourging and mocking, the cross – from all those occurrences friends in mourning should have reasoned: "He's been right so far! Let's wait to see what happens next; maybe God will raise him." It appears, however, that inside themselves they had not a prayer, let alone an expectation, of ever seeing Jesus again. Mildly put, Easter took them by surprise.

Although the "longer ending" of Mark's Gospel (16:9–20) is certainly a later addition,[18] the word at 16:11 about some of the disciples' skepticism regarding Jesus' resurrection probably derives from historical fact. Reported independently by Matthew (28:17) and Luke (24:11), the tradition of Easter skepticism would have been a queer invention. It casts aspersions on those disciples who, by the time such an invention could have succeeded, were thought to have been foretold of the resurrection by Jesus himself. Nor would the disciples, short of being masochistic, have fabricated the word themselves. But if they had *not* been foretold of the resurrection and of particular happenings allegedly preceding it, their reported skepticism makes sense. Whether coming from women or from some of their own number, the Easter declaration would then have seemed silly talk, a hitherto unspoken word that nothing save personal experience could enable them to believe.

Conclusion. Why such amazingly correct predictions, suggesting suprahuman knowledge for Jesus, were later put into his mouth is a complicated question. To answer it fully would involve the whole history of the Jesus-tradition. That tradition continues to be researched in necessarily small pieces, and findings are often less than certain. What we have noted generally of traditions about Jesus applies as well to the development of particular traditions giving him ability to predict the future. Within that development lively christological beliefs played a major role as did practical concerns of the

Church. Then, too, special interests of the Gospel writers came into play. Although examining all of that would exceed our limits, we shall consider why *Mark* relied so much on Jesus' allegedly marvelous predictions. But that must wait for this chapter's final major section – and there is still another to come.

In the meantime, a summary observation will conclude this section. A christology that imputes to Jesus suprahuman knowledge on grounds of his astounding predictions not only disregards the Gospels' postresurrection vantage point and historical-interpretive character. In taking those predictions as authentically his, it makes a shambles of Jesus' faithfully reported anxiety. That christology is then a violation of his humanity. Furthermore, it turns Jesus' disciples into a crowd of puzzling dolts, so impervious to all that supposedly was going on around them that one might seriously wonder if they ever got *anything* straight – yet on their testimony transmission of the gospel fundamentally depends! Such a christology, therefore, seems rather ill-equipped to serve either the search for Jesus of Nazareth *or* the welfare of Christian faith among judicious inquirers.

Self-Awareness as Messiah/Suffering Servant?

If surely not in his expectation of an early Eschaton, nor in the wonderfully accurate predictions that are assigned to Jesus, may we not find evidence of special knowledge at least in his self-understanding? Did he not certainly know that he was the Messiah who was to suffer and die for the world's redemption? Clearly, the Gospels depict him as thus aware of himself.

Take, for example, Mark 8:27–31. There, as we have noted, the evangelist places side by side Jesus' acknowledgment that he is the Christ and a saying attributed to him about his necessary suffering and death. Mark's implication is unavoidable: Jesus knew he was the Christ *and* what that would entail for him. Further, to cite the first Gospel clue to Jesus' mysterious identity, the Gospel of Mark begins in that vein. At his baptism by John, who functions as the Christ's forerunner (1:1–8), Jesus hears a heavenly voice telling him that he is the Messiah and the Isaianic Servant combined (1:9–11) – that is, the ideal Servant/King whose death will atone for the sins of all people. With texts like these in hand, no wonder the Church has traditionally viewed Jesus as one who was fully aware of his unique role in the accomplishment of God's saving purpose.

However, here again the predication of special, God-given knowledge to Jesus fares poorly against the findings of critical research. Granted, no amount of scholarly effort could conceivably disprove that he was actually God-inspired. The question reaches beyond the domain of the scientific critic. Moreover, Jesus surely believed himself to be inspired and, indeed, in a special relationship with God. He was to announce the coming kingdom of God, to summon men and women and even reprobates to join with him in recognizing its imminence, if not in fact its very presence in his own words and deeds. He spoke authoritatively of God's demand for radical obedience, more strict in its requirements than was the Law, and he dared to mention particulars. Not only that, he took it as his business to impugn the Law at points. And apparently he offered God's grace to simply anyone who would have it. Obviously then, Jesus was no ordinary rabbi or street-preacher. On this current scholars mainly are in wide agreement. Nonetheless, as most scholars see it, evidence indicates that Jesus probably neither understood himself to be the Messiah nor foresaw his own death as an atonement for sin.[19]

The messianic secret. At the forefront of evidence in this regard are matters concerning the so-called messianic secret – the idea issuing from the Gospel of Mark that Jesus commanded others to keep his identity as Messiah a secret. Of its eight appearances in Mark, six relate to miracles, which generally to early Christians were *signs* of Jesus' messiahship: healing the sick and casting out demons (1:34; 3:11–12); cleansing leprosy (1:44); curing the deaf and speech-impaired (7:36); restoring sight to the blind (8:26, where the command to silence is implicit); and raising the dead (5:43). The other two appearances are private directives to the disciples: on occasion of the Great Confession (8:30); and at the Mount of Transfiguration (9:7–9), where Peter, James, and John, in Jesus' glorified presence, are told by a heavenly voice, "This is my beloved Son." Although the Transfiguration story has been seen as legendary on every count – form, content, the disciples' subsequent unfaithful behavior – *its* authenticity is not at issue here. Rather, our concern is the authenticity of the messianic secret itself. This is also the case regarding the other incidents prompting its appearance in Mark. Were all of them merely legendary dramatizations of post-Easter beliefs, the messianic secret per se, if demonstrably or reasonably authentic, would be convincing evidence of Jesus' messianic self-awareness. When critically examined, however, the secret does not seem to

be that at all. It seems, instead, positive evidence to the contrary —
strictly a creation of Mark for purposes of his own.

To appreciate the critical issue here, one needs to consider the
difference between pericopes and ligatures. In scholarly parlance a
"pericope" is a single unit of the Jesus-tradition that circulated independently before it was eventually joined with other pericopes,
mostly in the composition of the Gospels. A "ligature," on the
other hand, is an editorial comment, a statement composed by the
Gospel writer himself to tie two or more pericopes together. This
distinction between pericopes and ligatures is especially important concerning the basic genuineness of Gospel items. In a word,
pericopes fare much better. True, some pericopes (e.g., the Transfiguration) need not have originated in historical fact. It is also possible
that a given ligature _might_ have originally come from authentic tradition. Still, basic authenticity is generally far more probable for
pericopes than for ligatures. In that regard the difference between
pericopes and ligatures can be put in two easy sentences. (1) The
pre-Gospel existence of a pericope is formally identifiable and therefore certain. (2) The pre-Gospel existence of a ligature's content
must at best be surmised.

The fact to note now is this: in every case of its Marcan appearance, the command to silence, whether implicit or spoken directly
about Jesus' messianic identity, is a ligature. It is Mark's own word,
with no formal evidence of its previous existence. That must be kept
in mind. And this also: from nothing else in the Synoptic accounts of
Jesus' ministry does it seem that he actually acknowledged himself
to be the Messiah, the Christ.

Readers familiar with the Gospels may want to question that last
statement, especially in view of Jesus' response to the high priest's
question whether he is the Christ. Most translations of Mark 14:62a
show Jesus giving a directly affirmative answer: "I am" (_ego eimi_).
However, two observations about that are in order here. _First_, what
Jesus actually said in his appearances before the Jewish authorities
and Pilate as well cannot be known. The meetings were secluded:
Jesus' followers were not privy to what transpired there. Scholars
may reasonably speculate about what occurred in general, but not
recover Jesus' verbal response(s) with any certainty. On the contrary,
it seems that Mark's descriptions of those meetings (14:55–65; 15:1–
5), which influenced later Gospel accounts of them, came largely
from his own hand.[20]

Second, regarding Mark 14:62a itself, we may also observe that
Jesus' response to the high priest's question whether he is the Christ

is debatable. The translation giving a directly affirmative answer ("I am") has difficulties working against it. (Those difficulties pertain to my general interpretation below of how Mark used the messianic secret, and this seems the easiest place to deal with them critically.) On the one hand, many Greek manuscripts contain a longer reading of Mark 14:62a which, in my judgment, is almost certainly to be preferred: "You say that I am" (or "Do you say that I am?"). The reasons for this preference are twofold. The longer, noncommittal answer to the high priest's question fits better with the rest of Mark's narration, as we are about to see. And the gist of the longer reading is also reported by Matthew (26:64) and Luke (22:70), each of whom used Mark as his major source. Were the shorter reading the original of Mark 14:62a, Matthew and/or Luke would likely have followed it for sake of a Christian confession from Jesus' own lips.[21] Would *neither* of them been attracted to that? On the other hand, if the shorter reading was in fact the original, I think Mark must have meant it as a question: "Am I?" Since the distinction between a declaration and a question in Greek did not depend on word order, *ego eimi* would permit either "I am" or "Am I?" That Mark would have intended it as a question and thus a refusal to answer directly seems clear from his presentation of Jesus as uncooperative with his accusers. In the preceding verse (14:61) it is said that initially "he was silent and made no answer" (like the Suffering Servant in Isa. 53:7). And in Mark 15:2, with Pilate asking Jesus whether he is "the King of the Jews," the question receives a noncommittal response: "You say so," or "Do you say so?" In all of it there appears a nuance that Jesus, far from claiming in public to be the Messiah, was being hit with a trumped-up charge of having done so. Interestingly, John's version of Jesus' response to the question from Pilate (18:34), though couched in a later embellishment, plainly suggests a counterfeit accusation: "Do you say this of your own accord, or did others say it to you about me?" In any case, to render Jesus' response in Mark 14:62a as a messianic self-assertion (as most critics do) needlessly entails an inconsistency in Mark's narration.

Two other Synoptic sayings might seem to be messianic self-references by Jesus (Mt. 11:27 = Lk. 10:22; and Mk. 13:32). In each of them he speaks of himself as "the son" in relation to "the Father" — a combination of terms that distinctly points to one who is "the son of God." Besides the fact that these sayings appear to be later formulations, it is certain that only in post-Easter, Christian usage was "the Son" or "the Son of God" a definite messianic title. In Jewish usage before and after Jesus' day, "God's son" had a variety of applications, some messianic, most of them not. Therefore, if Jesus ever alluded to himself as God's "son" — and there is other evidence to suggest that he did[22] — the term by itself would not have had a clear messianic import. For that to come across, he would have needed to explain it as such with regard to himself; but evidence that he did so is wanting.

So the consensus of current scholarship holds: the messianic secret aside, no saying of Jesus in the Synoptic Gospels provides historically reliable information that he acknowledged himself to be the Messiah or Christ.[23] And if my interpretation of Mark 14:62a is correct (I am indebted to others for it), the messianic secret is the _only_ Synoptic item wherein Jesus admits to being the Christ!

Since the nineteenth century, New Testament critics have been divided on the genuineness of Jesus' reported messianic self-awareness. The debate continues, at points much as it began, only now with more sophisticated critical tools. Understandably, once the messianic secret was shown to be a Marcan ligature (1901), a conservative reaction set in, especially among English-speaking scholars. In their view the secret, though reported in Mark's own words, nonetheless goes back to Jesus, who knew (or believed) himself to be the Christ.[24] He may not have made the claim publicly, which, as many recognize, would have been out of character. Yet he shared his messianic self-understanding with his disciples but cautioned them to keep it quiet, lest popular hopes for a Messiah be stirred and result in nothing good. Or because his being the Christ was a truth that each person had to grasp for himself. At the other extreme, the messianic secret was first explained as an inventive cover for the supposed, embarrassing fact that traditions about Jesus did not show him to be the Messiah during his lifetime. Throughout his narrative of Jesus' ministry, Mark used the secret to apologize for that "fact" and to give those traditions a messianic context, thusly: Jesus the Messiah desired silence of those who "knew" him to be the Messiah. Each of these positions has moderated with increased knowledge of the development of pre-Gospel and Gospel traditions.[25] But for over two decades now the pendulum has been swinging to the "skeptical" side — and there it is likely to stay.

To illustrate and summarize the problem, Mark 8:27–30 offers a nice avenue. It is the earliest Gospel report of the Great Confession of Jesus as the Christ (vss. 27–29) and his consent that he is such (vs. 30, the command to silence). Verses 27–29 derive from a pericope, but not definitely from a historically genuine remembrance. While the insignificant mention of Caesarea Philippi may hint at authenticity, Jesus' asking his disciples what others are saying about him seems artificial – as if he did not know that at least as well as they did. Artifice is also apparent in the confused assessments of Jesus by those other men, who say he is John the Baptist or Elijah or one of the prophets – figures with whom Jesus as the Christ was emphatically contrasted.[26] All told, the structure of verses 27–29 seems too neat to be coincidental. This unit therefore appears to be a post-resurrection story which properly affirms that only Jesus' followers, as opposed to other people, can correctly say who he really is (and from Mark's standpoint, as we will see, even they can say that rightly only after Jesus' death). If any particular occurrence underlies these verses, it may have been little more than a conversation between Jesus and his disciples about the reactions of other people to him, the details of which exceed our reach. But whatever occasion may lie beneath them, verses 27–29 came to Mark as a pericope, a unit of oral tradition. Verse 30, a ligature, was composed by *him.*

In view of the many Synoptic reports of Jesus' sayings, we now have only to ask a question of probability. With the possible exception of Mark 14:62a (itself historically unreliable), is it probable that Jesus' claim to being the Messiah would have been lost to oral tradition? That word would have been the most important of his words about himself or anyone else. Surely, a confessing church would receive and maintain it as such. Then how can it be that as the Great Confession began taking shape, Jesus' own agreement with its truth was, so far as we can tell, given no place in early traditions of his sayings? Extremely conservative scholarship has not been able to answer this question satisfactorily. Hence the pendulum's swing.[27]

In sum, when Jesus' response to the high priest's question is set aside as historically unreliable and even exegetically debatable, the messianic secret is the *only* Synoptic item whereby he admits to being the Christ. It thus must be reckoned as Mark's creation entirely. And Jesus must be seen, in all likelihood, as unaware of his messiahship. Some teachers (but no reputable critics) might argue that he kept the matter to himself, *ergo* the silence of oral tradition. Such reasoning, however, sniffs at evidence while favoring an *a priori* assumption which merely lines up with the post-Easter word that Jesus is indeed the Christ. One might just as well say that he also believed in the Trinity or the virginal conception but didn't let that out either. In any case it is a circular argument, beginning and concluding with the notion that Jesus had special knowledge in tune with later, Christian beliefs.

Atonement and the early kerygma. Direct inspiration from God, giving Jesus special knowledge about himself, does indeed appear in two Gospel items where he hears a heavenly voice: the account of his baptism and the Transfiguration story, both of which traditions were first recorded by Mark. As noted above, the Transfiguration "experience" – heavenly voice and all – lacks historical foundation. That leaves Mark's baptism account for us to consider here. Traditionally, readers may recall, the Church has taken the story to indicate that Jesus not only saw himself as the Christ but also knew that his death would be a sacrifice or atonement for sin. Having just dealt with his reported messianic self-awareness, we shall mainly concentrate now on the last half of that contention concerning his baptism, the part about foreknowledge of an atoning death.

The authenticity of the baptism itself is beyond any reasonable doubt – a widely shared position to be discussed in our next chapter. Not so, however, the heavenly voice telling Jesus he is Messiah and Servant of the Lord. That clearly seems a Christian formulation: a pericope, perhaps (if not Mark's own creation), but nonetheless a prophecy after the fact. Mark used the item, as I see it, to link Jesus' messiahship with a sacrificial interpretation of his death. (In the next section of this chapter, I will argue, against the view of most critics, that Mark's baptismal reference to Jesus as the Isaianic Servant, within the larger Marcan context, strongly suggests an "atonement" for sin like that of the *Suffering* Servant in Second Isaiah.)

For our present purposes, the essential authenticity-problem of Mark's baptismal narrative (1:9–11) is *not* in its "mythological" details: the opened heavens, the Spirit descending on Jesus like a dove, the heavenly voice. Among the very conservative of critical scholars today, few would insist that Jesus actually saw and heard *all that,* even in his own mind's eye and ear. Though apropos to Christian faith and Mark's intent, such details are usually conceded to be symbolic. Rather, the essential problem is whether Jesus, at his baptism or any other time, envisioned himself as the Messiah *and* the Suffering Servant. As the story suggests on its surface – and vividly, I think, by the time of Jesus' death in Mark's Gospel – did the Church's understanding of Jesus as the Christ who died for humankind's sins originate with Jesus himself?

The traditional, affirmative answer to this question is clearly presented for laypersons by John Wick Bowman.[28] We need not trace all or even most of the salient points in his argument since the general position that he represents has often been treated above in our discussion of various matters (Jesus' successful predictions, his rebuke of Peter, the messianic secret, etc.). One item, however, holds special interest here. It is his contention that the Christian concept of Jesus as "the Suffering Servant-Messiah," combining two Old Testament figures never before fully united in any known Jewish thought, is best explained as coming from Jesus' own ingenious reinterpretation of Israel's Scriptures. Such a reinterpretation, Bowman and others have reasoned in effect, was more apt to be the product of one man (Jesus) than that of a group (albeit Christian) especially since committees and their like are notoriously wanting in creativity.[29]

Well, an ingenious reinterpretation it was. And Jesus could *possibly* have come up with it by studying Old Testament prophecies and applying them anew to himself. That, at least, seems to be the implication of the heavenly voice in the baptism story (Mk. 1:11). The first half of it ("You are my beloved Son") comes from Psalm 2:7, a royal psalm used in enthronement ceremonies and eventually taken as messianic. Mark's inclusion of it seems obviously aimed to say that Jesus, already named "Christ, the Son of God" (1:1), is the long-awaited ideal king, the fulfillment of God's royal promises to Israel. The other half of the heavenly word ("with you I am well pleased") comes from Isaiah 42:1. Isaiah 42:1-4 is the first of four Servant-poems in Second Isaiah (that is, Isa. 40-55) that foretell of one who, in his self-effacing suffering and atoning death, will be God's agent for redeeming both Israel and all nations. In our next section we shall have more to say of that prophecy and Mark's own use of it. Enough to say here that its being joined with Israel's messianic hope was a stroke of genius indeed. Although each of these Old Testament figures related to the ultimate success of God's saving purpose, they were thoroughly dissimilar in identity, appearance, and fate. The Messiah was an individual, splendid in power and glory, destined to reign victoriously and make Israel great again. The Servant of the Lord, on the other hand, was a corporate entity, publicly shamed and disgraced, a set-apart people whose very success would necessarily issue in their own demise. Only from the standpoint of God's intent in Jesus, as Mark understands it, could these disparate figures of Israel's hope ever come together as one. The genius of their combined existence is therefore *God's* own genius. Hence, as we will see in Mark's Gospel, the "heavenly voice" alone can give this word first utterance, can make it a word that works. But – and no matter where or exactly when – someone had to "hear" it.

That the baptismal "heavenly voice," or better to say, what it suggests, was not transmitted via Jesus' own mind seems evident from Luke's "report" in Acts of the Church's early kerygma. At issue here are the alleged speeches of Peter and others during the Church's first days.[30] While the later, so-called Pauline kerygma (1 Cor. 15:3b–5) explicitly identifies Jesus' death as an atonement "for our sins," the purportedly early kerygma in Acts 1–12 does not. Curiously, the idea of Jesus' death being sacrificial does seem to be echoed in Luke's account of Paul's farewell speech to the Ephesian elders at Miletus — that is, in its reference to "the church of the Lord which he obtained with his own blood" (20:28). But no such suggestion is found in any of the other speeches in Acts, Paul's included. Further, forgiveness of sins is related to (_a_) Christian baptism, (_b_) repentance, (_c_) Christian belief, (_d_) the name of Jesus Christ, and (_e_) Jesus' resurrection and exaltation, yet _never directly to Jesus' death_.[31] Well now, if Jesus' disciples, on his own word to them, had believed his death to be a sacrifice for sin, it is not likely that Luke's reports of their preaching would have omitted specific mention of that idea. A unanimous belief from the first, the idea would have been of foremost importance in the Church's kerygma. "Without the shedding of blood there is no forgiveness of sins" (Heb. 9:22) was a dictum which, though an exaggeration, nevertheless reflected the Law's unflinching requirements for sacrificial offerings. And Christians with a Jewish background tended to put much stock in the Law. Hence, to the early Church, Jesus' _death_ effecting forgiveness could only have been a word to receive and proclaim with the greatest enthusiasm. So prominent and crucial a word in the Church's first preaching, its exclusion in subsequent traditions of that preaching would have been a strange reduction, to say the least.

Still, there is a critical problem to be reckoned with, particularly concerning the historical reliability of the speeches reported in Acts. Oddly enough, those who wish to defend Jesus' foreknowledge of his death as an atonement for sin may find some comfort in the severest skepticism: namely, the position that Luke's accounts of the Church's preaching are largely his own invention and so are not to be trusted. In other words, from Acts one cannot say with any certainty that the earliest Christians did _not_ preach the redemptive significance of Jesus' death. It is a sticky issue, the historical value of Acts, and heavy with unresolved questions. But for sake of our point here, we may pay respects to both sides of it, the most skeptical and the most conservative. In the long run, neither position offers much or any support for Jesus' sacrificial death being an item in the Church's initial preaching.

On the one hand, critical scholarship has increasingly come to recognize that Luke, in composing Acts, used his sources (whatever they were) quite freely in accord with his own special concerns. Describing a steady, God-empowered movement of the gospel from its beginnings among Jews in Jerusalem to the far reaches of the Gentile world (culminating with Paul in Rome), he was certainly creative. Furthermore, he was either apologetic regarding Paul's differences with leaders of the Jerusalem church[32] or fairly ignorant of Paul's message and ministry, or both apologetic and poorly informed. In any case, "kerygmatic" speeches seem tailored to Luke's own theological/historical purpose; ecclesiastical disagreements about Christians' observance of the Law are glossed over; and great motifs of Paul's preaching are absent – to mention only some of the difficulties attending the historical reliability of Acts.[33] Nevertheless, all commentators agree that Luke could not have written Acts without at least some sources at his disposal. And therein lies what seems an insuperable difficulty regarding the earliest Church's preaching forgiveness through Jesus' death. Were that Pauline word not even echoed in Acts 20:28, its absence in Luke's report of Paul's preaching would be easier to explain than its omission in the speeches attributed to Peter and company. Fragmentary materials about Paul's message, having come to Luke presumably late from Hellenistic Christendom, might conceivably omit the word. Gentile Christians, impervious to the Law's demands for atoning sacrifices, would not on their own be compelled to see forgiveness as necessarily related to Jesus' death. The case is far different, however, for sources about the Church's earliest preaching in Palestine. Originating in a Jewish Christian community, such sources (as already indicated) would surely have made Jesus' death "for our sins" unmistakably prominent, *if* that was part of the Church's initial understanding of his redemptive significance. Nor would the chance of its being subsequently omitted, either in Luke's sources or by Luke himself, seem very likely. In the development of Christian traditions, items of christological importance were customarily added to the traditions, not subtracted from them. Also, though Luke appears to have been unconcerned to present Jesus' death as a sacrifice for sin, there is positive evidence indicating that he did not find the idea offensive.[34] Best therefore to conclude that Luke's sources for the Church's earliest preaching did not refer to Jesus' death as a sacrifice *and* that those sources lacked the idea because it had not been part of the earliest preaching.

On the other hand, some scholars, holding a far more conservative view of the early speeches in Acts, recognize Lucan embellishments but still regard the speeches as essentially reliable materials for uncovering the Church's early kerygma.[35] In this view Acts 10:36–43, Peter's speech in the home of Cornelius, is especially pertinent. It is thought to be a kerygmatic formula derived from Aramaic (the language then of Palestinian Jews) and reflecting rather fully the basic beliefs of the young Jerusalem church. If that be so, its silence about Jesus' atoning death is, in fact, weighty evidence against the idea's having been among the Church's first confessions. Granted, one might argue that the idea seems to be _implicitly_ there, in verse 43: "To him [i.e., the crucified and risen Christ] all the prophets bear witness that every one who believes in him receives forgiveness of sins through his name." But such a circumlocutory reference to Jesus' death as a Servant-kind of sacrifice is highly improbable, scarcely to be found in a kerygmatic formula that emanated from Jerusalem. To the Christian community there, Jewish in makeup and mind-set, Jesus' _death_ effecting forgiveness of sins would, I repeat, have been beyond significant measure — and beyond any mention that was only vaguely implicit in a statement of basic beliefs. Had they initially believed Jesus' death to be atoning, Jerusalem Christians would have shouted the word. That they _eventually_ came to see it as a sacrifice for sin, given their belief in Jesus' fulfillment of the Scriptures, is understandable. But not their formulating a confession of faith that failed to mention the idea directly, especially if they had received the idea from Jesus himself!

Conclusion. Again we are compelled to conclude, this time concerning his messianic identity and unique role in God's purpose, that Gospel reports attributing special knowledge to Jesus are post-resurrection expressions. Rather than representing his own self-awareness or even originating all at once, they developed gradually as the Church, empowered to life through its Easter experience, increasingly came to a new understanding of Jesus' person and redemptive significance. This conclusion, incidentally, is further confirmed by the absence of any saying from Jesus designed to correct popular notions of the Messiah's splendor and nationalistic role, aligning the external appearance and fate of the Messiah with those of the Suffering Servant. However, to say that he did not perceive himself as Messiah and/or Suffering Servant by no means suggests that such designations failed to fit him. On the contrary, Christian faith is much obliged to affirm that Jesus of Nazareth was all that and more. Yet in keeping with the origins and growth of the Jesus-tradition, only from this side of Easter, and only through Christian eyes at that, can people not be confused about who he was and is.

The Mystery of Messiahship in Mark

While the main point of this chapter is made — Jesus apparently possessed no special or suprahuman knowledge — our discussion, necessarily, has been largely negative. Moreover, it has probably raised several questions which, for general readers, we would be unfair and misleading to leave unanswered. For one, why does Mark, in his use of received traditions, so regularly make the disciples look like numskulls, incapable of faith, as it were? For another, how is that related to the confession of Jesus' being the Christ and, especially, to the messianic secret? Indeed, why in Mark's account of Jesus' ministry should that confession be *kept* a secret? And what in the world are we to get from Mark today, given the realities of literary-historical criticism? Does a critical approach to Mark's Gospel merely dispel popular misconceptions about Jesus and events surrounding him? Or is that approach actually helpful in coming to terms with authentic Christian belief?

So we must attempt to fashion a positive word now, yet not too simplistic a one. Such questions ought to be answered, of course. But answers, if critically informed and presented clearly, can hardly be succinct. Moreover, from a scholarly viewpoint the thrust of this section is debatable; and matters discussed above will often be repeated or extended for clarity's sake. It is nonetheless hoped that the discussion here will bring things together and serve a positive end.

The messianic secret in Mark, an editorial creation as we have seen, must ultimately be understood in relation to the whole of Mark's Gospel.[36] When so viewed, the secret concerns not simply that Jesus *is* the Messiah but, more importantly, what *kind* of Messiah. Not just his messianic identity, but the nature of his messiahship is the ultimate mystery that is beyond even his disciples' comprehension. As Mark tells of Jesus' ministry, it is not too much to say that his is a messiahship which, however those disciples might be instructed by the "historical" Jesus himself, they *cannot* comprehend. Hence Mark's use of traditions in making the disciples appear thicker-headed than they no doubt were.

The disciples' dullness. Particularly in relation to the other appearances of the messianic secret and to Jesus' alleged predictions of his suffering and death and resurrection, the Great Confession that Jesus is the Christ (8:27–30, including the secret) is generally recognized as crucial in Mark's Gospel. In other words, the Great Confession of Jesus' messiahship, incorporating his Mark-initiated agreement with it, is the watershed of Mark's Gospel – the high or turning point to which all previous items lead and in "explanation" of which everything thereafter follows. Give or take critical qualifications, the observation seems rather safe. At the same time, outlines of Mark's Gospel, offered to elucidate his primary purpose in writing, have failed to produce a consensus. Scholars, who must work with their own critical inclinations anyway, are left in the lurch regarding the issue: Mark doesn't *say* what his purpose is. Instead, like many New Testament writings, his Gospel owns something of an esoteric quality. Though not intentionally arcane, as if to befuddle hostile readers, it assumes that readers will be "in the know." Mark's purpose in writing is a mystery today, much as Jesus' messiahship is always a mystery. Nevertheless, the disciples' inability to comprehend the nature of that messiahship was surely a significant motif within Mark's purpose. To put the matter as bluntly as he depicts it, those poor fellows never get the point. Accordingly, Mark's account of their relationship with Jesus can be divided into three major sections that present, overall, the disciples' progressive failure to understand who Jesus of Nazareth is.[37]

In the first section (1:16–8:26), prefaced by an introduction heralding Jesus as the Messiah/Servant of Yahweh and thus by implication the bringer of eschatological redemption (1:1–15), the disciples are at a loss regarding his identity and universal significance. This, in spite of a host of clues: Jesus' performing mighty works galore (signs of the messianic age), claiming authority to forgive sins and "proving" it (2:1–12), calling himself "lord even of the sabbath" (2:28), hauling Jewish customs and aspects of the Law itself into question (7:1–23), and so on. The *demons* recognize Jesus as the Messiah/Son of God (1:24; 3:11), but the disciples do not. Their best word, evoked by his having saved their lives at sea, is a question they cannot answer: "Who then is this, that even wind and sea obey him?" (4:41). Likewise, while speaking of it to all others only through parables, Jesus directly shares with the twelve "the secret of the kingdom of God," privately explaining everything to them (4:10–34) – but their dullness prevails. From the residue of his feeding miracles (twelve and seven baskets full, numbers signifying

Israel and completeness), they fail to perceive that the new people of God is being formed of Jews and Gentiles together (8:14–21). "Do you not yet understand?" Jesus asks them twice, as if amazed at their having eyes and ears for nothing (8:17, 21).

The next two sections (8:27–14:9 and 14:10–72) are marked by misconception and rejection, respectively. In these sections the evangelist makes it clear that the disciples, whose behavior and aspirations collide with Jesus' teachings, are not themselves to blame for their inability to comprehend his messiahship. Their comprehending it ever before Easter is simply not in the cards. With his own death approaching, Jesus assures them that they "will all fall away," *as indeed they must* (14:27). Consistent with that, though now confessing Jesus' messiahship (8:27–29), they do not understand his lessons concerning it (8:31–38) — namely, what it will mean for him (suffering, death, resurrection) and what it requires of them (self-sacrificial discipleship). Hence Peter's objection to Jesus' first Passion-resurrection prediction and Jesus' response: Peter, confessor of Jesus as the Christ, is "not on the side of God, but of men" (8:33). This, mind you, spoken to one who, all the same, is unquestionably on *Jesus'* side! So also Mark's ensuing treatment of the Transfiguration: *the* mountaintop experience goes for naught. "This is my beloved Son," the privileged three disciples are told from above; "listen to him" (9:7) — that is, instead of listening merely to the Law and the prophets (represented by Moses and Elijah, who appear with Jesus only to vanish). But, as Mark carries on, the disciples are unable to shake free of their religious heritage, particularly regarding the nature of Jesus' messiahship and its consequences for them. They can *only* listen to him, not understand his teachings as Messiah. Those teachings continue to baffle them (9:10, 32, 38; 10:13–15), they are concerned about which one of themselves is the greatest (9:33–34), and James and John want the best seats in Jesus' glory (10:35–37). Oh boy, oh boy!

To the disciples, as to every contemporary Jew with eschatological hopes, a Messiah who must suffer and die (without even a fight) is an impossible concept. So when Jesus' "hour" arrives at his being arrested, they all forsake him and flee (14:50). And in Mark's Gospel, save the following material regarding Peter's denial (14:54, 66–72), that is the last to be seen of them. Nothing — not even predictions which, we have seen, Mark has coming into reality right and left — *nothing* can bring those disciples out of hiding, still less make them look toward Jesus' resurrection. Rather, the mystery of his messiahship is beyond every one of them even as Mark's Gospel abruptly ends.[38] Only later will they understand and speak the good news (13:9–11).

Within the Marcan framework of Jesus' ministry, seeing is not believing. The disciples as well as the demons see Jesus of Nazareth, mighty works and all. Though both groups confess his messiahship, neither can penetrate its meaning. The trouble, as we shall observe, is that their confessions precede his death. Moreover, even the first witnesses of the empty tomb, informed by an angel that Jesus has risen, are struck dumb with astonishment and fear (16:1–8). None of it seems to make any sense. And that, precisely, is where Mark leaves it!

But yet...

A clue to the mystery. In recollection of how Jesus' experience *begins* in Mark's Gospel, with the heavenly voice addressing him as God's Son and Servant (1:11), a clue to the mystery of his messiahship may also be found at the *end* of his experience. It comes from the lips of a Gentile given to commanding attention. Mark tells that when Jesus "breathed his last" and "the curtain of the temple was torn in two, from top to bottom" (15:37b–38), the presiding centurion, observing that last breath, immediately said, "Truly this man was the Son of God!" (15:39).[39] The centurion's cry is the only explicit, public confession of Jesus' messiahship that Mark allows to stand uncontested – that is, without being silenced or qualified.[40] This seems to suggest that Jesus as the Son of God must be understood in relation to atonement or not be understood at all. Only when the Temple veil is rent asunder, the barrier of sin between God and humanity destroyed by God himself in Jesus' death – only then and there can the mystery of Christ, with all its awesome implications, unfold in eschatological triumph. To be sure, Mark could not have written apart from the Church's Easter experience. Christian faith as he knew it would not then have existed. Nonetheless, from Mark's point of view, the risen Christ is no Christ apart from his atoning death.

Is Jesus the Suffering Servant? Several New Testament scholars of high and worthy esteem have concluded that Mark had no interest in Jesus' death as an atoning sacrifice.[41] Distinguishing between pericopes (traditions received) and ligatures (editorial comments), they note, among other things, that the Marcan ligatures lack explicitly sacrificial connotations. To put it simply, Mark added no words of his own stating in effect that Jesus died for our sin(s). However, the intent of a Gospel writer is to be sought not only in his personal comments but also in his particular use of traditional materials. How he structures those materials, leading from one to another and thereby developing certain motifs, surely conveys his meaning at least as much as do his own words. And it goes without saying that a gifted writer/editor may well be subtle in this — and all the more when a *mystery* is being revealed.

So it is with Mark. The movement of his Gospel, relative to the mystery of Christ, seems sacrificial to the core. And, as mentioned above, such is the case from the start of it: in the heavenly reference to Jesus' being the Isaianic Servant (1:11b, quoting from Isa. 42:1). Admittedly Mark's only precise reference to Jesus as the Servant, it does not *by itself* indicate a sacrificial interpretation of his death. That is because the reference is to the first Servant-poem (Isa. 42:1-4), not the fourth (52:13-53:12) — and only in the latter is the Servant described as one who will suffer and die as an offering for sin. However, I find it difficult to imagine that Mark at 1:11 did not intend to *imply* a sacrificial meaning for Jesus as Messiah/Servant. Why? Because from there on a sacrificial death is artfully suggested at crucial points in Mark's Gospel.

For example, Mark 8:27-10:45, a section dealing with traditions of special revelation and private instruction to the disciples, begins and ends with teachings that Jesus, as the Christ and the Son of man, must suffer and die and be raised (8:27-32) and, having come as a servant, is "to give his life as a ransom for many" (10:45). Although "ransom" (*lutron*) appears nowhere else in the New Testament,[42] the external affinity of the saying with Isaiah 53:11-12 hardly seems insignificant in *Mark's* use of it.[43] For immediately thereafter he sets the stage for Jesus' entry into Jerusalem as the Messiah *whose business it is to be a sacrifice.*

Blind Bartimaeus, a beggar sitting by the roadside to Jericho, twice hails Jesus as "Son of David" (10:46-48). That is a royal "title" with nationalistic overtones. *Therefore,* Bartimaeus's exemplary faith notwithstanding, Mark sees it as a title in need of immediate qualification.[44] Hence his ensuing account of the Triumphal Entry, which in one stroke brings Jesus not merely into Jerusalem but, particularly, into the Temple, the house of sacrifice (11:1-11). Like Bartimaeus's bold greetings, the crowd's tribute to Jesus along the way bespeaks hope of a nationalistic Messiah, not a suffering one (11:9-10). So Mark, in distinction from Matthew and Luke, appends to the Triumphal Entry-tradition a statement (11:11, probably of his own making) tying the messianic entry with a visit of Jesus to the Temple. Significantly, Jesus does nothing in the Temple. He only looks around at everything and departs. But, the point is made! The Messiah is to be known in view of what the Temple distinctively is: namely, Israel's one and only lawful slaughtering place for sacrificial victims.

In this case, as so often is true of Gospel items, the meaning is in the action. Before Mark got his hands on it, the Entry-tradition simply reenacted the messianic prophecy of Zechariah 9:9:

> Rejoice greatly, O daughter of Zion!
> Shout aloud, O daughter of Jerusalem!
> Lo, your king comes to you;
> triumphant and victorious is he,
> humble and riding on an ass,
> on a colt the foal of an ass.

While that traditional reenactment dramatized Christian belief in Jesus' messiahship,[45] even pointing up its inherently humble character, Mark's extending the action into the Temple could scarcely have been aimless. With loud hosannas still ringing — "Blessed is he who comes in the name of the Lord! Blessed is the kingdom of our father David that is coming!" — and with Bartimaeus's confession only verses past, the "Son of David" hurries into the house of sacrifice. Thus begins Passion Week, according to Mark. And one is reminded of the heavenly voice as Jesus' ministry itself was about to begin, naming him God's Son and Servant joined in one person. If literary structure means anything — and additional evidence will appear below — the Marcan Messiah is the *Suffering* Servant, the sacrifice *par excellence*.

The Isaianic Servant who dies yet lives. There are other indications in Mark of Jesus' death as an atonement for sin: most noticeably, (1) the words of institution of the Lord's Supper (14:22–24), a post-Easter liturgical formula that speaks of Jesus' "blood of the covenant"; and (2) the crucifixion narrative (15:16–39), which culminates in the rending of the Temple curtain and the centurion's confession of Jesus as "the Son of God." To appreciate the eschatological force of these and still other Servant-like items, however, it is necessary first to consider the Servant in Second Isaiah itself — that strange, enigmatic figure of hope with whom Jesus is identified at the outset of Mark's Gospel.

According to the Servant-prophecies in Second Isaiah,[46] the "Servant of the Lord" will perform a mission of all-encompassing significance. When he is finished with it, nothing will remain to be done but for the world to stand in dumbfounded astonishment before him and his accomplishments (52:14–15). Though "despised and rejected by men; a man of sorrows, and acquainted with grief" (53:3a), he will establish "justice in the earth" (42:4a) and will bear "the iniquity of us all" (53:6b). Indeed, he will offer himself in suffering and death as a kind of once-for-all sacrifice for sin (53:10a, 12b). Through him will be redeemed not only Israel but "the nations" as well; salvation shall reach "to the end of the earth" (49:6). During the course of his mission, however, the Servant's identity and redemptive significance will be hidden from public knowledge, like "a polished arrow" tucked away by God "in his quiver" (49:2). Even those to be helped by him will not, at the time, esteem him (53:3b). Only when his task is completed, when the Servant is dead and referred to in the past tense – only then will his previously unheard-of significance be seen and understood (52:15b; 53:4ff.). *Yet,* while destined by God to die and be no more, the Servant will continue to live: "He shall see his offspring, he shall prolong his days; . . . he shall see the fruit of the travail of his soul and be satisfied" (53:10b–11a).

In the Servant-prophecies, therefore, one encounters a curious set of opposites, as if history and human thought were in for a turnaround. Through a violation of justice, justice will be established. Thus will the Servant be shamed but not shamed (50:7b), incognito in life but recognized in death, and, most curious of all, simultaneously dead and alive. It sounds like the end of the world – and so it is for the prophet. But to grasp even his barest meaning in these eschatological opposites, we must inquire of the Servant's identity.

Who then *is* this Servant of the Lord according to the unknown author of Second Isaiah (or, perhaps, the unknown author of the Servant-prophecies inserted in Second Isaiah)? Scholarly opinions have varied widely. They range all the way from (1) a historical individual (e.g., the prophet himself) to (2) a corporate figure (e.g., the city of Jerusalem) to (3) a mixture of the two (i.e., the so-called fluid concept, which maintains that the prophet had an individual in mind at times but, at other times, was thinking of a group of people).[47] Most recent opinions, however, seem to favor a wholly corporate interpretation, and rightly so. Although the Servant is depicted as an individual and, in the second and third poems, speaks in the first person singular, the only name given to him is "my servant,

Israel" (49:3) — and at that point the Servant is doing the speaking (telling what God has named him). Assuming single authorship of the poems, that name, Israel, seems sufficient to rule out a historical personage, either known or yet to arrive. Similarly, the fluid concept of the Servant's identity, while clever in itself, seems a bit too clever. It is unnecessarily complicated and, at that, largely a product of Christian exegesis. Believing that the Servant-prophecies have been fulfilled in an individual (Jesus), those scholars who initially fostered the concept appear to have read their own faithful inclinations back into the prophet's mind.[48] All of which is to say, there is no compelling reason to see the Servant in Second Isaiah itself except as a corporate figure, a personification of Israel, albeit a holy-remnant Israel. The Servant is an Israel within Israel: a faithful, obedient group through whom will be redeemed the remainder of Israel and all other nations besides. Precisely what group that is, and precisely how they will bring it off in a hostile, unjust world, the prophet doesn't say. But God, who is to fashion the Servant from the womb (49:1, 5), will see to it that his mission succeeds.

In this corporate sense of the Servant's identity, the eschatological opposites within the prophecy, especially the otherwise unthinkable ones of a simultaneously dead and living Servant, come together naturally, so to speak. As the Servant succeeds in his universal mission, bringing *all* nations into the fellowship of God's redeemed, *his* peculiar existence will, of course, end. For then, with salvation overtaking the earth, the erstwhile people of God will no longer be God's special people, set apart from everyone else. Suppose, for purposes of an analogy, that a college fraternity opened its doors to all students and that every student on campus became an active member of it. The fraternity as a fraternity, meaning an exclusive club, would then cease to exist, *even though* those members who voted to open the doors might still be around to see the results of their action. Likewise, the Servant's guaranteed success guarantees his own demise. The good elite people of God, despised and rejected by men, must therefore be struck down by God himself as their boundaries are enlarged to include all people among their number. And they, smitten thus by God and afflicted (53:4), will surely be satisfied to see their offspring as righteous and one with themselves (53:10–11).

This is to say, among other things, that the Servant's sacrifice in Second Isaiah is a bloodless sacrifice. It is not a man, much less a helpless animal victim, who must die to bear "the iniquity of us all." Rather, the completion of God's purpose will spell the death of a favored people by favoring, instead, all people. And that, indeed, will establish "justice in the earth." *For* "by his knowledge [Heb. *daath*, intimate relationship] shall the righteous one, my servant, make many to be accounted righteous" (53:11b). Ultimately united with the Servant, the many (i.e., all, as opposed to the few) are to share in his righteousness. What the prophet envisioned, therefore, was not atonement via bloodletting but atonement via suffering for righteousness' sake and, somehow inherent in that, the creation of a new humanity, the new people of God no less.

Jesus' Servant-messiahship and the end of the world. In the makeup of his Gospel, Mark's depiction of Jesus' ministry seems too closely aligned with the Servant-prophecies to be mere happenstance. Serendipity in writing occurs, of course, but not all over the place.

Having heard the heavenly voice at his baptism (1:11), Jesus alone knows his own true identity: the Messiah/Servant who has come, he says, "not to be served but to serve, and to give his life as a ransom for many" (10:45). Those who may *think* they know who he is — the demons,[49] the disciples,[50] people beholding his mighty works[51] — do not know that, in fact *cannot* know it, while Jesus is still alive. So they are directed to hold their tongues or, in one case of vociferous demons, are driven away into speechless pigs (5:13). Like faithful Bartimaeus's confession of Jesus' Davidic sonship (10:46–48), *whatever* those confessors might say about him is bound to be misleading, without knowledge of him as the Servant whose death brings salvation to Israel and the world (cf. 8:14–21). His messiahship must therefore be kept a secret until his death (and resurrection, in juncture with previous traditions, but Mark cannot wait for that!). And so it remains in Mark's Gospel, even when friends and foes rattle on about it.

None of this means that Marcan confessors of Jesus' messiahship are wrong in what they say of him. On the contrary, even those who mock Jesus as "King of the Jews" speak the truth about him (as would the Servant's detractors in deeming him "smitten by God"; Isa. 53:4b). Upon his being condemned, Roman soldiers hail and treat Jesus as a helpless king (15:16–20) — and so he is. The chief priests and scribes at Golgotha are even more articulate in speaking of "the Christ, the King of Israel" (15:32). They state: "He saved others; he cannot save himself" (15:31). Indeed. The fate of "Israel's" Servant/King, whose atoning role makes him die and also live, is not his own to manage. Similarly, *all* confessors of Jesus as Messiah in Mark, whether friendly or hostile or demon-possessed, are correct in their confessions. Like those who falsely accuse Jesus of threatening to destroy and replace the Temple (14:58), they bespeak his redemptive significance.[52] They tell the truth about him. But prior to his death they do not know the truth. The meaning of their words escapes them.

That predicament is what maintains the messianic secret in Mark, to the end of Jesus' life. Despite Jesus' repeated desire for silence, men rattle on concerning his being "the Christ," "the Son of God," "Son of David," "King of the Jews." When spoken of him by humans, these titles, in their Marcan contexts, betray a growing confusion about who the living Jesus is. Not surprisingly, confused utterance of them intensifies as he nears the city and the time of his death – the where and when of its public viewing.[53] To Mark, it would seem, the rattling can only intensify as the crucial moment draws nigh. For who the Servant is, and what his mission in suffering is, others can only mistake before the Servant dies. Hence, while the silence about Jesus' messiahship is broken time and again, the secret of it holds on.

His real identity thus hidden from everyone else – the polished arrow secreted by God in his quiver! – Jesus goes around teaching the kingdom of God's righteousness and doing good works, yet repeatedly he is "despised and rejected by men." Indeed, after the heavenly voice at 1:11, there follows in Mark a crescendo of pre-Passion clues and notes of rejection and suffering. The reader is thereby increasingly led to see Jesus, even before his arrest and death, as the "man of sorrows, and acquainted with grief."[54] To say the least, the frequency of such items is impressive: 2:15-17, 20; 3:2, 6, 21-22, 31-35; 5:40; 6:1-6; 8:11-13, 31-33, 34; 9:9, 11-13, 30-32, 35; 10:2, 32-34, 38-39, 45; 11:1-11 (as explained above), 18; 12:6-8, 10, 12, 13-15; 14:1-2, 7-8, 10-12, 18-21, 22-24, 27, 30, 32-36, 41-42.

While that crescendo builds toward its climax at the cross, only the apocalyptic discourse of chapter 13 offers pause concerning Jesus' Servant-like rejection and suffering. Yet what is said there about the end of the world is introduced by a saying *which Mark occasioned* to herald the end of Israel, itself a Servant-motif. Namely, the Temple will be destroyed (13:1-2), as surely it must be in Mark's understanding of Jesus' universal, eschatological role as Servant of the Lord. A building of perpetual sacrifice and Jewish religious exclusiveness, "a den of robbers" instead of "a house of prayer for all the nations" (11:17), it cannot be merely cleansed. Rather, in Mark's use of tradition, all activity there in behalf of Israel's sacrificial cult is brought by Jesus to a standstill (11:15-16)! Likewise, in what the

Temple represents, the structure has to come down, same as the barren fig tree, also representative of Israel, must surely wither and die (11:12–14, 20).[55] In God's creation of a new Israel in Christ the old Israel is to be destroyed completely, at its foundation and roots, according to the metaphors of Temple and tree. That the Temple had *been* destroyed by the time he wrote was, for Mark, an apocalyptic sign that the end of the world had already begun in the life and death of Messiah/Servant Jesus, which meant the death of old Israel as well. Or so it seems to me.

In any case, the similarities of Jesus to the prophesied Servant should hardly be dismissed in Mark. And it is in his mission as the *Suffering* Servant, culminating in his death and resurrection, that Mark's disclosure of the mystery of Jesus' messiahship seems most full of meaning. Smitten by God and afflicted, he cries with the psalmist, "My God, my God, why hast thou forsaken me?" (15:34; Ps. 22:1). Also like the psalmist, however, he only *appears* to be forsaken, just as the Servant in Second Isaiah was to be shamed but not shamed. Completing Mark's many crucifixion allusions to Psalm 22, Jesus' often termed "cry of dereliction" is instead the prelude to coming triumph, as in Psalm 22 itself. Mark uses the saying to highlight Jesus' own knowledge that his fate is controlled by God and is good. Like the Servant who alone would know that he was destined to die and yet live, Jesus is the only person in Mark's crucifixion story who understands his dying situation. In immediate contrast (15:35–36), some bystanders hear his cry to God and promptly mistake it!

Also like the corporate Servant in Second Isaiah, Jesus, though a victim, is neither a lost nor a lonely one. For in him all humankind seems to die in order to be re-formed. As the Servant named "Israel" was to be "numbered with the transgressors" in his atoning, once-for-all death (Isa. 53:12), Jesus, well before his own death, binds himself to the lowest of people. He *eats* with publicans and sinners (2:15–17) – an act which, according to the Semitic view of eating and drinking, makes him *one* with them. How early that action appears in Mark! And, notably, it appears in immediate preface to Mark's presentation of two sayings about (1) the bridegroom's (i.e., Jesus') death and (2) the inadequacy of old wineskins to hold new wine (2:18–22). This early clue to the mystery of messiahship is artistically subtle, yet nonetheless forceful: in Jesus Christ's Servant-sacrifice, which incorporates sinners in his own righteous person, the old becomes passé as the new is brought into being. *Publicans* even, the most despicable people and least likely candidates for rightful membership in the old Israel, are being accounted righteous in the New Israel of the Messiah/Suffering Servant![56]

This all-inclusive import of Jesus' sacrifice, involving his life as well as his death, perhaps best explains why no precise theory of atonement comes to the fore in Mark. A precise theory, especially one expressing penal substitution, or even forgiveness of sins via Jesus' _blood,_ would detract from the saving character of his entire ministry and from the all-embracing, eschatological significance of his Servant-suffering, -rejection, and -death. However that may be, when his mission is done and Jesus of Nazareth breathes his last, the Temple curtain is torn in two. Thus in Jesus' death the way is opened to the Holy of Holies, that innermost sanctum of God's presence into which Jews alone could gain vicarious entrance through the high priest's annual sacrificing there. At the sight of that last breath, only _then_ — and this one time from Gentile lips! — does Mark permit public confession of Jesus' messiahship to stand on its own (15:37–39). The mystery that began at 1:11 with the heavenly but ambiguous reference to Jesus as Messiah/Servant, the mystery that carried on with applications of the equally ambiguous "Son of man" title to him, the mystery that stumped his closest disciples, indeed the mystery that not even he could reveal to them in life — that mystery is full out for the reader at last. The Servant is dead and, yes, in a sense, old Israel and the old world too. Long live the Servant!

The meaning for faith. Let no one suppose, however, that the mystery of Jesus' Servant-messiahship is something merely to be explained or fully understood, as if christology might get by with a kerygmatic smugness or arid intellectualism. Of all responses to Jesus, Mark seems to condone personal indifference the least. Over and again in Mark's account of the public ministry, Jesus' words and actions properly evoke amazement or even fear.[57] Likewise, in parallel to the dumbfounded astonishment prophesied of those who would see the Servant and his accomplishments (Isa. 52:14–15), the first witnesses to the resurrection — and in Mark's abrupt ending, the _only_ witnesses to it — are amazed, in fact terrified, to the point of silence concerning it (16:6–8). Although directed by the angel to tell his disciples that they will see the risen Jesus in Galilee as promised (cf. 14:28), the women "went out and fled from the tomb; for trembling and astonishment had come upon them; and they said nothing to any one, for they were afraid" (16:8). While the silence of those women is surely no model for a confessing church, we can sympathize with their reported amazement and fear. For Jesus' mysterious Servant-messiahship, albeit revealed and alive among us, exceeds our ability to rationalize, much more our ability to confine or control. Just so, Mark leaves us to wonder about our own response to the gospel, to imagine what *we* should be doing, and doing in our weakness, to witness to its power.[58]

Conclusion

Weakness. Good weakness comes from human limitations. It can come from not knowing all, or even very much, yet knowing enough not to pretend otherwise. Hence, the summons to Christian disciple-ship levels a requirement that is anything but dissimilar to what was required of the historical Jesus himself. That is, well-placed commit-ment and trust — authentic faith which, while serving with limited knowledge and therefore anxious at times and capable of being mis-taken, nevertheless seeks the kingdom of God's righteousness in being with and for others and leaves the future to God. According to the author of Hebrews (1:1ff.), it is that kind of faith, uninhibited by suprahuman endowments, that made Jesus of Nazareth superior to the angels.

Chapter 3

Without Sense of Being a Sinner?

*For our sake he made him to be sin who knew no sin, so that
in him we might become the righteousness of God.*
— 2 Corinthians 5:21

*For we have not a high priest who is unable to sympathize
with our weaknesses, but one who in every respect has been
tempted as we are, yet without sinning.*
— Hebrews 4:15 (cf. 7:26–27)

Was Jesus of Nazareth guiltless in his own mind? To answer this
question affirmatively, as most Christians seem inclined to, would
suggest for him an abnormal human experience. Popular notions of
Jesus' divinity might be served thereby, but his common humanity
with us would not. The latter, in fact, would be tarnished since guilt
is a fundamental aspect of our human condition. Our sense of ought-
ness — "the moral imperative" it is sometimes called — takes care of
that. Whether believing in God or even in sin, we make demands of
ourselves that we fail to meet. We demand ourselves to be good and
to act in goodness toward others. When we behave contrary to those
demands, we experience guilt as persons self-accused. Forgiveness
or being accepted/loved by others may remove guilt as an emotional
burden, but not guilt as a personal fact. From that singular fact there
is no escape open to healthy, complete human beings. Happily for
his humanity as well as for the people around him, Jesus apparently
did not consider himself to be sinless. In that he was like us, despite
normal Christian thinking about him.

Ever since the divinity of Jesus took hold in Christian thought,
the doctrine has kept close company with the Church's regular confession that he was sinless. However, that does not appear to have
been the original function of the confession. In relying on it, Paul

and the author of Hebrews were primarily interested not in Jesus' divinity but in his having effected an atonement for sin that entailed a perfect sacrifice – a sacrifice of self in utter obedience to God. So, too, its use in 1 Peter 2:22–24, where Jesus' significance as sinless is given in terms of the sacrificial Servant of Isaiah 53. Similarly, the only other explicit New Testament reference to the matter is sacrificial: "He appeared to take away sins, and in him there is no sin" (1 Jn. 3:5). Early interest in Jesus' sinlessness, it therefore seems clear, was concerned with his making atonement, not with his being divine. Even so, the latter connection was bound to be made as christological developments turned increasingly toward the divine. In a word, if the historical Jesus was divine, he would surely have been sinless as well.

No doubt the idea of Jesus' utter righteousness preceded that of his thoroughgoing divinity. The former idea, but not the latter, could have been inferred from the Church's early belief that Jesus was the Christ. For the promised Messiah was described as specially righteous yet was expected to be completely human. At the very least, therefore, Jesus' sinlessness would have been a relatively easy inference from Old Testament promises concerning the Christ (even though faithful imagination was needed in that). On the other hand, thoughts about his unique divinity would require the influence of additional and later factors.

But we need not engage here in a circular debate. It is enough simply to observe that no christology heralding Jesus' own divinity could have well run the race of Christian tradition minus the supporting idea that sin had no part in him. To a church informed by the Scriptures, divinity implies moral perfection. And that spells *sinlessness*. Was Jesus of Nazareth really divine? If so, according to Western Christendom's logic, he was really and thoroughly good – all good in word and deed and good to the core of his being.

To that assumption we must soon return, especially as it conflicts with what appears to be Jesus' view of himself as a sinner. The evidence for Jesus' self-image in this regard has been an embarrassment to Christian faith. But it need not be, as I intend to show along three lines. (1) Jesus' sense of being a sinner attests to his authentic humanity as a historical figure – a man in his own time and long-standing culture. (2) It actually reflects his goodness, particularly as he brought a "new" goodness to bear against what Jewish culture had largely become. And (3) the very traditions that suggest Jesus' self-image as a sinner provided Mark with acute opportunity to depict him as the utterly righteous man – a use to which Mark faithfully and properly put those traditions, yet without shading them to play down their embarrassing suggestion.

Before looking at the pertinent evidence, however, we must qualify our comments concerning it.

God Alone Is Judge

Was Jesus of Nazareth a sinner?

An *absolute* answer goes begging. Assuming the existence of God who demands righteousness of people, one's answer to the question depends, in the first place, on a set of values that cannot be demonstrated scientifically. And in the second place, even if such values could somehow be agreed upon, the reliable evidence in Jesus' case is so very limited that a "factual" answer escapes historical speculation.

Human values and the will of God. In the final analysis, whether a person is or ever was a sinner is not for us to say absolutely. In heaven and on earth (especially on earth where we have eyes to see) the question involves definitions of terms that are determined arbitrarily. By that I mean the definitions cannot be empirically verified, as can be the valence of iron or the overspin on a tennis ball. They are posited in conjunction with *a priori* assumptions about the nature of reality and the character of good and evil. As such, they serve as myths — necessary myths, of course, if social chaos is to be avoided; but they are locked to assumptions that cannot be proved, whatever their social worth.

Take, for example, the term "sin" and one of its counterparts, "love." While a general definition of sin might gain widespread acceptance (e.g., "any want of conformity to the will of God"), its particular applications are loaded with value judgments regarding God's will, and those values do not sit still. Is God against divorce or, for that matter, penny-ante poker? It all depends on whom you are talking with and, quite often, when and under what circumstances. Similarly, the command to love, in and of itself, lacks specific gravity. Though all Christians hold it to be binding, we must pump particular content into what "love" means concerning particular issues and moments. And so we do. Yet we do so from varied standpoints that bespeak different, often contradictory views of reality, both perceived and imagined. Hence the conflicting positions one readily finds among sincere, serious ethicists regarding such matters as abortion and euthanasia. The basic problem is not that one position is more realistic or better informed than another (however sophisticated or silly any one of its forms might be). It is rather that none of them is, or can be, value-free. Should the quantity of life take precedence over its quality? And how is one to tell? When in fact does human life begin? Indeed, what kind of life deserves to be called human? Answers to these and other ethical questions, like the values attending them, stand arbitrarily, by fiat. Not one of them can be argued absolutely, except via some cosmic "Because" or supposed earthly Authority – and It cannot be proved either.

This all means that the will of God is fundamentally a problem for people of faith and always a risk for those who try to do it. In no case will our value judgments necessarily be God's. Or, to paraphrase Isaiah 55:8, God's ways and thoughts are anything but ours. Who then are we to say *factually* that Jesus was, or was not, sinless?

The problem of insufficient facts. Persons of faith do, of course, make value judgments about human behavior: whether this or that action is good or bad, typically decent or sinful. Within the context of a religion that is ethically concerned, one's failure to do so would itself be a show of bad faith. What's more, there usually exists a consensus about the meaning of justice and righteousness that allows many, if not all, of such faithful judgments to elicit significant agreement. As an example, the condemning words of the prophets were most often rejected but, at the same time, honored. The prophets spoke not in a moral vacuum but in terms of specific values that their hearers would have seemed fools to question. To stone a prophet is one thing, to debate with him is something else. Still, the prophets made their judgments in sight of easily recognizable facts. There were particulars, and the particulars were common knowledge. Not so, however, concerning any factual judgment *we* might make about Jesus' sinlessness. In this case the evidence is largely irrelevant. It is severely limited and, for the most part, simply beside the point.

In the biblical and Christian view, sin relates both to external behavior and to internal attitudes. Yet on each of these counts the Jesus-traditions come up short – and not just in their being christianized traditions aligned with post-Easter faith. On the one hand, they leave great voids in Jesus' life. They tell us nothing reliable about experiences prior to his baptism or public ministry;[1] and, to make matters more uncertain, they report his doings thereafter only in the most fragmentary fashion. On the other hand, available Jesus-traditions, while containing much of his teaching, do not zero in on his innermost thoughts. That kind of biography, we have noted, was not the concern of those who formulated the traditions that the Gospel writers transmitted. This is all to say that the historical critic is stymied on the question of Jesus' sinlessness. She or he lacks sufficient facts to offer even a guarded opinion.

An apology. The matter must now be put theologically. Whether Jesus was without any sin is a judgment reserved for God alone. Pulpit pounding to the contrary, one must seriously wonder, certainly from a Christian standpoint, who else but God *could* make such a judgment. Granted, one may affirm Jesus' sinlessness as a legitimate item of faith, but not as an arguable fact. Besides, the confession that he was indeed sinless is a word to which Jesus would have strenuously objected. And that, after all, is our primary concern here: what Jesus thought about himself in this matter and why. I have no interest in questioning the tradition of his sinless existence, much less any stomach for refuting it. Personally, nothing in my being will let me call that man a sinner. Nor does anything I know about him (or think I know about him) warrant my doing so. At the same time, it does seem clear that the Church's time-honored esteem of Jesus as one without any sin reflects nothing of his own self-image.

The Evidence

We turn now to the pertinent evidence of Jesus' self-image as a sinner. That evidence, I admit, is sparse. Nonetheless, while it comprises only two traditions underlying the Gospel of Mark, the evidence itself is compelling. Both of the oral traditions are so offensive to early Christian faith, so out of line with beliefs that developed about Jesus' righteous messiahship soon after his death, that each of the traditions must be deemed as basically valid. Neither of them can be dismissed out of hand, nor can its embarrassment to Christian faith be convincingly explained away.

God alone is good. Directly to the point is the incident recorded in Mark 10:17–22, where Jesus objects to being called good. "Good Teacher," a man asks him, "what must I do to inherit eternal life?" Jesus prefaces his answer with a question and comment of his own: "Why do you call me good? No one is good but God alone" (10:18). While Luke substantially follows Mark in this, recording the appellation, the man's question, and Jesus' initial response almost verbatim (18:18–19), Matthew makes convenient changes:

> "Teacher, what good deed must I do, to have eternal life?" And he said to him, "Why do you ask me about what is good? One there is who is good." (19:16b–17b)

Obviously, Matthew's intent was to remove the offense that the Marcan wording immediately suggests: Jesus viewed himself as one with all other humans in falling short of being good. And just as obviously, the tradition beneath Mark 10:18 is so contrary to the early Church's esteem of Jesus that it would not have come out of thin air.

Matthew's emendation of what seems a vivid confession of sin on Jesus' part has been joined by exegetical efforts to eliminate the offense in Mark 10:18 itself. From early church fathers to modern commentators one finds various explanations of Mark 10:18 involving, so to speak, a double take — as though to say there is much more here than meets the eye and what does meet the eye is absent.[2] In short, Jesus was not professing to be a sinner. Instead, he was claiming to be Good God (not Good Teacher); or he was repudiating his questioner's flattery; or he was saying in effect that, while God's goodness is absolute (i.e., independent per se), his own goodness had yet to grow and be proved in the trying situations of his God-incarnate life; and so forth.[3] All of this seems to suggest that words may mean whatever one wants them to mean.

Even when tacitly made, the assumption behind such interpretations ridding Mark 10:18 of its immediate offense is that Jesus knew himself to be the Messiah and was aware of his peculiar, redemptive significance in line with later, Christian faith. As we have observed, however, that most probably was not the case.[4] The contention that Jesus had such special knowledge fails to pass critical muster. Therefore, the surface import of Mark 10:18, embarrassing though it may be, should be left to stand on its own. Not that Jesus *was* a sinner, but that he *regarded* himself as one. In recognition of that, by the way, Christian faith has lost not one thing essential to itself.

Jesus' baptism by John. The other tradition pertinent here concerns Jesus' baptism by John. First recorded for us in Mark 1:9–11, the tradition was christianized before Mark put his hand to it. It conveyed post-Easter faith about the unique significance of Jesus within God's redemptive purpose. The authenticity of the baptism itself, however, seems beyond question. For the word that Jesus was baptized by John, of all people, straightly implies a consciousness of sin in Jesus, a feeling of *being* a sinner. Once again, it is not the kind of word that the Church would have manufactured.

According to early tradition, as reported in Mark 1:4, John preached "a baptism of repentance for the forgiveness of sins." Although his ministry was eventually embellished beyond histori- cally agreeable facts — Mark 1:5 has it that John baptized as penitents "all the country of Judea, and all the people of Jerusalem"(!) — there is no reason to question its essentially penitential character. Those who came to John for baptism did so "confessing their sins" (Mk. 1:5). Further, from the tradition behind Mark 11:28–30, it is clear that John's administration of baptism was widely known and that Jesus approved of it. So the first impression one gets from the mere fact of Jesus' own baptism at the hands of John is well-nigh unavoid- able. Whether beheld in the flesh from the banks of the Jordan or viewed two thousand years later, the event seems to say that Jesus believed himself in need of forgiveness.

As in the case of Jesus' objection to being called "good," Matthew was also uneasy with this immediate suggestion of the baptism tra- dition. Though he largely followed Mark's report of it, he inserted in his own narration an item about John's reluctance to baptize Jesus. According to Matthew's additions, John needs to be baptized by Jesus, not vice versa, and says so to him. Jesus, in turn, does not deny that assessment but convinces the Baptist to get on with it anyway in order "for us to fulfill all righteousness" (3:14–15). The comple- mentary character of that insertion is indisputable. Whatever else he meant by it, Matthew apparently felt a disclaimer was needed for the pressing implication of Jesus' baptism.

Except for the consensus among current New Testament critics, interpretations have not changed much in this regard. Established Christian faith still wants Jesus to have seen himself as the Church has come to see him. One often hears from the pulpit that Jesus, far from confessing any sin of his own, let John baptize him for other reasons — to give people a leading example of what *they* ought to do; or to indicate his approval of baptism as a valid Christian sacra- ment.[5] Indeed, it was not too long ago that scholars of the greatest repute continued to defend a "respectful" explanation of Jesus' bap- tism experience. Vincent Taylor, for one, in surely the finest English commentary on Mark at the time it first appeared (1952), argued that Jesus' inner experience as the Christ, not any consciousness of sin, best explains his submission to baptism by John.[6] Like many of ancient Israel's leaders who are repeatedly described in the Old Testament as endowed by the Spirit of the Lord for special purposes, "it is natural that on the eve of His ministry Jesus should look for such an endowment."[7] Taylor's position requires that Mark's story of the baptism is basically authentic in its details that are particularly meaningful to Christian faith: the Spirit descending upon Jesus like a dove, the heavenly voice telling him he is the Messiah and Servant of the Lord (and at that, in Taylor's opinion, most probably the *Suffering* Servant). However creative those details, they reflect Jesus' self-understanding at the time he accepted baptism. Additionally, that he approached baptism not as a penitent is confirmed "by the entire absence of the consciousness of sin in His personality, as it is revealed in the Gospels."[8] And the evidence of Mark 10:18 to the contrary, in Taylor's discussion of that text, must somehow be turned on its head.[9]

Anyone familiar with Vincent Taylor's commentary on the Gospel of Mark knows what a masterpiece it is. After four full decades now scholars continue to consult it, so rich and lucid is its erudition. Their debt to him can hardly be overstated. But, to repeat, the assumption that Jesus saw himself as the Messiah/Servant, which is crucial to the exegesis of Taylor and others who deny to Jesus a sense of sin, sells nowadays only with great difficulty. For reasons already indicated in these pages and more, scholarship has mainly abandoned that assumption as critically untenable.

Conclusion. We must conclude that Jesus, in all probability, thought of himself as a sinner. To reason otherwise from the pertinent evidence would be laborious indeed, if not patently biased. Further, when one attempts critically to explain Jesus' apparent consciousness of sin, this conclusion becomes even more compelling and finally, in my judgment, not at all unattractive. We are speaking here of a *good* man.

Jesus' Sense of Being a Sinner "Explained"

"Explaining" Jesus' consciousness of sin may sound contradictory, particularly since we have often noted that Gospel traditions about him were not designed to answer such questions of modern biography. I must therefore stress that nothing along a line that plumbs the intricate depths of an individual approaches my concern here. Routine biography is out. And psychohistorical analysis, sometimes an amusing business in current history writing about persons of the near and distant past, would be immeasurably more laughable regarding Jesus of Nazareth. No half-serious student will ever attempt it.

Even so, something of an explanation is allowed by the limited facts available to us. While those facts raise more questions than the Jesus-traditions were meant to address, they help us at least to appreciate Jesus' apparent self-image as a sinner. Two matters of fact are especially in mind here. One concerns his Jewish heritage, the other his "understanding" of the radical righteousness that God requires of people.

The Old Testament's teaching. That Jesus knew the Scriptures and was influenced by them is, of course, a truism. As a devout Jew, he could not have ignored them; and Gospel reports of his sayings, even when purged of later additions, are replete with references and allusions to Old Testament materials and ideas. The fact that he sometimes took issue with a scriptural word is important for us, to be sure, but beside the point just now. What we wish to note here is that Jesus was in obvious agreement with the Old Testament view (reflected in Mk. 10:18) that everybody is a sinner before God.

Often misconstrued as a low view of humanity, that teaching coheres with just the opposite esteem. Scriptural "man" (*adam*) is a marvelous creature, splendid in ability and enterprises. Indeed, *adam* is made "little less than God," crowned "with glory and honor," the summit of all creation and given dominion over it.[10] On the other hand, for all its complaints about sin and its system of atoning sacrifices, the Old Testament sees the human person as susceptible to God's good influence. He/she can be enabled through any number of means to hear and do God's will or at least to seek it and *try* to do it. Only *adam*, the finest of creatures, has that in his résumé.

But if man's ability toward righteousness is to his credit, his failure in achieving it is his undoing. And the more one knows of God's demand for righteousness — a righteousness like his own! — the more one is apt to cry with Isaiah:

> Woe is me! For I am lost; for I am a man of unclean lips, and I dwell in the midst of a people of unclean lips; for my eyes have seen the King, the Lord of hosts! (Isa. 6:5)

Hence — rather than offering a systematic view of human nature, much less theorizing about man for theory's sake — the Old Testament considers human goodness in practical terms, in sight of *God's* goodness, and draws conclusions accordingly. The verdict: human goodness is relative at best. Some people seem better than others, and much is made of the differences between "the righteous" and "the wicked" (e.g., Ps. 1). But even that prideful distinction evaporates when their failures before God are commonly reckoned: the sacrifices of atonement are for *all* the people. For, as the psalmist said of the race,

> They have all gone astray, they are all alike corrupt;
> > there is none that does good,
> > no, not one. (Ps. 14:3; cf. 53:3)

Given the Old Testament's view of human goodness and sin, Jesus' evident self-image as a sinner is hardly surprising. Only the alternative would be difficult, in fact too far-fetched, for us to comprehend. We would then be looking at a devout Jew who obviously treasured his heritage of the Old Testament, who agreed with its teaching that God alone is good, yet who regarded himself as sinless, even though he evidently did not think himself to be the righteous Messiah. Such a Jesus would seem either less than human — immune to major cultural influences whose assumptions he shared — or else split in personality. Neither view is reasonable.

God's demand for radical obedience. The other matter in "explanation" of Jesus' apparent self-image as a sinner concerns his understanding of what God wills for people. And here particularly, assuming the reality of his human makeup, we may observe that Jesus' sense of being a sinner was unavoidable. Not just allowable, but existentially inevitable. To appreciate that fully, however, we must recognize a tension that existed for Jesus between the will of God and the Torah or Law, especially as these were regularly viewed by the Jewish rabbis. (We shall consider this matter in greater detail than is needed to "explain" Jesus' consciousness of sin; our treatment of items here is a prelude to this chapter's next sections.)

In describing Jesus' understanding of what God requires of us, recent commentators have employed a variety of terms: "radical obedience," "a new righteousness," "kingdom of God ethics," and so on. Each of the terms implies innovation and bespeaks a new condition that goes to the heart of a person. The terms suggest something so radical and existentially intense that no set of rules could ever confine it. In short, according to Jesus, God is concerned not only with what people *do;* God is basically concerned with what they *are.* We may cite one example immediately. Whereas Jewish dietary regulations were full of prohibitions, Jesus taught that what comes *out* of a person defiles him, not what goes *into* him (Mk. 7:15).[11] Righteousness, in other words, is first and foremost a matter of being.

Although the saying in Mark 7:15 was indeed revolutionary, its concern with being was scarcely new. Rabbinical teaching often voiced such concern, as well it should have. For the Old Testament recognizes in a variety of ways that one's deeds relate to the heart. God wills that his people *be* holy, as he is holy (Lev. 19:2). Yet their holiness (*other*ness) is to exceed mere form or external identity. Redeemed and set apart from others, which is what they observably are on the surface, they are to serve as his "image" in the world. Being his people, they are to reflect in their social relations what God himself is like as a social being (Gen. 1:26–27).[12] His "mercy-and-justice," as they have experienced it, is thus to be theirs as well. It is to be manifest among themselves and in their treatment of outsiders. Human action and being, therefore, are ultimately inseparable. Hence the prophet Micah's eloquent linkage of them, in terms of doing and attitude:

> He has showed you, O man, what is good;
>   and what does the Lord require of you
> but to do justice, and to love kindness,
>   and to walk humbly with your God? (Mic. 6:8)

And witness but one fact more in this vein. When fed up with Israel's sins and devoid of hope that the people as they were would or could repent, prophets looked for God to change their nature. On the brink of unmatched doom, for instance, Jeremiah stopped his weeping long enough to deliver God's word of a coming new covenant between him and all his people: "I will put my law within them, and I will write it upon their hearts" (Jer. 31:33). Habitual disobedience called for a radical change in the people's being.

As for the Law itself, some details of which Jesus dared to impugn, it was supposed to implement Israel's holiness. It was to make the "otherness" of God's people a righteous reality in formal and in daily affairs. Accordingly, the Law, originally and for centuries, was a flexible, growing corpus. As the people's socioeconomic and political situations changed — say, from a seminomadic to a settled, agrarian life or from a tribal confederation to a national monarchy —

new regulations were devised to deal with newly encountered problems. After all, righteousness must be detailed and up-to-date if it is to have any practical meaning. In time, however, that malleable character of the Law proper disappeared. After Assyria's deathblow to the Northern Kingdom of Israel (721 B.C..) and upon Babylon's *coup de grâce* for the Southern Kingdom of Judah (587 B.C.), the people of God were left without a national identity. From then on their "otherness," no longer joined with a political reality,[13] would largely or wholly depend on their common submission to the Law. Of necessity, the Law increasingly took on a central importance that made it, eventually, the sum and substance of Jewish religious obligation. The upshot of all this was that the Law came to be regarded as sacrosanct — too holy to be altered — and righteousness became a matter of strict adherence to all its many details. Consequently, prophecy for the most part vanished (save in apocalyptic form). There seemed to be no need for its fundamental service — that is, an updated, on-the-spot announcement of the word of God. Instead, God's will for every conceivable situation was thought to be contained in, or at least deducible from, the Law itself (i.e., the Law proper, the Pentateuch). As one might expect, differences arose within Judaism concerning the Law's interpretation. That, coupled with situational change, gave rise to a variety and plethora of regulations involving the minutest details. On one fundamental, however, all devout Jewish groups agreed: the people of God must live by the Law's many precepts. Righteousness was legalistic.

Into that kind of atmosphere Jesus of Nazareth came as a breath of fresh air. While he respected the Law, often following its formalities (e.g., Passover) and speaking of its "weightier matters" (Mt. 23:23), he would not be its slave. If sabbath observance stood in the way of human need or even decent pleasure, evidently his habit and advice were to break the Law as it was commonly interpreted. Hence his reported healings on the sabbath (e.g., Mk. 3:1–5), which, by Jewish tradition, should have been postponed were life or pain not at issue. Hence also Jesus' apparent nonchalance about his disciples' needless plucking of grain on the sabbath (Mk. 2:23–24) and his acute remark about the day itself: "The sabbath was made for man, not man for the sabbath" (Mk. 2:27). True, sabbath traditions in the Gospels frequently show signs of embellishment and the inclusion of secondary materials; and they often lack technical details that demonstrate sabbath violation.[14] But so widely attested is the word that Jesus broke the sabbath, whatever the details of that may have been, that his disregard of sabbath rules seems beyond much doubt. Also, his saying about the sabbath being made for man not only appears to be genuine on its own. It is typical of a "liberated" Jesus whose remarkable freedom permeates the traditions that we have of him.

Critically speaking, were we to ask what accounts for Jesus' peculiar freedom in the midst of devout legalism, only speculative answers could be given. To say that he learned from Old Testament lessons begs the question at once, for all other Jews had the Old Testament too. The purpose of the Law, the relation between being and doing, the prophets' protestations and promises regarding the will of God – these were common property to Jesus' contemporaries. Why *he* broke away from the accepted legalism of his day remains a mystery to us. Rather, our concern here is his "definition" of righteousness and what he thought it entails for people. In other words, how is the Law's purpose to be fulfilled? What is its summation? And, specifically, what led Jesus, free-spirited though he was, to conclude from his understanding of righteousness that he was a sinner along with all others?

As already indicated, Jesus believed that God's will for people focused on their being as revealed in their actions, not simply on their actions alone. To be sure, one might satisfy details of the Law or, as in the case of the Pharisee in Jesus' parable, even go beyond those details (Lk. 18:10–14). However, it is the publican in that parable who comes off as the hero. While the Pharisee has every good reason to be thankful that he has not fallen into heinous crimes but, instead, has lived a Law-abiding life and more, the publican's prayer is the one to be emulated: "God, be merciful to me, sinner that I am!" (18:13). Which is to say that meeting the Law's requirements, however helpful they may be, cannot fulfill the righteousness God demands of all people.

So what of God's intent in giving the Law? How is one to meet *that?* According to Jesus, the Law's foremost commandment is that you love God with all that you are; and on its heels is the second one, that you love your neighbor as yourself (Mk. 12:29–31).[15] Although Jesus' combination of the separate commands to love God and to love neighbor may have been a first in Jewish teaching (the question is moot), that would only begin to reflect his insight. Much more to the point is his understanding that one's commitment to God (i.e., loving him) is to be at the deepest level of one's being *and,* concurrently, is to be self-sacrificial. All self-reliance must be aborted and with it all trust in the things of this world. For only as one loses his life can he save it (Mt. 10:39 ≈ Lk. 9:24); and no person can serve two masters, God and mammon, but rather he will love the one and hate the other (Mt. 6:24 = Lk. 16:13).

Yet it is in this world, with generous attention to people's immediate needs, that obedience to God's demand for righteousness displays itself. Love for the neighbor, which follows love for God, means *being* a neighbor, as vividly enacted in Jesus' parable of the Good Samaritan (Lk. 10:30–35). A traveler is robbed, beaten, and left half-dead on a country road. The victim is then seen in turn by three others going down the road: a priest, a Levite, and, so to speak, a mongrel Jew — a Samaritan, whose credentials for goodness were habitually held in contempt. At once the Samaritan has compassion for the victim. He binds the man's wounds, delivers him to town, and sets him up in an inn to recuperate, no costs barred. Precisely in its lack of such immediacy, and in its native inability to command *radical* obedience to God, the Law fails. The priest and the Levite, men committed to the Law, passed by on the other side!

According to antithetical sayings of Jesus collected in Matthew 5:21–48, that is also the shortcoming of those details of the Law which actually need correction. They reflect customary ways of behavior, not obedience to God at the heart of one's being, and so they do not serve love immediately in daily affairs. Contrary to such traditional precepts — "an eye for an eye," to cite the worst of them — Matthew's summary of Jesus' teaching is that God's people must be "perfect" as God is "perfect" (5:48). The Greek word is *teleios,* meaning in this case "complete" or "whole." While that summary appears to be Matthew's own, it is nonetheless fitting. As many of Jesus' sayings in Matthew 5 indicate, as do his sayings elsewhere, the goodness called for is to be evidenced in a thoroughgoing, God-like love for others that permits no trace of selfish confusion. So radical is God's will for people! (And as we shall see, so radical is his grace!)

Now we must ask, who among this world's people has it within himself to bring off completely such unselfish love for others? One specific teaching of Jesus will suffice to highlight the difficulty here — no, the impossibility, for him as well as for us. Though recorded solely in Matthew 5:27–28 and paralleled in rabbinic traditions reported later, its genuineness is readily conceded by most commentators.

You have heard that it was said, "You shall not commit adultery." But I say to you that every one who looks at a woman lustfully has already committed adultery with her in his heart.

Is there a righteous adult in the room? The lustful moment, when one finds oneself regarding another individual not as a person to be served but as a thing to be used for self-satisfaction, how suddenly it arrives! And must we suppose that Jesus never experienced a lustful moment of his own? Just because there is, understandably, no evidence one way or the other? To answer affirmatively, in defense of a self-righteous Jesus, would be to deny that human biology was fully part of his makeup. And that would deny, by present scientific knowledge, that Jesus was fully human. We should then even have to correct the assertion in Hebrews 4:15 that he overcame every temptation that faces us.

Let no reader get carried away with the program. Anyone who objects (to my argument here) that Jesus would then have been a common sinner needs to think more carefully—about scientific findings and Jesus' own teaching as well. Lust is a by-product of the sexual drive in us. It occurs not as a matter of will, as if one had to find time for it in a busy schedule. Rather, it appears as a "happening," whether one goes on to cultivate the urge or puts it out of mind. This much we know about lust, and nothing can remove it from normal human experience. Nor may it be argued that Jesus, in speaking of lust as adulterous, was thinking merely of the cultivated kind – the look that is willfully continued or even premeditated. Such a distinction is an affront, robbing from the radicalness of a goodness that is to emulate *God's*. In Jesus' view any want of love, however explained, falls short of what God wills that people *be*. Nor may one suppose that Jesus viewed God as a "realist" whose judgments make allowances for unavoidable faults. To the contrary, as Jesus saw it, a *new* reality is dawning – the kingdom of God is at hand! – and not even *Moses* escapes criticism for having compromised God's will (concerning divorce, Deut. 24:1–4). Moses allowed divorce, Jesus taught, because of men's "hardness of heart," but "from the beginning" God willed otherwise: no divorce, period (Mk. 10:2–9). And now is the time for God's radical will to be radically spoken and faithfully heard: You must love as God does! Certainly, in the context of such understanding, no kind of lust could be regarded by Jesus except as a manifestation and reminder of sin.

So, assuming Jesus' condition as a man in the flesh, we have all the more reason to appreciate his apparent self-image as a sinner. The demand for radical righteousness, as he understood it, left no one any room to justify oneself before God. Hence, in Jesus' parable the publican, a swindler by vocation and hated for it, beats his breast and seeks the forgiveness that he and all others so terribly need. The best of people, like the Pharisee in that parable, must learn to pray with the worst of people: "God, be merciful to me, the sinner!" (Lk. 18:13). And for his own part, we know, Jesus objected to being called "good." Indeed, it seems he had already joined in the publican's prayer when he went to John for baptism.

Toward a righteous Jesus. The fact that Jesus considered himself to be a sinner doesn't trouble me as a Christian, nor should it trouble the Church. Earlier I said that nothing will allow me to call him a sinner. That still holds, notwithstanding my comments about lust as a natural occurrence in normal human experience. As a person of this century, I can blame people no more for hormones than for the color of their eyes. Yes, I know the *logical* implication of matters discussed within this chapter's present section. Namely, if Jesus was correct about all humans as sinners before God (or correct only about lust as a sin), and if he was fully human (or experienced lust), it follows that he was indeed a sinner before God. But that conclusion, though demanded by logic, includes the term "God." And "God," in Jesus' usage and ours, connotes One who is free — the Creator who is over all, human logic included, and whose ways and thoughts are not ours. Therefore, we say that God alone is Judge. Which means that, given no evidence otherwise, the refusal of Christians to call Jesus a sinner is not only faithful but also linguistically proper.

Even more important to the Church should be the fact that we cloud the attraction of a good person's life when we erase his or her confessions of imperfection. By whatever criteria goodness is defined, and however relative its existence among us, this much is clear: those who profess to be good *are not*, and those who seem to be good *do not think they are*. Imagine going camping with the former! Rather than finding offense in Jesus' apparent view of himself as a sinner, Christian faith might thus be grateful for it. Mark, at least, wasn't bothered by the two traditions he received to that effect. Instead of attempting a cover-up as Matthew would do, he used both of them, the baptism tradition especially, to invite his readers to see Jesus as *the one in whom righteousness has finally become a reality for all people.*

That is a splendid word in Mark's depiction of Jesus, and I invite my own readers to pause with me now and look at it. The leading question of this chapter has been settled: Jesus, in his humanity and unavoidably, considered himself a sinner. However, limiting discussion of his goodness to his own negative self-assessment would be unfair to general readers and to the historical Jesus alike. As in our previous chapters, there is another side to the coin. In this case — and not just from the standpoint of post-Easter faith — the other side offers a positive word about Jesus' *real* righteousness.

The Historical Jesus and Traditions of His Righteousness

As I argued in chapter 2, Jesus' baptism in Mark is the first clue to his mysterious identity. He is, as Mark's readers are meant to see eventually, the Messiah/Suffering Servant in whom all Israel and "the nations" are made righteous and one. That special use of the baptism tradition will receive additional attention in this chapter's next section. But to get there honestly we must go by way of the historical Jesus himself.

Often it is not enough merely to recite Christian faith about Jesus in the words of some New Testament writer. Lest such confessions seem little more than mythmaking, one must ask, wherever possible, whether the writer's meaning seems historically warranted. Nowhere is this more necessary than in Mark's use of the baptism tradition. His meaning there can hardly be seen, much less appear to be credible, apart from Jesus' real righteousness. Worse than a clever cover-up of his own, Mark's re-view of Jesus' embarrassing baptism would then be like a snapshot so out of focus that the camera ought to be tossed. So we will take time here to observe how Jesus, in his concern for what he believed to be God's demand for radical obedience, actually resembled the two righteous figures with whom Mark begins to identify him in the baptism story: the Messiah and the Suffering Servant.

General observations. From what we have seen to this point, Jesus' self-understanding, though not obliterated in the Gospels, was often reworked to express postresurrection faith. But this does not mean that the Church's faith about him bore no significant relation to Jesus himself. On the contrary, as Günther Bornkamm has shown, the Church's messianic titles for Jesus, while charged with new understanding of his importance, nevertheless befit the historical Jesus.[16] Such titles, issuing from Old Testament figures and given new meaning in Christian usage, were apt descriptions of him — that is, as early church people recalled how Jesus had been. This, Bornkamm believes, is because the historical Jesus, whose uniqueness is revealed *in* his words and deeds, and the risen Christ, who led his once brokenhearted followers into new understanding of his person and significance, are one and the same.[17] With that I wholly agree. I would only add specifically that this historical fitness of the messianic titles given to Jesus also holds for Mark's implied designation of Suffering Servant.

Within the framework of Israel's eschatological hope, we have noted, the Old Testament figures of Messiah and Suffering Servant were thoroughly dissimilar in identity, appearance, and fate. Still, as agents in the final working out of God's purpose, they owned corresponding marks of distinction in terms of righteousness. Each of them, it was said, would be righteous himself *and* would effect a reconciling righteousness among others.[18] Given the essence of traditional Yahwist belief, that correspondence is not surprising, even for such disparate figures as these. What rather commands our attention is that Jesus, in devotion to the new righteousness he saw as demanded by God, brought together the most obvious yet contrasting characteristics of these two Old Testament figures. Where the Messiah and the Servant differed in visible attributes, Jesus acted and appeared like both of them simultaneously—and he did so in the conviction that the long-awaited kingdom of God was near, indeed was already dawning.

This striking similarity by no means disturbs the consensus that Jesus most probably neither claimed messianic titles for himself nor understood his significance as either the Messiah or the Suffering Servant. But it does help explain how the Church, under Easter's influence and prompted by recollections of him, came to see him as the once-for-all realization of both those promised "persons." In Jesus' words and deeds expressing God's demand for a new, end-time righteousness, outstanding yet disparate traits of the Messiah and the Suffering Servant were actually combined.

The righteous Messiah, the righteous Suffering Servant. According to popular Jewish thought, readers may recall, the Messiah was to be a splendid and mighty ruler, a gloriously triumphant sovereign whose power in restoring Israel to greatness and establishing justice in the land would be unmistakable to all. Contrariwise, the Servant, whose identity and success would be evident only when he had died, was to be a lowly and seemingly defeated figure, one who would freely and literally spend himself in bringing salvation and righteousness not to Israel exclusively but to the Gentiles as well. On the one hand, then, we have the Messiah: a person of authority in his own right and immediately recognized as such. On the other hand is the Suffering Servant: a self-effacing figure, unappreciated in life yet succumbing to no discouragement in his zeal for others for righteousness' sake. How these contrasting characteristics break forth in Jesus of Nazareth! Consumed with the demand of radical obedience to God, he was both (1) a person of inherent authority and (2) a man who, though misunderstood by "his own" and opposed by others, spared himself no hardship in being *with* and *for* all people beside him. Since our knowledge of Jesus is limited, we do not speak thus of him absolutely. But neither do we speak sentimentally. Virtually all the Jesus-traditions in our possession are laced with these distinguishing traits. Throughout his words and deeds reported in the Gospels there marches a concern for righteousness that is, instantaneously, manifestly authoritative and widely compassionate, inescapably judgmental and teeming with liberating grace, beyond his opponents' ability to refute and yet open to their frontal attack — in short, a spoken and enacted righteousness that is both self-authentic and self-denying.

Apropos here is Mark's early comment about people being "astonished" at Jesus' teaching: "For he taught them as one who had authority, and not as the scribes" (1:22). Whether emanating from eyewitnesses or coming from the evangelist himself, it is doubtlessly a valid observation, richly attested to in reliable records. For example, consider the "directness" of Jesus' teaching (to borrow Bornkamm's well-advised term). Whereas Jewish scribes customarily appealed to Scripture and tradition to uphold their teachings, Jesus announced God's will *on his own* and, we have noted, even criticized Scripture and tradition at times. Thus run the antitheses in Matthew 5:21–48, at least half of which seem basically genuine:[19] "You have heard that it was said...But I say to you... " So too Jesus' personal judgment that Moses' permitting divorce was in violation of God's will from the first (Mk. 10:2–9) — unthinkable talk for a rabbi! In that instance, as we will see, Jesus did appeal to Scripture but used scripture *against* scripture, and against its most revered "author" by name. But the clearest evidence of Jesus' inherent authority is in the fact that he attracted numerous followers, no doubt many times the symbolic number "twelve." Even so, the authoritative character of his mission, especially as it called attention to the coming rule of God, evoked more than astonishment and a following. It inspired men in *positions* of authority to seek his destruction.[20] Like those he named "blessed" in the Beatitudes (Mt. 5:3–12), he too, in his own commitment to righteousness, would suffer for its sake.

This combination of Messiah-like authority and Servant-openness to rejection and death is notably revealed in Jesus' reported dealings with his opponents themselves. Nowhere in Gospel traditions does he lose control, however pressed with criticism or shifty questions aimed at putting him on the defensive. Instead, he takes charge of the situation completely, particularly in view of who and what his critics are. He responds with a word which, while possible to deliver those critics from habitual enslavement, they would be embarrassed to contradict. For instance, consider Jesus' word when Pharisees are said to have "watched" to see if he would heal a man on the sabbath: "Is it lawful on the sabbath to do good or to do harm, to save life or to kill?" (Mk. 3:4) – so much then for legalism versus good works. Likewise, recall Jesus' response to the Pharisees' question regarding his disciples' "unlawful" sabbath grain-plucking: that is, his word about the sabbath being made for humanity, not vice versa (Mk. 2:27). So consistent was that with the traditionally viewed purpose of the Law as a whole, any opponent's rejoinder would have seemed picayune.

But the most remarkable of Jesus' responses to hostile questioners is his unprecedented, explicit criticism of Moses, through whom, tradition asserted, God had given the Torah (the Law proper, the Pentateuch). Authentic beyond much doubt[21] – especially since the earliest, Jewish Church largely honored "Mosaic" teachings – this incident provides the example *par excellence* of Jesus' cool authority in an otherwise defenseless situation:

> And Pharisees came up and in order to test him asked, "Is it lawful for a man to divorce his wife?" He answered them, "What did Moses command you?" They said, "Moses allowed a man to write a certificate of divorce, and to put her away." But Jesus said to them, "For your hardness of heart he wrote you this commandment. But from the beginning of creation, 'God made them male and female.' 'For this reason a man shall leave his father and mother and be joined to his wife, and the two shall become one.' So they are no longer two but one. What therefore God has joined together, let not man put asunder." (Mk. 10:2–9)

Every reader of the Torah knew that divorce was lawful (Deut. 24:1–4). The question put to Jesus must have been to entrap him, perhaps in the current rabbinical controversy about *which* conditions justified divorce. Or else his position was already known and his answer would supposedly incriminate him as one who disrespected the Law proper. In either case, it seemed a no-win situation. Yet he turned the tables on his questioners, confronting them with a word (from the Torah!) concerning God's primordial will (Gen. 1:27b; 2:24) — that is, a word they could not contest without even greater self-incrimination than they may have hoped for him. It was all to say in effect: "Yes, Moses permitted divorce, but his making that compromise misrepresented what God had given him to write in Genesis; and now will you side with that part of Moses' teaching that you like, or with God?"

These and other descriptions of Jesus' interaction with the people around him certify his inherent authority. Not that all such descriptions are basically authentic. But so varied and widespread are the reports that the image of him as a Messiah-like, authoritative person in service of the reign of God cannot be overshadowed. Yet that fact about him, so attractive to the helpless and to people of low estate, would eventually make him seem helpless and low — a loser in his arrest, revilement, and death. And not just to his opponents would Jesus thus appear, but to his disciples as well.

One other Suffering Servant quality, manifest in Jesus' authoritative words and deeds, calls for attention here. Namely, he taught and acted as one who would have Israel's bounds enlarged — and enlarged immeasurably beyond traditionally accepted limits. This is evident, for example, in what we have already observed of Jesus' story of the publican at prayer (Lk. 18:10–14). Although its concluding homily seems a later addition ("For every one who exalts himself will be humbled, but he who humbles himself will be exalted"), the point of the parable itself is clear: God's grace is open and operative for all who recognize their need of him, including the worst of sorts with no claim whatsoever to membership in God's people. Accordingly, one must love even one's enemies. One must give oneself to their welfare, because that is what God does (Lk. 6:27–36). And the *lex talionis,* "an eye for an eye and a tooth for a tooth," rehearsed in the Law itself — let that law of retaliation be forgotten![22] God doesn't act that way. Instead, he embraces the Law-condemned, maybe penitent, sinner. He is like the father who, totally shamed by his wayward and homeless son, runs out to greet the returning lad at a distance and, before the son can even finish his prepared confession, falls upon him with kisses and then throws a party for him. Thus with joy, indeed merriment, is the New Israel to come into being (Lk. 15:11–24; cf. 15:3–9). In Jesus' words, therefore, was a grace of God as radical as God's demand for righteousness. The two were not to be separated. Rather, the grace was to prompt God's people, in self-sacrificial obedience, to emulate God's own right-eousness; and the righteousness demanded of those favored people was for them to recognize God's grace toward all — publicans, ne'er-do-well rebels, whatever. So Jesus taught: in order to explode Israel's self-containment.

And so Jesus acted. Time and again in the Gospels, self-righteous isolation is countered by Jesus' freewheeling association with the so-called godless: publicans, sinners, outcasts — to repeat, people whose right to be numbered with the elect is nil. Like the prom-ised Suffering Servant, he numbers himself with them, takes them to himself most intimately. As previously noted, Jesus ate with them — an act that, in Semitic thought, meant he was joining himself to them in a binding fellowship, the ties of which were unthinkable to break.[23] Recorded first by Mark (2:15–16) and frequently men-tioned in other Synoptic materials,[24] Jesus' eating with "publicans and sinners" seems certainly authentic. It runs true to form of one who, according to Gospel traditions, welcomed close association with such people and even sought them out. Moreover, while of no interest to Hellenistic Christianity per se, it surely was not the inven-tion of a Palestinian church in which Judaizers prospered and would criticize Peter (and *another* "Cephas"?) for eating with Gentiles.[25] Nor was Jesus' eating with the ungodly any less offensive to his own opponents who were upset with him *because* they understood the meaning of that action (Mk. 2:16). Here then was a devout Jew, a member of Israel's select fellowship with God, who would open up that prized communion to the likes of publicans. And in his zeal for such "justice in the earth" he would willingly, like the Servant, pay a dear price rather than be discouraged.

Christian traditions of Jesus' utter righteousness. The Church's iden-tification of Jesus with the disparate figures of the Messiah and the Suffering Servant was a natural, so to speak. Not that we can un-cover the steps by which this was done, nor must we. It is enough for us to recognize that whoever effected this complete, hitherto unheard-of union had prompting aplenty in traditional recollections of how Jesus had actually been. He resembled the promised Mes-siah, with whom he was first identified, and resembled the promised Servant too.

So also came into being traditions of Jesus' thoroughgoing right-eousness, a distinction held in common by those two promised figures. From every early tradition we have — and thus we may speak here without fear of contradiction — Jesus seemed to be a man utterly committed to God, and in the most urgent and wide-hearted terms. As none other in the Jews' rich history of heroically faithful men and women, he reflected a brand new righteousness that turned all self-righteousness on its head. He was one who seemed to embody the radical obedience which he taught that God demands. He acted it out, plainly for others to see, and with an astounding freedom toward friend and foe that made all that we know of his life (not just his death) a sacrifice. So the Church, empowered to faith and life through its Easter experience, praised Jesus of Nazareth with such descriptions as one "who knew no sin" (2 Cor. 5:21) and "one who in every respect has been tempted as we are, yet without sinning" (Heb. 4:15). And never mind that he objected to being called good or that he submitted to John's baptism of repentance. His followers had seen the man himself, how he was with them and others, and it was that same historical Jesus, they believed, whom God had vindicated.

Utter or perfect righteousness is, to be sure, beyond the historian's confirmation. Still, the appearance of righteousness in Jesus is indispensable to Christian faith and to a Christian theologian like Mark. With historical assurances of that righteousness in hand, we may therefore proceed to consider how Mark points to its all-encompassing significance in his re-view of Jesus' baptism.

Jesus' Baptism Re-viewed in Mark

In Mark's account of Jesus' baptism by John, where the Synoptic fusion of Messiah and Servant of the Lord is first recorded for us, Jesus' identity as such seems specially related to the meaning of his righteousness. Succinctly stated, Jesus is the Messiah/Suffering Servant who makes all people righteous, in that his righteousness becomes theirs as well. Mark links the tradition of Jesus' baptism (1:9–11, including the heavenly voice bespeaking who Jesus is) with John's preaching of repentance (1:2–8). In that linkage Mark suggests, as we will see, that the world's repentance has become a reality in the man Jesus of Nazareth. Granted, this is a strange word, and not just because sin has failed to exit from the world stage left. Attributing such far-flung significance to one man's life, however righteous he might have been, it involves a concept of human corporateness quite foreign to Western thought. We shall have to make some sense of that, from a biblical perspective at least. But first let us recall (from our previous chapter) some aspects of Mark's christology, particularly now as it bears on his introductory connection of John the baptizer and Jesus the baptized.

Jesus' secret identity and the summons to repentance. Mark's story of Jesus' baptism, in its reference to the heavenly voice, is the first of several clues he gives to the secret of Jesus' messiahship – a secret that cannot be fathomed until Jesus has died and is to be resurrected. While many seem to recognize him in life as the Christ, the Son of God, the Son of David, their confessions at best are confused and therefore unacceptable. For as the voice informs Jesus alone, he is the Messiah who must ultimately be understood in the role of the Servant – and *Suffering* Servant at that, if my interpretation of Mark is correct. Accordingly, not until Jesus breathes his last does Mark allow any public confession of his messiahship to stand on its own. But then, with the Temple curtain torn in two and the Holy of Holies exposed, the end of the world seems to have arrived in the creation of a new people of God. Through the fulfilled promise of the Servant's life and death, the wholesale sacrifice of one who would nonetheless survive, the way into God's holy and saving presence has now been opened to all. Thus in the Servant-Christ, as Mark presents his significance with subtle yet increasing force, is the old Israel destroyed and the New Israel begun. For as was prophesied of the Servant's universal effects, "the many" (i.e., all, as opposed to the few) share in his righteousness. Like that prophesied also of the Messiah, it is a reconciling righteousness. But it so extends Israel's boundaries that the old people of God are dead and gone, as it were, supplanted by God's new people brought together in Jesus Christ.

I think it was such a christology that led Mark, in the introduction to his Gospel (1:1-15), to link Jesus' baptism directly with John's call for repentance and to do so without embarrassment. We have seen that Matthew had to modify the baptism tradition (and Jesus' objection to being called "good") in order to keep him from looking like a self-confessed sinner. But Mark was spared that necessity by his using the baptism tradition itself, in conjunction with John's preaching, to point to Jesus as the Messiah/Suffering Servant whose utter righteousness is effective for others. Not surprisingly, this meaning of the baptism story does not immediately surface – a fact I may now enlarge upon. The baptismal heavenly voice, Mark's only precise reference to Jesus as the Isaianic Servant, alludes to the first Servant-poem (42:1-4), not the fourth (52:13-53:12); and only in the latter is the Servant described as the suffering, righteous one who will "make many to be accounted as righteous." At the same time, the first poem does say that the Servant will establish "justice in the earth" (42:4a) – a crucial item for the Servant-poems and for Mark as well. In Second Isaiah itself that reference to "justice in the earth" is ambiguous. What "justice" will mean for the world *and* for the Servant is yet to be revealed in the three poems that follow. Likewise, Mark's reference to the first Servant-poem is ambiguous. In order to understand, the reader must keep on reading! And that ambiguity keeps ever so neatly with the esoteric character of Mark's Gospel, in which Jesus' significance as Messiah/Suffering Servant is a secret to be fully disclosed only upon his death.

All this is to say that Mark, from his first description of Jesus' experience, artfully invites the audience to ponder Jesus' significance, who he is and what his righteousness means, and to enter into the new reality freely and faithfully themselves. And there, at the outset of Mark's Gospel, stands *this* command: Repent! Preached by John as the Christ's forerunner, it is reiterated in the first words Mark assigns to Jesus (and their mention of the *euangelion,* meaning the "gospel" or God's "good news" in Christ, rings clearly of Christian reflection, in this case Mark's own reflection): "The time is fulfilled, and the kingdom of God is at hand; repent, and believe in the gospel" (1:15).

"Repent," "repentance." In Synoptic usage the verb (*metanoeō*) and its corollary noun (*metanoia*) connote an about-face. They signify a turning away from sin and, concurrently, a turning toward God in obedience and reliance upon him. While appearing only three times in Mark (1:4, 15; 6:12) – each time, significantly, from Mark's own hand! – these words are weighted there with eschatological import and bespeak God's demand for the kind of new righteousness which Jesus repeatedly taught and enacted. That righteousness, we have seen, constitutes a profound reversal in customary being and behavior: a commitment to God so radical, and a trust in divine mercy so thorough, that one sacrifices everything, oneself included, to participate in the fellowship of God's kingdom that is now "at hand."

Repentance: an impossibility? Nice words they are – "repent" and "repentance." Every decent person, one way or another, longs for the virtuous life that they seem to suggest. God knows, the heart wants to hope. But who among us (except Jesus, says Christian faith) has ever come close to living such a life? Well, we must answer with Mark right off, certainly not Jesus' disciples (who, in Mark's Gospel, seem a model of both the Church and the world). Those disciples amount to twelve (3:13–19a), a number signifying the New Israel that is being created in Jesus Christ. For their own sorry part, however, the disciples look more like *old* Israel, incapable of becoming what they *ought* to be. So pronounced is this resemblance in Mark that it warrants some looking into.

Like clockwork, and with threats of judgment if God's word fell on deaf ears, the prophets had called Israel to repentance, to return to the Lord in obedience and faithful trust. But with enough regularity to break a Yahwist's spirit, the nation failed to repent; and, as a matter of fact, the threatened disasters arrived, culminating in Israel's collapse. To be sure, in the Old Testament's view, Israel *is* God's people, elected and brought into being by him; and according to Yahwist belief, God's covenant-loyalty guarantees his chosen people's future. But Israel must also *become* God's people — another aspect of Yahwist faith to which we have paid some notice. Those people are to reflect in righteous behavior what God's election of them means. However, for all its promises and faithful heroes, the Old Testament in no small way is a history of Israel's inability to realize that high calling. And in Mark's Gospel the twelve, elected by Jesus himself, cannot realize it either. The kingdom of God is at hand; but the people of New Israel, on their own steam, simply cannot get going.

Significantly, this fact of the disciples' inability to repent is, upon later reflection, suggested at the very beginning of Jesus' ministry in Mark. The fact seems clear when Mark's first two items of that ministry are seen in relief of his narration as a whole. Jesus summons Galileans generally to repentance and belief "in the gospel" (1:14–15). Then he issues a particular call to Simon Peter and his brother Andrew and another call to the brothers James and John to follow him — and the four of them do (1:16–20). Hence, with Jesus' preaching of repentance still ringing the air and with John's preaching of it only a few verses past, Mark assembles the most intimate of Jesus' disciples — Peter, James, and John, the privileged three. Readers of these pages will recall how *that* trio fares in Mark's Gospel! The old, self-serving ways are so ingrained in them that they seem, if anything, excellent examples of how *not* to repent.

Similarly, the disciples as a whole cannot meet the demand for repentance. In Jesus' commitment to do God's will by serving a new righteousness, they side with him, yes, even pledge him their allegiance to death (14:31), but only at last to forsake him and flee (14:50). Along the way, moreover, the twelve even go out themselves and preach that "men *should* repent" (6:12); yet the subjunctive mood of the statement, itself a Marcan composition, ironically reflects their own incapacity to do so. Proleptically, those disciples display a pettiness that flies in the face of their particular calling, as though Jesus' own lead meant nothing. Privy to his special instruction and encouragement (4:1–12, 33–34), and having heard his public call for self-denial and cross-bearing (8:34), they nonetheless fall into a discussion about which of them is the greatest (9:33–34). Evidently, the required new righteousness, present among them in Jesus himself, is beyond the disciples' reach, so far in fact that repentance for them seems out of the question.

In his depiction of the disciples, however, Mark doesn't aim to make them whipping boys or mere object lessons.[26] *Jesus* chose them. Rather, especially in line with the eschatological thrust of his Gospel, Mark's "low" view of the disciples exemplifies what he holds to be true for all people: (1) they cannot comprehend Jesus' identity apart from his death; and (2) they can try to repent, as indeed they should, but they cannot themselves succeed at it. This latter impossibility is highlighted, dramatically and with kerygmatic force, in Mark's introduction. He describes John's preaching of repentance as having been incredibly successful: *all* the people of Judea and Jerusalem confessed their sins and were baptized by him (1:5). Yet the Baptist says publicly,

> After me comes he who is mightier than I, the thong of whose sandals I am not worthy to stoop down and untie. I have baptized you with water, but he will baptize you with the Holy Spirit. (Mk. 1:7–8)

Obviously a Christian addition to John's actual preaching, this word was to say, in effect, that his "baptism of repentance" (for all its unparalleled success!) could not bring off what it seemed to promise. It could not usher in the God-directed righteousness which lies at the heart of repentance. Instead, that new reality for people had to await their being "baptized" by Jesus. Through him alone, Mark immediately hints in his story of Jesus' baptism (1:9–11), was to be established the all-embracing righteousness of Israel's end-time hope. Thus, in Mark's Gospel the impossibility of repentance is part and parcel of the good news that the world's repentance has been achieved.

The corporate significance of Jesus' righteousness. No less a word than that — the achievement of repentance as a new reality for humankind – seems adequate to convey Mark's meaning in his use of the baptism tradition. The baptized Jesus is not only the Christ, the righteous and triumphant Messiah. He is also the Suffering Servant, the righteous one in union with whom all others are to be made righteous themselves. As such, Jesus is the one participant in John's baptism of repentance who has truly repented. Like no one else before or since, he turned completely *away* from sin and completely *toward* God in obedience and faithful trust. And precisely in doing that, he turned the word around with him. Hence, as Mark understands Jesus' Servant-sacrifice, the end of the world is present, is knocking at the gate; and the new age of the victorious Messiah has arrived, bringing into being the kingdom of God's righteousness for all. In other words, as Mark's correlation of the baptism story and John's preaching of repentance suggests, *in and with Jesus we have repented!*

"Jesus has truly repented, and so have we in and with him." At first sight, that word might seem also to suggest that Jesus himself was a sinner, one who needed to confess and turn away from sins of his own. Nothing, however, could be farther from Mark's intent or farther from his dramatic disclosure of Jesus' secret identity. To be sure, Mark reports without apology Jesus' objection to being called "good" – and readers must decide for themselves whether this man was "good" like God (10:17–18). Similarly, Mark records the fact of Jesus' baptism with no attempt whatever to deny explicitly Jesus' need of the forgiveness that John's ministry offered to people – a denial which, while appearing in later reports, would have detracted from the artistry of Mark's Gospel and, particularly, its "mysterious" character. At the same time, there can be no doubt of Jesus' utter righteousness as Mark takes care to present him. That is certain in Jesus' identity alone: the promised Messiah and the Isaianic Servant, both of which figures, we have noted, obtained an inherent righteousness fully consistent with God's purpose for Israel and the world. Further, Mark's Gospel is replete with traditions of Jesus doing the kind of good works that God's demand for radical obedience immediately bids. Without thought for his own security, his every deed mirrors the new, end-time righteousness of the kingdom of God at hand. For Mark, as for the Church apparently from its earliest days, all recollections of Jesus of Nazareth are of one whose actions were righteous indeed. Not without cause, the righteousness of Jesus was taken as historical fact. And since Mark took it as fact, he was able to suggest that repentance is now a reality for the world. Because Jesus lived the kind of God-directed life that lasting repentance entails, his righteousness/repentance becomes humanity's common property.

What we meet here is, again, a concept of human corporateness which, while foreign to the Western mind, is taken for granted in much of biblical thought.[27] Often referred to as "corporate personality," the idea is that the individual and the group to which he or she belongs are so inseparably related that one member's actions can implicate all others of the group. No mere rule, say, of guilt by external association, this ancient Semitic concept plowed to the heart of human existence. Personality was thought to be corporate in essence: the group rather than the individual constituted personality's basic unit. The individual self was viewed as essentially a corporate being, one whose existence and very life were tied up in that of the group. This did not preclude him or her from genuine importance, as Old Testament faith attests with its multitude of individual heroes and villains, each of whose contributions for better or worse was taken quite seriously. For all their vitality, however, indeed even their ability to commune with God, individuals were not held to be entities in themselves. In Greek thought one's body (*sōma*) sets one off from others, allowing the possibility of being a hermit. But old Hebrew does not even have a word corresponding to *sōma* in that sense. Instead, as ancient Semitic thought had it, the individual and the group, the one and the many, were bound together in a real and effective unity. Hence, one person's actions could be regarded as really involving all other members of the group. They could act in and with that one person.

Much has rightly been made of the prophetic emphasis on individual responsibility before God. The New Testament shares that emphasis. Nevertheless, the idea of human corporateness had scarcely disappeared by the time of the Church's Palestinian birth. It comes across most explicitly in Paul's writings, yet it thrives elsewhere as well. The Church is the body of Christ whose members are as inseparably related as are the members of an individual's body — hands, eyes, ears, and all (1 Cor. 12:12–26). Just as redemption in the Old Testament is corporate, meaning membership in the people Israel, salvation in the New is only within the body of Christ. This is not because God is fussy about one's "joining" the Church, but is simply the fact of the matter. The redeemed person is *in* Christ with all the rest of the redeemed; they *are* members of one body. As such, they participate in a reality that is ever fresh. Their inheritance of redemption is imperishable, undefiled, unfading, for in and through Christ they have been born anew (1 Pet. 1:4, 23). In that one man has been mediated a new covenant, a new relationship between God and his people. It is a relationship established in forgiveness and justification (= righteousness), and a relationship that nothing in all creation can shatter.[28] If one like Adam could formerly engulf others in his guilt, no longer is such the case, as Paul reasons in his letter to the Romans. Taking for granted the universal effects of one man's sin (i.e., "Adam's" — admittedly a strained exegesis of the Hebrew *adam* = mankind), the apostle argues therefrom the similar effects of another man's righteousness — "the one man Jesus Christ" (5:12–21):

> Then as one man's trespass led to condemnation for all men, so one man's act of righteousness leads to acquittal and life for all men. For as by one man's disobedience many were made sinners, so by one man's obedience many will be made righteous. (Rom. 5:18–19)

Thus in the resurrected Jesus Christ, himself the Second Adam (1 Cor. 15:45–47), human corporateness meets its master — not to be replaced by an "enlightened" individualism, rather to be redeemed.

The above New Testament citations assigning corporate importance to Jesus' life, death, and resurrection could be added to many times, both in the Gospels (where it is often dramatized) and in other writings (where it is usually engaged propositionally). As much as anything else that is apt to be missed by most readers today, Semitic corporateness helps unlock the wealth of Mark's Gospel, especially his re-view of Jesus' baptism against the backdrop of the Baptist's call for repentance. That Gospel teems with Semitisms. We have seen this, for example, in the meaning attributed to Jesus' eating with sinners — itself a Marcan clue that Jesus is the righteous Servant who, being "numbered [i.e., united] with the transgressors," is to make them righteous.[29] What a splendid word indeed we therefore encounter in Mark's treatment of the baptism, where Jesus is first identified, albeit subtly, as the Messiah/Suffering Servant. It is as though to say, "Read on, and see that in that one man, thoroughly righteous and baptized by John, you have done what you could not do. You have repented!"

Postscript. We must add a postscript which may seem anticlimactic, but it is not of our making. The word that humankind has repented in Jesus Christ, that *his* turning away from sin and toward God in trustful obedience has turned the world around with him — that eschatological word is not to relieve people of any effort in repentance themselves. Paul, for one, having asserted the corporate effects of Jesus' righteousness, put the screws to that possibility posthaste. "Are we to continue in sin that grace may abound?" he asks rhetorically. "By no means!" he crisply answers and then goes on to explain why not. Those people who know the depth of their own involvement in Jesus' accomplishments cannot enslave themselves to sin; instead, by the power of the resurrection in which they share, they are to walk in newness of life as slaves of righteousness (Rom. 6:1–19). Likewise, Mark's two uses of the verb "repent" are in the present tense, indicating habitual or continuous action. "Be repenting and be believing in the gospel," he has Jesus preaching at the start of his ministry (1:15). And "men should be repenting," according to Mark's summation of the disciples' preaching as they were sent out by Jesus (6:12). All of which is to say that the people of New Israel, as was intended for those of old Israel, must attempt to become what they already are. We *are* righteous in Christ; in him we *have* repented. Therefore, we should *be* repenting, and all the more if we think that Jesus was good like God.

So we are returned by the nape to where we began with Mark in this chapter (10:17–22). A rich man, Law-abiding and honorable, calls Jesus "Good Teacher," only to be faced with a greater goodness, more immediate and loving, than he has ever willed for himself. "Go," Jesus finally tells him, "sell what you have, and give to the poor." To try to be repenting must surely mean something like that.

Conclusion

What a good person thinks of him- or herself is never the end of the matter. Rather, that person's life — or better to say in this case, what one man's actions seem to reveal about him — must be allowed to speak for itself. Hence this chapter's two points of view: (1) Jesus' negative self-assessment, inevitably the outcome of his humanity in relation to what he believed to be God's demand for radical righteousness; and (2) Mark's historically based and faithful "correction" of that assessment. Both points of view reflect something of Jesus *the man* and therefore, I think, belong together. And each of them is good news.

Chapter 4

Able to Do Miracles at Will?

I've heard of having your faith tested, but this is ridiculous.

—Tandy, in Bruce Jay Friedman's *Steambath*

Can Morty, the Puerto Rican attendant in a steambath somewhere between death and eternity, really be *God?* Young Mr. Tandy, a new arrival whose womanizing career was cut short without warning, doesn't think so. Morty barks orders into a tacky-looking console, directing everything from freeway wrecks to giving "that girl on the bus a run on her body stocking." Tandy, the principal character in Bruce Jay Friedman's play,[1] remains to be persuaded that a steambath operator is God. So Morty, who takes a momentary liking to the rascal Tandy, deigns to prove his deity through a series of miracles, the first of which is a card trick!

While offering a hilarious commentary on human pettiness, Friedman is playing with popular ideas about what God Almighty is (or should be) like. Not the least of them is the notion that divinity is certainly manifest in mighty works which otherwise go unexplained. To his credit in that regard, Tandy persists in his skepticism. Morty's stunts get progressively better. The last of them, majestically transforming Morty to the accompaniment of deafening organ music, brings Tandy himself down to one knee, albeit begrudgingly. Nevertheless, for all his spoiled ambition and self-deceit, Tandy seems to know that a miracle here and there will not authenticate God to humankind. And never mind that Tandy has a completely self-centered view of what God *ought* to do. Miracles in themselves prove nothing.

That simple point, comically made by Friedman, is the immediate point of this chapter. Miracles, regardless of who performs them, do not demonstrate divinity. Nor can they verify the uniqueness of any historical figure. That holds for Jesus' miracles, even though his performance of miracles may be established as a reasonable fact.

The Church, for a large part, has tended to disagree with this evaluation of the miraculous in the ministry of Jesus. According to popular Christian thought, not to mention occasional arguments from the theologically trained, the miracles of Jesus provide data to support his divinity. He was able to do miracles at will, which meant that he was actually divine.

Such thinking is unfortunate for Christian faith. Besides rendering to Jesus a sort of omnipotence that shatters his genuine humanity, any argument that his miracles indicate divinity for him falls heir to two fallacies: (1) it entails circular logic, in that it begins with an assumption which the argument is supposed to prove; and (2) it banks on a historically naive understanding of Gospel traditions about Jesus' miracles. The first of these failings we shall examine forthwith. The other one should become apparent in our discussion of the miracle-tradition itself: that is, as it was both rooted in historical fact *and* subsequently embellished.[2]

Apologetics Running in Circles

Christian apologetics, whenever it tries to prove the truth or demonstrate the general reasonableness of any Christian doctrine, degenerates into a futile and logically illegitimate business. It becomes futile because articles of faith cannot be proved, not even to believers; else they would not be articles *of faith*. And it is logically illegitimate because the so-called demonstrated proof is unashamedly based on one or more unprovable assumptions. Although this criticism applies to theistic apologetics as a whole, it is all the more acute for apologetics of the Christian or Bible-related variety. The latter variety attempts to do exactly what Christian or biblical faith suggests can never be done: that is, to make the tenets of a faith which God reveals only to believers "reasonable" or "acceptable" to the public at large. Though perhaps issuing in false comfort to believers (especially if their doctrines are under attack), such an enterprise offers nothing but propaganda. The sophisticated or simply the alert viewer will see it as poor propaganda at that.

Nowhere is this inadequacy of Christian apologetics more glaring than in arguments that present Jesus' divinity and his miracles as necessarily or reasonably interrelated. Those miracles, it is often maintained, both attest to and result from his being divine. To wit:

Jesus did miracles, *therefore* he was divine; conversely, Jesus was divine, *therefore* he did miracles. The circular character of such logic is so transparent that only people who hunger for persuasion would ever be moved by it. It is the logic of Eric Hoffer's "true believer," one whose mind-set lets *a priori* assumptions control whatever may pass for acceptable evidence in order to arrive at conclusions which are already in tow. Granted, as we will see, Jesus of Nazareth did some things that were deemed miraculous by friends and foes alike and by himself as well. Nonetheless, the connection of that with his being divine weaves together so many unverifiable assumptions that guarded skeptics are then prompted to throw up their hands in yet greater disbelief. Consider three such interlocking assumptions, not one of which has the slightest chance of ever being proved in this world.

1. God exists. This one we treated in our introduction. Were it within the realm of empirical demonstration, all informed persons would be theists, save some in the clutches of severe emotional/mental disorder.

2. God alone causes miracles to happen. This second assumption, so essential to extrapolating Jesus' divinity from his miracles, has often been qualified by the ambiguous term "good." God alone causes *good* miracles to happen — which all the more rests the matter not on measurable ground but in the eyes of the beholder. In any case, the assumption here imposes an arbitrary explanation on all humanly confounding (yet good?) phenomena. Moreover, it goes against New Testament items. On the one hand, if such phenomena *must* be regarded as directly wrought by God, the door is slammed shut to all other possibilities, including scientific explanations from newly gained knowledge. Informed reason in the twentieth century cannot agree to that. Nor, on the other hand, could first-century reason specifically informed by certain Jewish or Christian traditions. According to those traditions, finitely inexplicable phenomena might be the doings of Satan. For instance, consider the tradition underlying Mark 3:22 (reported independently in Mt. 12:24 = Lk. 11:15). Scribes from Jerusalem are said to have charged Jesus with being "possessed by Beelzebul" and casting out demons "by the prince of demons." Whether the accusation itself is authentic, or whether Satan and demons exist, makes no difference. Even if this tradition arose after Jesus' ministry, its appearance clearly tells that interpretation of his mighty (and good) works could be decided only by faith, either faith "in" Jesus or faith "against" him, not by unbiased reason faced with "miraculous" data. And that leads to the third assumption in apologetic attempts to link Jesus' miracles and his divinity.

3. God became a man in Jesus Christ. Solely a Christian belief about God, this assumption has no apologetic force at all outside the Christian community, however many and varied the miracles that might be attributed to Jesus. Nor should it be used incidentally to bolster Christian acceptance of his miracles: that is, on the grounds that he was unique. For in that linkage of miracles and divinity, Jesus' uniqueness gets lost in a sea of other miracle-workers.

The pitfalls of laying the divinity of Jesus at the feet of his miracles are plain to see in early Christian apologetics. As G. W. H. Lampe has carefully shown,[3] fourth-century apologists like Arnobius, Athanasius, and Eusebius were playing against a stacked deck. Using his miracles to demonstrate that Jesus was God, those apologists were brought up short by a world in which miracles were commonplace. Stories about miracle-workers abounded not only among the Jews, whose tales of such persons often reached far back into Old Testament times, but also among the Greeks and others. In Hellenistic thought particularly, miracle-workers were sometimes called "divine men." The term signified unusually gifted persons who, in their special wisdom or their ability to do miracles, shared in a divine nature or relationship. The divine man was "a mixture of the human and the divine," in the citation of Hans Dieter Betz.[4] As such, according to Betz's description of Hellenistic anthropology, the divine man was man in the fullest sense: one who, in attaining his possibility for being divine, had become more than his merely animal possibilities allowed. While that may overstate the case, "divine men" were often known to work miracles.

Given that kind of intellectual environment concerning the miraculous (which vacillated from time to time), Christian apologists were bound to fail in verifying Jesus' uniqueness or his being God on the basis of his miracles. But how they tried! With "divine men" all around, apologists sought to make Jesus' miracles incomparable and superior to anyone else's. For example, besides citing traditionally affirmed healings and cures, Athanasius ascribed to the divine Logos, "who is Christ, the formation of his own body from the Virgin and the raising of it from the dead."[5] Agreeing with Athanasius that his resurrection and ascension were of Christ's own doing, Eusebius further announced that the moment of Jesus' death came exactly when he willed it.[6] Not even those wild claims, however, persuaded Hellenistic thinkers to see Jesus as distinct from other allegedly power-filled men. Nor could the public mind, on its own, regard his miraculous deeds as having any special import. Eventually aware of this, Christian apologists appealed to the idea of Jesus' being *uniquely* divine. In other words, they came full circle, predicating as an assumption the very article they were trying to prove. Lampe's summation puts the dilemma nicely:

> Miracles might commend Christ, but Christ was first needed to commend the miracles. It was not enough to ask men to believe in Christ's divinity because of the miracles; they had to be asked to believe the miracle-stories because they first accepted his divinity.[7]

Most Christians today are apt to smile at the shenanigans of Athanasius and company, but shuddering is more in order for the apologetics they represent. Their boldest claims concerning Christ's divine power made a joke of early traditions indicating his real humanity. Although one who forms his own body from the womb or raises it from death is certainly *more* than a man, it is equally clear that he is also *less* than a man. Nor is Jesus' divinity itself served by an argument from miracles. Rather, it is thereby denigrated and his uniqueness thereby denied. Not even the contention that he raised people from death will work in favor of his being divine or unique. According to ancient stories that circulated alongside the Jesus-traditions, resurrections were also performed by other miracle-workers — Hellenistic "divine men," Jewish rabbis, the Old Testament figures of Elijah and Elisha, and so on. One can scarcely say, except by fiat, that the traditions of Jesus' raisings are surely valid whereas all other like stories are not. Thus, the argument from miracles suggests divinity here, divinity there, divinity just about everywhere. It is not a promising logic.

In order to avert confusion, I should interject that nothing within these pages is meant to minimize the uniqueness of Jesus. Still, that uniqueness must ultimately be seen in what *God* is said to have done in and through him, not in what Jesus himself did. That he seemed one of a kind in his own day and place, particularly in his active concern for righteousness, was stressed in our previous chapter. It is also true that history moves on and, therefore, permits no clones. Nevertheless, who can say factually that Jesus' concern for righteousness, or his performance of miracles, is *sui generis* in humanity's life? *Faith* should well say so, especially in terms of

Jesus' redemptive significance. But that word cannot rightly come from any historian who stakes a claim to objectivity and who must avoid making God's judgments. We Christians can't convince the world of Jesus' uniqueness. What's more, our faith wants joy if we must convince ourselves of it. The gospel, however theologians may formulate it, is something to be proclaimed, not something to be proved.

The Miracle-Tradition: Rooted in Fact

Did Jesus of Nazareth perform miracles? Or at least some things that seemed to be miracles?

The question is by no means unimportant in Gospel research. True, as we have often noted, the good news itself does not hinge on the Gospels being factually authentic at every turn, but on the reality of Easter. Within the light of Easter the Church came to an increasingly new understanding of Jesus' significance and thus, amidst practical concerns of its own, "retold" the incidents of his ministry. That was faith speaking for faith, and not for historical accuracy. All the same, the question of historicity is thrust upon us by the Gospels themselves. Purporting to deal with the redemptive consequence of an actual man, they force us to ask whether the figure presented bears any semblance to Jesus of Nazareth as he actually was. A completely negative answer would throw the Gospels, and the Christian confession as well, into wholesale disrepute. We would then be left with an anomaly: a faith which, while touting God's redemptive action in history, has nothing historical to commend it; or, in other terms, a Church which, supposedly remembering how Jesus had been, remembered not at all but instead created a total myth.

The importance of Jesus' miracles in this regard stems from the fact that they play so large a role in the Gospels — most of all Mark, the earliest Gospel. According to the calculations of Alan Richardson, 200 of the 425 verses in Mark 1–10 are involved directly or indirectly with the miraculous.[8] That is nearly half of Mark's account of Jesus' ministry prior to Passion Week! The authenticity of the miracle-tradition, therefore, can hardly be by-passed in the larger question of the Gospels' historical worth.

But note that we are speaking of the miracle-tradition in the singular. Whether Gospel reports of Jesus' miracles (plural) derive from authentic traditions (plural) is a question that can only be answered (if at all) one reported miracle at a time. Although several of

Jesus' miracles will hold our attention, a detailed study of the numerous traditions underlying them is beyond what we can or need do in this chapter. Rather, the immediate question here concerns the *general* tradition that Jesus worked miracles. Namely, was there such a tradition that was rooted in historical fact?

The answer to this question is, most assuredly, yes. Three kinds of testimony dictate it, even for critics whose personal beliefs rule out divine intervention in earthly affairs.

1. Extrabiblical attestation. One kind of testimony comes from a Jewish source. Actually, aside from Christian literature, there are two principal references to Jesus as a miracle-worker—in Josephus's *The Antiquities of the Jews* (18.3.3) and in the Jews' Babylonian Talmud (Sanhedrin 43a). The reference in Josephus is widely recognized as part of a later addition, favorable to Jesus and surely the result of Christian influences. Not so, however, the Talmudic reference, regarded by many critics as a product of early rabbinic tradition. Significantly, it charges one named "Jesus" with wrongdoing:

> On the eve of Passover they hanged Yeshu [of Nazareth] and the herald went before him for forty days saying, "[Yeshu of Nazareth] is going forth to be stoned in that he hath practised sorcery and beguiled and led astray Israel. Let everyone knowing aught in his defence come and plead for him." But they found naught in his defence and hanged him on the eve of Passover.[9]

Notably polemical in its general accusation of defenseless guilt, this reference grants Jesus' doing of miracles, yet calls it "sorcery" (black magic). If authentic and referring to Jesus of Nazareth, it seems clear evidence that he had a solid reputation for miracles. This is particularly so in the desire to smear rather than refute that reputation. The Jewish charge of sorcery, by the way, is also indicated in second-century Christian writing (e.g., by Justin Martyr, c. A.D. 155). Moreover, as Reginald Fuller observes, if the Talmudic sorcery-charge is independently reminiscent of the Gospel accusation that Jesus cast out demons by the power of Satan (Mk. 3:22), it suggests a genuine reputation that specifically included exorcisms.[10] And exorcisms would be among the easiest of Jesus' miracles to explain today. Seizures and other displays of uncontrolled behavior, which we attribute to neurological and biochemical factors, were widely taken then as evidence of demon-possession. When such factors allowed a person's behavior to return to normal, an exorcism was thought to have occurred.

2. Multiple attestation of Gospel forms. Certainly the strongest testimony for the essential historicity of the miracle-tradition is located in the Gospels themselves. It comes from the fact that Jesus' having done miracles is expressed in multiple forms or kinds of Gospel traditions, not just in one such form. However, before we proceed to the principle at work here, some remarks are in order about form criticism – an aspect of literary study that is especially pertinent to the remaining concerns of this chapter.[11]

A translation of the German word *Formgeschichte* (literally, form-history), the term "form criticism," when applied to Gospel research, denotes scholarly concern with the history of traditions related to Jesus. Where did they come from, how did they develop, and why?[12] Since the pioneering form-critical studies of Karl L. Schmidt, Martin Dibelius, and Rudolph Bultmann first appeared in the years 1919–21, it has been an axiom that oral traditions about Jesus assumed a variety of forms. Recent study tells that, because of the interplay between speaker and hearers, oral communication of those traditions no doubt varied; and some stories likely changed on occasion from one general form or kind to another.[13] Even so, distinct forms of Jesus-traditions are discernible. Each such form, like its counterparts in ancient cultures, has characteristics of its own, allowing the trained eye to identify that form in the Gospels. Among the different forms thus identified (with occasional overlapping) are: pronouncement stories (providing settings for sayings of Jesus); miracle stories (focusing on miracles themselves); parables; other sayings of Jesus (several types, orally transmitted with or without a narrative setting); historical stories (sometimes biographical); legends; and, some would say, myths.

Now this: ancients habitually credited made-up deeds and sayings to historical personages. Therefore, whether an item in any of the Gospel forms is to be deemed probably authentic depends on how well it meets such criteria as we have often employed in this study. First, is the item not likely a product of the early Church[14] (or of contemporary Jewish influences?)?[15] Or, second, is it somehow consistent with other items that meet the test of authenticity? Or, third, the principle before us here: Is the item attested to in a multiplicity of Gospel forms?[16] To understand this criterion, one must appreciate that no form in and by itself lends historical value to any saying or fact reported about Jesus. The saying or fact could have been invented either to serve a speaker's or the Church's particular concerns or else simply to fit the form. However, to quote Edgar McKnight's general observation regarding scholarly judgment, "When a teaching or purportedly historical fact occurs in more than one form the possible authenticity of that teaching or fact is increased."[17] And, I may add, the more forms the better. The reasoning here is that an item's appearance in multiple forms suggests that it likely existed before the forms were composed, rather than its having been invented to suit the forms and, say, the Church's interests.

Such is the case with the reported fact that Jesus performed healing miracles. The fact occurs not only in miracle stories (where it is to be expected) but in pronouncement stories, historical stories, and gathered sayings of Jesus as well. In every instance of a miracle story proper, save one semiexception (noted below), the miracle is obviously essential to both the form and the Christian intent of the story.[18] A miracle, however, is not essential to a pronouncement story. The tradition reported in Mark 3:1-5 offers a vivid example.[19] Whereas Jesus' sabbath healing of a man with a withered hand provides the context for a confrontation with his Jewish opponents, his word to them is the story's primary concern: "Is it lawful on the sabbath to do good or to do harm, to save life or to kill?" (3:4). That saying, so typical of Jesus, could have held in any number of settings or, for that matter, could have stood on its own. It didn't need a miracle for support. Given the indifference of Gospel traditions to modern biography, we may not assume that the saying's actual occasion was necessarily similar to the one provided in Christian oral transmission. Nevertheless, that context, nonessential to the saying itself, does indicate that Jesus' reputation as a miracleworker was extant before this pronouncement story was formulated. Significantly in that regard, the story may have been one of the earliest Jesus-traditions. Concerned with sabbath observance, it probably originated in the Palestinian church, where the question would hold special interest. Also to the point of genuineness, the story lacks a christological thrust – that is, does not express Christian faith per se (the first criterion noted above regarding an item's authenticity).

A similar word, incidentally, may be said of the one semiexception to what we have noted generally about healing miracle stories in the Gospels. That semiexception is Jesus' healing of Simon Peter's mother-in-law, reported from oral tradition in Mark 1:29-31. Although it follows the threefold pattern of most ancient miracle stories – description of sickness, cure of sickness, proof of cure – the story has no point whatever, Christian or otherwise. The woman is lying sick with a fever, is healed by Jesus, then rises to serve those who are present. Period. While some critics see it as nothing more than legendary, a reflection of the ancient love of storytelling, others regard the tale, particularly in its pointlessness, as a genuine memory.

Multiple attestation applies not only to the variety of *stories* of Jesus' miracles but also to his several alleged *sayings* about himself as a miracle-worker. Whether they are likely authentic will be of paramount interest to us. However, the salient fact here is the widespread appearance of such sayings. They are found in independent traditions underlying Mark (3:23) and Luke (4:23; 13:32) and in traditions coming from so-called Q, a source commonly used by Matthew and Luke in addition to their reliance on Mark.[20] Moreover, those sayings circulated in a wide variety of forms themselves: (*a*) conflict-sayings; (*b*) eschatological sayings; (*c*) a woe-saying; (*d*) a proverbial saying set in a particular context; and (*e*) sayings contained as part of a historical or biographical story.[21] Scholars often differ regarding the origin of these sayings, but that in no way detracts from their remarkably widespread appearance.

What therefore can we say at this juncture? Simply this: if the multiple attestation of Gospel forms lends a degree of authenticity to any purported item about Jesus, then his reputation as a miracle-worker seems unquestionably secure. Miracle stories, pronouncement stories, historical stories, plus several kinds of his reported sayings – this multiplicity of forms concerning Jesus' performance of miracles can ill be dismissed. With a specific gravity of its own, it suggests that his reputation for miracles was grounded in his deeds (whatever those deeds may have been).

3. Authentic sayings of Jesus. Are at least some of Jesus' sayings to which we have just referred authentic themselves? If so, as Fuller remarks, "They contain pretty nearly firsthand evidence that Jesus did perform miracles."[22] That they are *essentially* authentic – meaning that Jesus somehow alluded to his own working of miracles – is, I think, clear enough, although the evidence may not be quite as extensive as Fuller and others have argued.

At issue here are sayings of considerably different historical value. With one exception (Lk. 4:23, treated in our next major section), most likely authentic are those reflecting conflict between Jesus and his opponents: that is, (1) one or more variations of the Beelzebul controversy and (2) Jesus' response to the news that Herod wants to kill him. The other sayings in which Jesus refers to his own miraculous activity are, at best, suspect – a fact to be considered later.

Regarding the Beelzebul controversy (the accusation that Jesus performed exorcisms in association with Satan), three independent traditions come into play, one reported in Mark, the other two standing side by side in Q:

1. "How can Satan cast out Satan?" (Mk. 3:23b)

2. "And if I cast out demons by Beelzebub [Matthew: Beelzebul], by whom do your sons cast them out? Therefore they shall be your judges." (Lk. 11:19 = Mt. 12:27)

3. "But if it is by the finger [Matthew: Spirit] of God that I cast out demons, then the kingdom of God has come upon you." (Lk. 11:20 = Mt. 12:28)

How is the authenticity of these sayings to be settled, especially in a way that makes sense to the general reader? Four preliminary observations will put the matter into easier focus. *First,* it is certain that the Q-sayings (nos. 2 and 3 above) did not originally belong together, since the deeds of exorcists generally (not just those of Jesus) would then have to be seen as manifestations of God's final reign breaking into the present. Rather, because of the similarity of their dependent clauses, one of them probably spun off from the other. *Second,* although the traditions represented in Mark and Q predicate a conflict between Jesus and his Jewish critics regarding his exorcisms, the historical situation(s) that prompted their formulation cannot be determined with certainty. Conceivably, any one of these sayings could have originated in the Church, particularly when Jews countered the Christian belief that miracles performed either by Jesus or in his name were incidents of God's special action. But, *third,* even if the Beelzebul controversy was a later, Christian invention (which seems unlikely in view of its extrabiblical and Gospel attestations), a miracle-worker in Jesus' milieu might well see his own deeds as God's redemptive action overpowering demons.[23] This means that the second Q-saying (no. 3 above) does not intrinsically depend on the historical validity of the Beelzebul controversy. Jesus could have spoken such a word on any appropriate occasion, not just in response to a charge that he was acting in league with the devil. And, *fourth,* the upshot of all this highlights what is the essential authenticity-question for each of these reported sayings. Namely, from what we critically know about Jesus, would the saying have been especially characteristic of him? More likely, therefore, his own than a creation of the Church? In each case, though not for all the same reasons, critical analysis allows an affirmative answer.

The saying most esteemed by nearly every critic is the second one from Q: "But if it is by the finger of God that I cast out demons, then the kingdom of God has come upon you" (Lk. 11:20 = Mt. 12:28). Rudolph Bultmann, the father of severest form-critical skepticism concerning the historical value of Jesus-traditions, nevertheless saw it as claiming "the highest degree of authenticity which we can make for any saying of Jesus."[24] The major reasons usually cited for this kind of assessment are threefold: the saying (1) neither reflects the Church's faith, (2) nor derives from contemporary Judaism, but (3) instead reflects Jesus' sense of eschatological power. More precisely, it lacks explicit reference to Jesus as the Christ, and it characteristically speaks of the kingdom of God contrary to Jewish expectation (i.e., as a present reality, not a reign of God that is wholly in the future).[25] Also, as noted, the genuineness of this saying does not entail the Beelzebul controversy during Jesus' own ministry. Hence its being held in such wide and high esteem.

Now a word to support the first Q-saying: "And if I cast out demons by Beelzebub, by whom do your sons cast them out? Therefore they shall be your judges" (Lk. 11:19 = Mt. 12:27). The reference to the second generation of Jesus' opponents (i.e., sons whose exorcisms will judge their fathers' logic) smacks of Christian polemic. It sounds like an argument against Jews who belittled the Church's exorcisms. But if that is why the saying received its present form, was there an earlier form of it? Change "your sons" to something like "your own" or "others," and delete the second sentence. The saying then vividly exemplifies what we have seen of Jesus' cool control in conflict-situations.[26] When confronted by Jewish hostility to what he was teaching or doing, he regularly turned the tables on his critics, putting them in an exposed position with a word they had not expected. So, too, here. Jesus bares the Beelzebul accusation for the hollow thing it is — prejudiced from the start and applicable to every exorcist in sight, those in good standing included.

My suggestion for a possible earlier form of the first Q-saying is pure conjecture, of course, but only to point out that the saying is the *kind* of response Jesus would make if accused of working through Satan. Mark's independent tradition of Jesus' retort to the charge is also typical: "How can Satan cast out Satan?" (3:23b). In other words, talk about nonsense, are the forces of Satan in civil war?

So each of Jesus' reported sayings that were traditionally linked with the Beelzebul controversy sounds like Jesus. Regardless of which one may be closest to his actual words, it would seem far-fetched to suppose that none of them came from Jesus, so enveloped are they in an aura of authenticity.

Turning now to the conflict between Herod and Jesus (Lk. 13:31–33), we meet another tradition that may be essentially genuine. Some Pharisees urge Jesus to flee for his life with the warning that Herod wants to kill him. Jesus answers,

> Go and tell that fox, "Behold, I cast out demons and perform cures today and tomorrow." (Lk. 13:32a)

The last clause of verse 32 ("and the third day I finish my course") looks like a Christian interpolation pointing to the resurrection. But nothing in verse 32a indicates a post-Easter creation of the Church. True, one may see the whole incident as a fabrication, with the Pharisees "treated as lackeys of Herod, passing on their master's threat and bidden to carry back the scornful reply of Jesus."[27] That view, however, requires nuance of the tradition and thus disregards the early Christian tendency (which actually increased as time passed) to put the scribes and Pharisees in a *strikingly* bad light. On the surface – and that's all we have to go by here – the Pharisees of this incident seem genuinely concerned for Jesus' welfare. They encourage him to flee for his life! Moreover, Jesus' response in verse 32a bears no trace whatever of Christian faith – no implication of his messiahship, not even a hint that his mighty works possess a special importance. Instead, the saying coheres with Jesus' determination to continue his ministry, come what may. Its essential authenticity, therefore, is at least viable.

Conclusion and caveat. The conclusion to be drawn from the testimonies above seems inescapable. Behind the various Jesus-traditions reported in the Gospels there was a firm miracle-tradition, a reputation for mighty works that basically derived from Jesus' own deeds. He most certainly performed exorcisms and, perhaps, healings as well, especially if the healings were originally understood as a release from demonic power. The evidence for this conclusion comes from a Jewish source, from independent Gospel sources, from nearly all the different kinds of Jesus-traditions, and from apparently genuine sayings of Jesus himself. Indeed, did he not perform miracles, we should then have to confess to yet a greater wonder – a historical attestation so rich that its origin defies explanation.

With that said, a twofold caution must be posted against taking the fact of Jesus' miracles too far. On the one hand, as already indicated, miracles were commonplace in the first century, if only because scientific explanations of routine and abnormal occurrences were still centuries to come for the people in the street. Their view of reality was far from ours. This is not to say that Jesus did nothing which would qualify as a miracle today. That contention, though perhaps correct, stems from an *a priori* assumption which cannot be proved anyway – the idea that the natural progression of things is never violated, not even by an act of God. At the same time, it would strain the imagination to suppose that differences between first- and twentieth-century views of reality played no part in the origin of the miracle-tradition. For that supposition not only predicates the real existence of Satan and countless minor devils. It removes the deeds of the historical Jesus – in fact, removes Jesus himself – from his own historical environment.

On the other hand, among the ancients, the deeds of miracle-workers were speedily and greatly enhanced.[28] Once such a person's reputation came into favorable view, his miracles were customarily multiplied, often several times over and not seldom without any substantial evidence to support the deeds newly assigned to him. To say that nothing of the sort could have happened concerning Jesus' reputation as a miracle-worker is, in the long haul, a rather credulous and naive proposition. It would be as if first-century Christians, unlike all other Christians, were insulated people, totally unaffected by the customs of their world.

But more directly to the point is the critically ascertainable fact that Gospel traditions often reveal an enhancement of the miraculous. That Jesus did some things which could be seen at the time only as miracles is, I repeat, beyond reasonable dispute. Yet equally clear is the fact that the miracle-tradition, whatever its original content, had taken on significant embellishments by the time it reached the Gospel writers. It is an important fact. Important for understanding Gospel traditions. Important for understanding Jesus of Nazareth in the weakness of human flesh. The fact is important, therefore, for historians and Christians alike.

The Miracle-Tradition: Subsequently Embellished

"Embellishment" is not used here to suggest a willy-nilly expansion of the miracle-tradition, as though the thing got out of hand. The term denotes, instead, a purposeful enhancement of the miracle-tradition, carefully in line with Christian faith and practical concerns of the Church. Granted, in Gospel narratives of Jesus' miracles one frequently detects products of the art of storytelling: for example, picturesque details or incidental items that would capture or focus attention. That kind of innovation by itself, however, is not what we have in mind. Rather, the embellishment to be observed here involved fundamental changes — alterations of the original tradition that were both radical and historically creative. Radical in the sense of redefining the miracle-tradition from the vantage point of post-Easter faith: Jesus is the Messiah, and the Church is his people called to be faithful in the world. And historically creative in the sense of reworking and enlarging the miracle-tradition to express that new found faith and existential obligation.

For sake of discussion, we may put that embellishment of the miraculous into sharper focus. *Jesus' reported words and his reported deeds were, in great degree, faithful and proper inventions of the Church.*

Invented words/meanings assigned to Jesus. Generally, we have seen, Jesus' conflict-sayings regarding miracles seem characteristic of him. The one exception is the saying reported in Luke 4:23:

> Doubtless you will quote to me this proverb, "Physician, heal yourself; what we have heard you did at Capernaum, do here also in your own country."

The authenticity of this saying appears next to impossible — on two grounds. First, the saying itself is incongruous. The spoken challenge for additional miracles comes as a *non sequitur* to the proverb quoted. That is blatantly artificial construction and anything but calm — not the kind of word a man in control of himself would offer in the give-and-take of public debate. And, second, the saying proposes that Jesus viewed his miracles as a means of proving himself to his opponents. According to independent reports from Mark (8:11–12) and Q (Lk. 11:29 = Mt. 12:39), Jesus adamantly refused to accommodate his opponents with any such sign — and that refusal has the earmarks of being genuine. For these reasons the saying in Luke 4:23 must be regarded as a Christian invention. Awkwardly setting a Jewish proverb in a conflict-situation, it was apparently designed to support the presumption that Jesus' mighty works ought to be sufficient to evoke Christian faith.

A similar conclusion seems required for Q's conveyance of Jesus' woe-saying upon three Galilean cities where, supposedly, he received a frosty reception:

> Woe to you, Chorazin! woe to you, Bethsaida! for if the mighty works done in you had been done in Tyre and Sidon, they would have repented long ago in sackcloth and ashes. But I tell you, it shall be more tolerable on the day of judgment for Tyre and Sidon than for you. And you, Capernaum, will you be exalted to heaven? You shall be brought down to Hades. (Mt. 11:21–23 = Lk. 10:13–15)

Though consistent with Q's understanding that Jesus' miracles imply his messiahship (noted below), this saying would have been dull and simplistic on the lips of Jesus. It suggests that his miracles in themselves should have led people to repentance – that is, at very least, to acceptance of him as one who was doing God's will. However, with other wonder-workers aplenty, could Jesus really have expected his miracles alone to effect wholesale repentance or to commend him so widely to people? Besides that obvious difficulty, two Gospel facts in particular impugn the genuineness of the saying: (1) nowhere else are Chorazin (otherwise unknown in the N.T.) and Bethsaida mentioned as sites of Jesus' mighty works; and (2) independent reports indicate that he got an enthusiastic response in Capernaum (Mt. 9:8; Mk. 1:27–28). This woe-saying, therefore, seems best explained as a prophecy after the fact. Reflecting the Church's own unsuccessful mission in Galilee, it makes that failure a matter of destiny. Hence, what we have in this saying is a practical, strictly apologetic enlargement of the miracle-tradition – not exactly inspirational reading today.

Far more substantial and interesting, particularly as confessional embellishments, are two similar sayings from Q. Each of them refers to things "seen" and "heard" as manifestations of eschatological realization, the dawning of God's new reign. Taken together they connote, *in Q,* that Jesus' mighty works reveal him to be the Messiah. That was a standard Christian interpretation flowing through the miracle-traditions directly beneath the Synoptic Gospels.[29] Jesus is the Promised One in whom, for instance, God's deathblow to Satan has been, and is being, delivered. Only one of these sayings, though, seems basically authentic. Furthermore, apart from Q's implication for it, it has nothing to do with Jesus' messiahship and, originally, perhaps nothing to do with miracles either. That is the blessedness-saying to those who have received timely knowledge:

> Blessed are the eyes which see what you see! For I tell you that many prophets and kings desired to see what you see, and did not see it, and to hear what you hear, and did not hear it. (Lk. 10:23b–24 = Mt. 13:16–17)

Typical of Jesus' perspective that God's final rule was invading the present as a brand-new reality, this saying most probably originated with him. But what observable things did he have in mind? The saying does not detail them, so that the particulars alluded to here need not be confined to, or even include, his miracles. Other possibilities are certainly available: Jesus' teaching about God's demand for a "new" (i.e., radical) righteousness in contrast to the old constraints of Jewish legalism; the opening of God's saving fellowship to "publicans and sinners" through Jesus' own acceptance of them; his attraction of such ne'er-do-wells in contrast to the limitations of customary Jewish exclusiveness; his word itself, in concert with any one or more of his own activities, that the dawning of the Eschaton is already in sight; and so on. In Q's presentation of Jesus' response to a query from John the Baptist (whether Jesus is the Messiah, addressed by the saying below), the things "seen" and "heard" are identified in a list of miracles. That may seem to suggest that miracles are meant in this blessedness-saying as well. However, only if the response to John is authentic may one surely suppose that here too is a word from Jesus about the revelatory significance of his mighty works, and with a messianic implication at that. Otherwise, Q's messianic understanding of the blessedness-saying seems most likely a post-Easter development, assigning to Jesus' miracles a meaning obtained from the Church's faith. By itself, the blessedness-saying does not offer a messianic meaning for any of the things seen and heard, whatever they might have been.

We turn then to Jesus' response as to whether he is the one "who is to come" — the question carried to him through John the Baptist's disciples. Jesus answers (Lk. 7:22–23 = Mt. 11:4b–6):

> Go, report to John what you hear and see:
> the blind see,

> the lame walk,
> lepers are cleansed,
> and the deaf hear,
> the dead are raised,
> the poor are preached good news,
> and blessed is he who is not offended in me.[30]

So very much has been made of this saying in both scholarly and popular writing, not to mention homiletical use, that we must consider it in greater detail than is customary for general readers. Besides the fact that laypersons are regularly spared its historical fuzziness, the skillful composition of the saying merits attention itself.

In the context Q supplies for it (Lk. 7:18–19 = Mt. 11:2–4a), the response to John, more than any other saying, provides a striking clue to Q's commonly shared Christian understanding that Jesus' miracles have messianic import. By itself, the phrase "he who is to come" (Lk. 7:19 = Mt. 11:3) need not connote the Messiah. It could signify anyone whose arrival was thought to herald the Eschaton – say, Elijah redivivus, the Messiah's forerunner. However, in the Q material following this saying, the role of eschatological messenger is assigned to John himself (Lk. 7:27 = Mt. 11:10). Converting Malachi 3:1 into a messianic prophecy by substituting second person pronouns,[31] Q identifies John as forerunner of Messiah Jesus. Therefore, John's question about the one "who is to come" concerns not merely Jesus' eschatological significance in general but his messianic identity in particular. And Jesus' response, in cataloging marvelous things that are heard and seen, thus gives to his miracles the function of messianic signs. Yes, those miracles indicate, he is indeed the Messiah. It is not an outright messianic claim by Jesus, yet a clear-cut implication for his wonderful deeds; and John should ponder them as such himself. Least of all, the saying in Q finally suggests, should he be offended by the wide-hearted mercy of Jesus' gospel, itself antithetical to the fiery judgment that John had expected (Lk. 3:16–17 = Mt. 3:11–12).

But is Q's presentation of this saying historically genuine? More exactly, did Jesus actually enumerate his miracles as the saying lists them, either in response to a question from John or in any other circumstance? The introductory line quoted above – "Go, report to John what you hear and see" – is pointless, except in relation to the larger context provided by Q. As we have just observed, however, that context in Q is messianic, unmistakably a reflection of the

Church's christology. So both John's question and Jesus' allusion to it (referring to things being heard and seen) clearly seem a Christian invention. This means that the similar but ambiguous reference to things "seen" and "heard" in Q's blessedness-saying continues to be ambiguous. Even if that saying came from Jesus, it cannot be taken certainly to denote his miracles, let alone imply a messianic import for them or for any observable thing. One cannot remove the ambiguity of a genuine saying by appealing to the clarity of a similar yet fabricated word.

Now to the other half of our question. Apart from allegedly responding to John (i.e., drop the introductory line), did Jesus ever speak of his miracles as this saying indicates? Those scholars who think he did have correctly observed that the saying (1) in alluding to end-time salvation as "already in process... is characteristic of Jesus" and (2) lacks "the *explicit* Christology of the post-Easter church."[32] The authenticity of this saying, however, cannot be settled so easily. As a scripturally coherent and metrically balanced recitation of various miracles that were making the rounds about Jesus, it is unlike any other saying attributed to him. Furthermore, while no such listing could be expected to mention every kind of miracle assigned to Jesus, curiously absent here is the one kind that seems authentic in his self-references elsewhere — namely, exorcisms.

In enumerating traditionally affirmed miracles of Jesus, this saying assembles, quite nicely, Day-of-Salvation deeds prophesied in the book of Isaiah (26:19a; 29:18; 35:5–6a; 61:1a). Admittedly, as champions of the saying occasionally argue, none of those prophecies is quoted verbatim. But that may be readily explained by a combination of four exigencies: (1) a change in perspective, from what will occur to what is occurring; (2) an economy of words, to make the saying manageable; (3) inclusion of deeds not mentioned in the prophecies (i.e., cleansing of lepers), to make the list of Jesus' miracles fuller and thereby balanced;[33] and (4) an obvious desire for poetic symmetry. Nonetheless, the wording is undeniably close to that of the Septuagint — and regarding Isaiah 26:19a (the dead), 29:18a (the deaf), and 61:1a (the poor), it could not be closer and still be symmetrical and present tense! Indeed, the Septuagint must have been lying open-at-hand when this saying was formulated.[34] That would not be unusual. For one of the early Church's basic beliefs was that Israel's Scriptures (O.T. promises, requirements, events seen anew) are fulfilled in Jesus Christ. The idea permeates the New Testament, Gospel traditions especially, and Old Testament texts are often alluded to without restraint to make the point. With that belief and practice backstage, the *implicit* christology of this saying seems to wave at the audience. Be that as it may, the extreme care and dexterity with which this saying was no doubt composed, joining traditions of Jesus' miracles to prophecies from Isaiah virtually word for word (see note 34), can only suggest a Christian origin for it. Although individual coincidences may sometimes occur, an extended series of them strung in a concise, adroit listing like this one exceeds the realm of probable chance.

We may now summarize these findings concerning embellishments of the miracle-tradition in Jesus' alleged sayings. Of the four sayings we have considered, three appear beyond question to be creations of the Church. And the other one, if it originated with Jesus *and* if he was alluding to his miracles, most certainly did not carry the messianic sense that Q implied for it. Such embellishments of the miracle-tradition, even when they arose for purely practical reasons, reflected postresurrection faithfulness – and in that, I should add, they were honest creations. For in the early Church's view, it was the risen Christ who was leading his people into new understanding; and the risen Christ was believed to be one and the same person with Jesus of Nazareth. What better way to express that belief than to put post-Easter meanings back into Jesus' own mouth? According to early Christian faith, embellishments like that were inspired.

Invented deeds assigned to Jesus. However good a miracle-worker may be with words, it's the miracles that draw the crowd. Similarly, the deeds assigned to Jesus are the main attraction of the miracle-tradition's embellishment. Even should none of his miracles be written off as the airy invention of a Gospel writer, it is clear that the traditions which the evangelists received were chock-full of embellishments. Virtually all the stories involving miracles provide evidence of Christian embellishment. Three groups of them should suffice to illustrate the fact: nature miracles, cleansing lepers, and raisings of the dead.

1. NATURE MIRACLES. Time was when Jesus' nature miracles[35] were subjected to rational explanation. Influenced by a renewed scientific and philosophical emphasis on cause-and-effect relationships, Protestant liberalism, especially of the late eighteenth century, often sought down-to-earth reasons for the origin of such stories that appear in the Gospels. Hence, for example, Jesus did not actually walk on water. Rather, he was walking in the shallows, and it was a very

foggy day. Likewise, his feeding of five thousand people, allegedly with only a couple of fish and five loaves of bread, was in truth a chain reaction among the crowd to a boy's example of sharing.

Contemporary scholarship smiles. Not because it always disagrees with the proposition that the nature miracles so-called were not actual violations of natural processes, but because of the naïveté inherent in any attempt to turn unsubstantiated "events" into credible occurrences. Wanting to have its cake and eat it too, old theological liberalism assumed that no such miracles ever happen, yet it strove to preserve a historical basis for Gospel accounts of them. Nowadays, scholarship in the main approaches the matter from a different angle – in view of evidence. It tries to get at the intended meaning of the nature miracles, not to make the stories of them more or less believable history. Two related generalities then emerge.

On the one hand, the nature miracles, without exception, have nothing to commend them beyond Christian testimony – and relatively meager testimony to boot. Unlike the healings and exorcisms, they are not mentioned in Q or in any of Jesus' reported sayings; nor are they even included in Mark's own summaries of Jesus' mighty works (1:32–34, 39; 3:7–12; 6:53–56). Moreover, none of the traditions of the nature miracles puts them in public view. Instead, only Jesus' disciples (plus the servants, in the case of water being changed into wine at the Cana marriage feast) are said to have witnessed them.[36] According to all the traditions and Gospel accounts of the nature miracles, their every performance was a private affair, unobservable, as it were, except to the eyes of faith.

That fact about them comes as no surprise. For, on the other hand, the pre-Gospel traditions of the nature miracles are loaded with Christian interests. Indeed, every detectable form of them reflects some aspect(s) of the Church's faith or life-situations. Three of the traditions focus on practical concerns: (1) the shekel in the fish's mouth (Mt. 17:24–27); (2) the cursing of the fig tree (Mk. 11:12–14, 20–24); and (3) the great netting of fish (as found in Lk. 5:1–11). Taken in order, how do these stories address such concerns of the Church? (1) The shekel in the fish's mouth suggests an affirmative answer to a question about Roman taxation. Addressed initially to Peter, the foremost church pillar, the question is unmistakably rhetorical in form: "Your teacher pays the tax, doesn't he?" The implication then is that Christians should pay the tax too. (2) The cursing of the fig tree, at least in the form that Mark received it (but see below), stresses the efficacy of expectant faith among Christians, particularly in the practice of prayer. And (3) Luke's version of the miraculous netting of fish is related explicitly to the Church's evangelistic mission.

Purely Christian interests are even more pronounced in the christological concerns of the nature miracles. Aside from the three "practical" ones just noted, all traditions of them display the bright and unique light of post-Easter eschatology – the Church's hearty belief that the new age of salvation has arrived in the resurrection of Jesus Christ. For instance, John's version of the miraculous draft of fish (21:1-14), no doubt a variant of the tradition reported in Luke, makes the miracle's occasion an appearance of the risen Lord!

Similarly, the story of Jesus' changing water into wine at the Cana marriage feast (Jn. 2:1-11) is so laden with Christian thought and symbolism, not to mention Johannine nuances, that its being wholly a Christian invention seems almost irrefutable. Jesus is the Messiah. He is the one who, in keeping with symbolic expressions of Israel's hope for future salvation, provides an overabundance of the choicest wine and, in doing so, replaces the Jewish rites of purification.[37]

Turning to the stories of Jesus feeding thousands of hungry people from but an armful of bread and a handful of fish, we again encounter the motifs of messianic plenty and newness,[38] not to mention eucharistic overtones. Variants of the same tradition (indicated by their similarity of details), the feeding of the five thousand (Mk. 6:30-44; Jn. 6:1-13) and that of the four thousand (Mk. 8:1-10) are primarily dramatic expressions of Christian eschatology. The so-called Messianic Banquet, or the uninterrupted feasting that would signify end-time salvation, has already begun through Jesus, whose provisions far exceed people's needs. Symbolized by the respective "twelve" and "seven" baskets of food remaining, the New Israel, the complete people of god, is being created in Messiah Jesus. What once was only a far-flung hope is now a reality in him.

The other two nature miracles, though maybe not so clearly to the modern eye, are no less Christian in their sense of eschatological accomplishment. Perhaps variants of the same tradition, Jesus' stilling of the storm (Mk. 4:35-41) and his walking on water (Mk. 6:45-52; Jn. 6:16-21) dramatize his victory over the power of Satan – that is, his victory over death. Dignified by such appellations as "the prince" or "the god of this world,"[39] Satan was thought by many to be the power behind humanity's besetting ills, both the dark alleys of routine evil and the unavoidable wrecks of nature – and his last blow to strike was death. In each of these stories the disciples of Jesus are fearful for their lives, and, in each case, he saves them from the wind and the sea. In rebuking the wind and commanding the sea to be still, Jesus is not meant to be someone who goes around talking to the forces of nature. Rather, he is the one who silences Satan![40] Likewise, in his walking on water Jesus is depicted as the one whom Satan's power could not control. Formulated by the Church, these stories enact the victorious import of Good Friday and Easter. Otherwise they are less than strange; they are then simply inconsequential.

Concerning the question of where the nature miracles came from, two sources appear in tandem — one plural, the other singular. A plurality of sources is evident in the stories themselves. Some of them, as noted, are variants of the same tradition. Additionally, at least two of the nature miracles strongly appear to have been developed from reported sayings of Jesus: (1) the great netting of fish, which recalls Mark 1:16–20 and Jesus' words about his followers becoming fishers of men; and (2) the cursing of the fig tree, which is a miraculous enactment of the parable found in Luke 13:6–9 and perhaps was originally designed (in a shorter form) to lend force in applying that parable to the Israel that rejected Jesus. In the same vein, the story of the marriage feast at Cana seems reminiscent of Jesus' sayings about (1) wedding guests not fasting until the bridegroom is taken away from them and (2) the necessity of putting new wine into new wineskins (Mk. 2:18–22). Further still, besides Day-of-Salvation themes (like "messianic" feasting), Old Testament legends occasionally had a role in the formulation of the nature miracles: for example, Elisha's more than ample multiplication of barley loaves (2 Kgs. 4:42–44). Hence, there was a plurality of sources indeed.

But all of that is secondary to the singular source of the nature miracles — the Church's life and faith. To hear the Church tell it, that life and faith developed in correspondence with the risen Christ. The fact that none of the nature miracles can be critically grounded in Jesus' ministry should, therefore, pose no embarrassment to Christian faith. For they were not meant to say how things once were but, instead, how things now are.

2. CLEANSING LEPERS. While only two Gospel stories depict Jesus removing leprosy (Mk. 1:40–45; Lk. 17:12–19), they also well exemplify that the miracle-tradition was embellished beyond his actual deeds. Did he ever cleanse a leper? Maybe so, maybe not. But certainly not in accord with either one of the Gospel stories. Nor, incidentally, did any such cleansing likely entail the kind of cure that most readers today are apt to associate with it.

What we customarily refer to as leprosy, a terribly disfiguring disease in its chronic and severest forms, does not appear in biblical usage of the term. There it signifies a variety of less critical, though distressing, ailments: boils, burnings, spottings, discolorations, itchings, exposures of raw flesh. From the descriptions of it in Leviticus 13 and the rites prescribed for declaring a leper cleansed (Lev. 14), it is evident that leprosy could simply disappear – a healing effected by body processes. That, however, does not detract from the miraculous element in either of the Gospel stories. Like Elisha's legendary cure of Naaman (2 Kgs. 5:1-14) – the only Old Testament story of a miraculous deliverance from leprosy – each of the Gospel stories involves an instantaneous healing, not a gradual one.

The story reported of Jesus in Mark 1:40-45 is a confusion of embellishments, so much so that popular translations must gloss over its difficulties to make the story intelligible. The Greek text that I prefer (see note 41 below) reads as follows (my translation, with RSV felicities in brackets, verse numbers in parentheses):

> (40) And a leper came to him beseeching him, and said to him, "If you will, you are able to cleanse me." (41) And provoked to anger [Moved with pity], stretching out his hand he touched him, and said to him, "I will; be cleansed." (42) And immediately the leprosy departed from him, and he was cleansed. (43) And having censured [sternly charged] him, he immediately cast him out [sent him away], (44) and said to him, "See that you say nothing to any one; but go, show yourself to the priest, and offer for your cleansing the things which Moses commanded, for a testimony to them [the people]." (45) But he who departed [he] began to proclaim freely and to spread the word, so that he [Jesus] was no longer able to enter a city openly, but was out in the country, and people were coming to him from every quarter.

Verses 42b, 44a, and most of verse 45 (beginning with "so that") can be set aside as typical Marcan additions (as can perhaps all of vs. 45). But what then remains in 1:40-44 makes sense only if it is seen as a combination of items from two earlier traditions – one in the way of an exorcism, the other concerned with keeping the Law.

Apart from a tradition of exorcism, Jesus' angry reaction to the leper's humble plea is patently absurd.[41] So too his censuring the man and driving him out by force, as if the leper himself were a demon! Significantly, the Greek verbs "to censure" and "to cast out" were typically used to denote exorcisms. In their original setting, no doubt, these aspects of the story did not convey hostility toward a leper. In that earlier story, it was a demon, perceived to be lurking behind the disease, that riled Jesus. Thus, it was one of Satan's agents whom Jesus rebuked and expelled. In fact, so awkward and piecemeal is the composition of the Gospel story, the original tradition of exorcism underlying it may not even have related to leprosy. In any case, whatever its details, that tradition's incorporation in this story suggests Jesus' victory over the demonic. He can do what the Law cannot — cleanse a leper! overpower Satan!

Mighty as that last word is, it is not the point of the story which Mark received. That point is sounded in verse 44b: "Go, show yourself to the priest, and offer for your cleansing the things which Moses commanded." What we have here is a pronouncement story, albeit put together none too neatly. Minimizing the element of exorcism to the extent of confusion about it, the story simply uses the cleansing of a leper to set the stage for a saying ascribed to Jesus: the Law should be obeyed! It was a matter of concern to Jewish Christians. Among most of them legalism continued to thrive, yet not absolutely. Should the Church keep Jewish customs intact? Paul described Cephas as hypocritical about this, and it is hard to imagine Cephas (Peter?) being alone in that ambivalence.[42] So it seems, in this story as elsewhere, Jesus was brought into the fray to "settle" the question. That he actually told a leper or anyone else to seek ceremonial cleansing is questionable. For he is said to have lambasted observance of rules for special purity as self-deceiving and insignificant (Mk. 7:5–8). Such an outbreak makes me wonder if Jesus put much stock in *any* nonpenitential rite of cleansing, whether assumed voluntarily or required of all by the Law (cf. Mk. 7:15).[43] However that may be, the miraculous setting for Jesus' alleged saying in this story is so clumsy that it must have been contrived.

The other Gospel story about a removal of leprosy, although simpler in development, is just as clearly an embellishment of the miracle-tradition. Found in Luke 17:12–19 alone, it tells of Jesus cleansing ten lepers, only one of whom, a Samaritan, returned to thank him. Whereas verse 19 is a Lucan addition (influenced by Mk. 5:34; 10:52),[44] the tale itself moves smoothly to the point of gratitude versus ingratitude. However, it seems manifestly a fiction derived from the story reported in Mark 1:40–45. Having pled for Jesus' mercy, the lepers are told by him, "Go and show yourselves to the priests" — precisely the same command given to the leper in Mark's earlier pronouncement story — "and as they went they were cleansed," this story says. Yet here, in the case of the eventually grateful leper, obedience to the command lacks historical sense. As Bultmann asks, "What could a Samaritan want with Jewish priests?"[45] The Samaritan heads off toward the priests with the other nine lepers because, of course, the point demands that he be with them. So what we meet in this story is a cleansing issuing from another story of cleansing, but with a different focus in the creation of an ideal scene. We are shown "this foreigner" whose thanksgiving for Jesus' ministry puts Jewish ingrates to shame.

3. RAISINGS OF THE DEAD. If the nature miracles and cleansings of lepers are obvious embellishments of the miracle-tradition, the reality of Jesus' raising dead people seems to fare no better. But this is not because one must go on principle that no such resurrections could have occurred. Rather, the Gospel stories in particular, and church tradition in general, fail to generate any serious degree of authenticity for the raisings. On the one hand, each of the stories sounds fictitious, either too modeled or situationally unreal to command historical value; and, on the other, raisings of the dead had a tenuous place at best in the Church's early recollections of Jesus. In question here are three alleged raisings: of Jairus's daughter (found in all three Synoptics), of the widow's son at Nain (only in Luke), and of Lazarus (only in John).

Alongside entanglements of its own, the Johannine story of Jesus' resurrection of Lazarus (Jn. 11:1–44) is a showcase for the kinds of difficulties that the raisings present individually and generally. Its peculiar problem for scholarship concerns the tradition that John received. Departing from his customary practice of interpreting a miracle by way of an ensuing discourse or dialogue, John laced the narrative with interpretive additions. So thorough are those insertions that most critics have washed their hands of trying to uncover the precanonical story. But for sake of judging its historical worth, the attempt must be made. For our purposes, Fuller's "tentative reconstruction" is representative and surely adequate:

> Now a certain man was ill, Lazarus of Bethany, the village of Martha and her sister Mary. So the sisters sent to him, saying, "Sir, he whom you love is ill." When Jesus heard that he was ill, he stayed two days longer in the place where he was. Then, after this, he said to his disciples, "Let us go into Judea again." Thus he spoke and then he said to them, "Our friend Lazarus has fallen asleep, but I go to awaken him out of sleep."
>
> Now when Jesus came, he found that Lazarus had already been in the tomb four days. Many had come to console the

sisters concerning their brother. When Jesus saw the sisters weeping, he was deeply moved and troubled; and he said, "Where have you laid him?" They say [*sic*] unto him, "Sir, come and see." Then Jesus, deeply moved again, came to the tomb and said, "Take away the stone." Martha said to him, "Sir, by this time there will be an odour, for he has been dead four days!" Jesus lifted up his eyes to heaven and cried with a loud voice, "Lazarus, come out!" The dead man came out, his hands and feet bound with bandages, and his face wrapped with a cloth. Jesus said to them, "Unbind him and let him go."[46]

In a heroic effort to make this story plausible, some commentators have opined that Jesus' words about Lazarus being asleep are ambiguous, indicating perhaps that he had been buried prematurely and, therefore, that the miracle was the restoration of a man who (for four days!) had been *as good as dead.*[47] Likewise, with his ankles tied together and his arms secured to his body, admittedly not conditions for walking, Lazarus is said to have "struggled" out of the tomb.[48] Such are the vagaries of shuffling fiction into fact. As in the story of Jairus's daughter (Mk. 5:39), Jesus' reference to death as "sleep" makes sleep a proleptic word of what he is sure to do in "awakening" Lazarus to life. But Jesus takes his time, delaying his trip two days and thereby prolonging Mary's and Martha's grief. However, in a fiction designed to *dramatize* the Church's kerygma, none of these existential oddities is artless. To the contrary, a realistic story would not convey nearly so well the redemptive significance of Jesus – a significance which, in his own death and resurrection, addresses life as it is in order to go clean beyond it. In that sense, Jesus must dally two days, to let death do its malodorous work. And the dead are merely asleep, waiting to be roused. And Lazarus must come out of the tomb with his hands and feet still bound, to show that the bonds of death mean nothing anymore. "Unbind him and let him go," says Jesus – not to make him alive, rather to make him free. Stimulating fiction (at least before John added to it), this story throbs with the gospel's power and promise.

External difficulties also weigh heavily against the story's authenticity. Some scholars object that, if authentic, Lazarus's resurrection should have appeared in the Synoptic Gospels, especially since John cites it as the immediate cause of the Sanhedrin's decision to arrange for Jesus' death (11:45–53). However, John has ordered events to suit his own scheme, and his editorial arrangement is not apt to be any more accurate than the Synoptic sequence. The problem, simply, is the utter silence of all traditions other than John's concerning Lazarus's resurrection and its consequences for him and his sisters. Only in this story is Lazarus said to be the brother of Mary and Martha. In fact, nowhere outside John's Gospel is he even mentioned as a historical person. Nor, by the way, are Mary and Martha identified as members of the early Church. If there had been a real raising of Lazarus, alleged friend of Jesus and his disciples, imagination would strip a gear trying to explain why traditions concerning him and his sisters did not swarm in the Church and show up in other reports.

For those not bent on defending the Fourth Gospel's depiction of Jesus, the origin of John's story of Lazarus's resurrection finds a ready explanation. Critics have long noted its affinities with two traditions reported only in Luke: (1) the parable about a rich man and a beggar named Lazarus, the latter of whom, were he raised from the dead, would not be able to persuade the rich man's brothers to repent (16:19–31); and (2) the story of Mary who listened to Jesus' teaching and her sister, Martha, who was distracted with practical matters (10:38–42). Significantly, the Johannine Martha is also concerned with practicality (the stench from an opened tomb). Further, aside from John's Gospel, New Testament mention of Mary and Martha is confined to Luke's story about them. All of this suggests that the original story of Lazarus's resurrection was prompted by items from Luke's special source. With a possible resurrection in hand for Lazarus of the parable, the resurrection of a historical Lazarus came to be presented as an actual fact. Thanks to help from accompanying tradition, a parable was converted into an event for sake of Christian preaching. That seems far more probable than a real occurrence leading to a parable,[49] especially in this case since the reality of Lazarus's resurrection is so weighted with difficulties.

Turning now to the Synoptic raisings, we need only cast lots for their order here. Each of them shares authenticity-problems with Lazarus's resurrection. One represents the storyteller's art, while the other appears to have been influenced by widely circulating stories. Additionally, both of them reflect Christian faith and interests.

The lot falls to the raising of the daughter of Jairus, a synagogue ruler. Recorded first in Mark (5:21–23, 35–43) and retold by the other Synoptists (Mt. 9:18–19, 23–26; Lk. 8:40–42, 49–56), the original story has been interrupted with the insertion of another miracle — Jesus' healing of a woman with a hemorrhage (Mk. 5:24–34). Probably effected in oral transmission, the insertion was to create a delay in Jesus' arrival at the ruler's house, as if a girl on the verge of death needs more time to die than one verse allows. The clumsiness of that insertion has been matched by attempts to remove the story's unrealistic air concerning death versus sleep[50] – but let art be art, even when it is Christian. For the thrust of this story, particularly in its bold and unrealistic strokes, is that Jesus alone can speak of death for what it truly is. His word (coming from Easter via the Church and "demonstrated" in the girl's resurrection) is the only one that matters. By contrast, the other speaking characters in the story, though sane and down-to-earth, are shown to be in a fog without even knowing it.

Actions and emotions move rapidly in the story, with a clue to its meaning ushered into the narrative early. No sooner does the ruler request help for his dying daughter than messengers come with word of her death and with advice of their own that he should trouble "the Teacher" no further. It is a word that Jesus ignores, telling the ruler to "fear not, only believe." Is she really dead? the reader then wants to ask. (The question has been raised by some commentators in pedestrian speculation that the girl was merely comatose.) Upon arriving at the house, Jesus sees a crowd of loudly wailing mourners and promptly asks them why all the fuss, since, as he says, "The child is not dead but sleeping" (Mk. 5:39). Straightway they laugh at him. One would expect actual mourners to groan even more at Jesus' suggestion, made within earshot of the dead girl's parents. But laugh they must for the story to work best. These people know death when they see it, same as does the world; and the gospel, which exceeds the wisdom of mortals, is outrageous when heard apart from faith. Hence Jesus' first word to the ruler: "Do not fear, only believe" (Mk. 5:36). Besides the fact that it has typical marks of the ancient miracle story in abundance,[51] this story moves as only inspired fiction can move. It dramatically overrides the routine in the interest of a reality more deeply perceived. Hear then "the Teacher."

The other Synoptic raising by Jesus, that of the widow's son at Nain, is less artful than the two already considered. We find it transmitted in Luke 7:11-17 from a special source. Even when its Lucan additions are left undisturbed,[52] the story is so relatively tame that one might regard it as a genuine memory. Upon critical inspection, however, it is clearly a mix from (1) pagan stories[53] and (2) a legendary raising attributed to Elijah (1 Kgs. 17:8-24). In contrast to his other raisings but in line with pagan stories, Jesus performs the miracle without being asked for help. Also, he stops the funeral procession near the city gate – another characteristic of pagan resuscitations. On the other hand, as in the Elijah story, the deceased is the young son of a widow. Moreover, after Jesus raises him, it is said that "he delivered him to his mother" — verbatim, the Septuagint description of Elijah's action (1 Kgs. 17:23). Additionally, if verse 16b was part of the pre-Lucan story, acclaiming Jesus as "a great prophet," the Elijah connection is even more pronounced (cf. 1 Kgs. 17:24). Most likely, therefore, the story originated in a Hellenistic-Jewish milieu, yet certainly a Christian milieu. For Jesus speaks the word of God — "*I say* to you, arise" — and his speaking, like God's speaking, is the same as acting! Thus comes God's word of power, in and through the risen Christ.

The general question remains. Did Jesus raise anybody from the dead? We must answer, "Apparently not." To say otherwise would seem to require critical disregard of the pertinent facts. We have considered the canonical evidence for an affirmative answer and found it to be consistently wanting. It consists, on the one hand, of three remarkably fictitious stories, each of which drives on post-Easter faith. On the other hand is Jesus' response to John in the saying from Q (including mention of the dead being raised), a saying so adroitly composed that it seems to shine as a Christian creation. And that is *all* of the so-called positive evidence. No other references to Jesus' raising of dead people are to be found in the New Testament.

Furthermore, the tradition of Jesus' sending the twelve out to preach, first recorded by Mark (6:7-13) and enlarged in Matthew (10:1, 5-23) and Luke (9:1-6; 10:2-12), patterns their commissioned works after his. It includes exorcisms and healings for them, but neither cleansing lepers nor raising the dead. The latter two works appear only in Matthew's version (10:8), and he had to add them on his own initiative. Such a patterned tradition, lacking those particular works, witnesses against their appearance in the original model.

Finally, the New Testament never mentions the resurrection of Jesus and his previous raising of others in the same breath, much less distinguishes between the nature of them. Paul, for instance, despite his association with leaders of the Jerusalem church (Gal. 1:18-2:10), seems to have known only of Jesus' resurrection. Writing to the Corinthians in the mid-50s, Paul spoke of it as "the first fruits," with the resurrection of all others being yet a future event (1 Cor. 15:20-57). Nor will it do to argue that the previously raised people eventually died, making Jesus' resurrection unique and, therefore, Paul's and the Church's only pressing concern. Precisely that distinction, if the earlier raisings actually occurred, would have demanded clarification. Unless, of course, neither the disciples nor anyone else who knew of those raisings bothered much to talk about them.

Conclusion

When the Gospel miracles are taken as utter fact and without question, the impression conveyed is that Jesus could perform a miracle whenever he pretty well chose — like Morty, the steambath attendant. That ability, if not genuinely proving his divinity to the Christian faithful, would at least help bring it home. Such is not to be, however, when Jesus' reported words and reported deeds are examined critically. Particularly in view of how the miracle-tradition was time and again embellished, we must acknowledge that his original reputation for miracles, though rooted in his own deeds, is beyond our recovery in all but one or two general regards. As we observed from a variety of testimonies, Jesus most certainly performed exorcisms and perhaps healings, especially if the healings were originally understood as a release from demonic power.[54] But that is all we can say with confidence. We cannot tell which exorcisms or healings are authentic, if indeed any one of them is. Nor does it profit to speculate. If first-century Christian faith could create stories about Jesus raising dead people, it could surely create numerous other stories to dramatize the kerygma or somehow else serve the Church's interests. With only one exception,[55] that is exactly what the Gospel stories containing miracles do.

This is *not* to say that Jesus did nothing that would appear to be a miracle today. (No historian knows enough to say *that.*) But it *is* to say that his miracles are grossly misused when taken to demonstrate his Godness. Or when taken to make him seem less human than other persons are. Or when taken without regard to the lively Christian faith which those miracles so richly convey. We do not, for example, celebrate the resurrection of Lazarus. When reading of it we celebrate instead the resurrection of Jesus Christ. In our better moments then, we let his miracles preach, not prove.

Chapter 5

Immortal?

All flesh is grass,
  and all its beauty is like the flower of the field.
The grass withers, the flower fades,
  when the breath of the Lord blows upon it;
surely the people is grass.

— Isaiah 40:6b–7

Was Jesus, like God, immortal? No, the Scriptures resoundingly tell, he was not. Whereas God is eternal, man is like withering grass, defenseless and doomed under heaven's hot breath. God lives and does not die, say biblical and Christian traditions in harmony with all but the strangest theologies. Men, however, are born to die. . . . Jesus of Nazareth died.

So we come to the *coup de grâce* for any popular notion of Jesus' divinity that would minimize his humanity. It is a deathblow struck by the gospel itself — a killing word, yet a word of uncontained grace, pressed down, shaken together, and running over. We shall come to that grace soon enough, shall meet it at nearly every turn. But, at this early moment, the matter of Jesus' death should be put more sharply, if only to call attention to the thoroughness of his humanity.

With all who had gone before and with all who would appear after him, Jesus of Nazareth shared *in toto* the inescapable mark of mortality. So indelible is that Good Friday mark, one could hardly be faulted, except by heresy hunters, were one obliged to affirm the humanity of Jesus at the expense of his divinity. Or at least to admit that the latter seems to pale in the former's stark reality. For whatever may be claimed for Jesus' divine nature, it, too, died on the cross. The death there was complete.

The Perspective of Faith

With that last sentence delivered, let me acknowledge that it is not a strictly factual statement or one that historical criticism might establish as reasonably sure. On the contrary, the totality of Jesus' death is a kerygmatic item, an item of Christian faith and of early Christian faith at that. Those who first announced it for others to hear were speaking historically, yes, but certainly not as historians, much less as scientists whose findings are verifiable. They were speaking as proclaimers of the resurrection. Moreover, their beliefs about the death of Jesus and about his resurrection were inextricably interrelated. By the same token, what we have to say in this chapter, though it concerns the historical death of the historical Jesus, will be said from the perspective of faith. It cannot be said otherwise.

History and kerygma. Jesus of Nazareth died. Regarding no other secure fact about him are history and the kerygma so intertwined and yet, at once, so torn apart.

On the one hand, to recall the leading questions of our previous chapters, they can and must be answered without evoking Christian faith. Was Jesus conceived of a virgin? Was he endowed with suprahuman knowledge? Did he think of himself as sinless? Was he able to perform miracles at will? Concerning those questions and others like them, historical evidence exists for consideration and for the construction of reasonable answers. Granted, the pertinent facts almost always appear incidentally, and the scholar is required to dig. Still, such evidence as there is calls for critical examination, not pronouncements of Christian faith, if solid judgments are to be made about Jesus as he actually was.

Not so, however, the question whether Jesus was immortal. That is, did he die completely? Or was it just his body that suffered death, not, say, his pre-existent, eternal being? To this question the most erudite scholarship can offer no definitive word. Employing the critical tools available, one may suggest an answer that seems evident, for example, in Pauline writings or in earlier Christian traditions. But that answer will nevertheless derive from the early Church's preaching. While Jesus' death was no doubt historical – in Jerusalem, by crucifixion, under the management of Pontius Pilate, likely in A.D. 30 and on the eve of Passover – its "known" nature is a faith proclamation. In that sense, as in no other matter concerning him, history and kerygma go arm in arm.

On the other hand, that is also where they part company. For in the view of the kerygma, the historical death of Jesus is inseparably tied to his resurrection. Binding them is a Gordian knot that even Alexander the Great's sword cannot sever. To wit: he who died is who was raised.[1] Jesus of Nazareth — alive, then dead and buried — is one and the same person with the risen Christ. Kerygmatically understood, his death is linked with an act of God that is, in a sense, outside history. God's raising of Jesus is an _un_historical act in that nothing historical produced it. One may say, as many have, that the resurrection happened _in_ history. And first belief in it was, from any angle, an "event" with ensuing historical results. There were particular effects readily manifest in the behavior of Jesus' disciples, who were turned from frightened followers on the run into public preachers of the gospel. But one may not say, from the kerygma's angle, that the resurrection was an event _of_ history, as though Easter were the outcome of preceding occurrences. In that distinction, the resurrection seems singular among the so-called acts of God in history.

The Bible habitually regards important historical events — meaning here significant events for faith that appear to have been genuine occurrences — as acts of God. Among them, to cite major Old Testament examples, are the exodus, the conquest of Canaan, the establishment of Israel as a nation under Kings Saul and David, the fall of the Northern and Southern Kingdoms, and the Jews' deliverance from Babylon. Even though biblical accounts of these events are often embellished, most famously in descriptions of the exodus, their basic authenticity can be validated through canons of historical investigation.[2] In other words, the reality of such alleged acts of God is confirmed by combinations of reliable evidence — archaeological data, linguistic details, corresponding records independent of Yahwist influences. What is more, if one has a mind to, each of those events can be explained a-theistically, like the bombing of Hiroshima or the discovery of the Salk vaccine. The event can be seen as resultant of human activity, without necessary reference to God, and its reality in history remains. Such is not the case, however, with the resurrection. If that event occurred as early Christian faith proclaimed it — the raising of Jesus Christ from the dead — then it was God's act alone. History played no role whatsoever, except to set the stage for its own invasion. Thus was history robbed of its force, or better to say, was Jesus' death robbed of historical meaning. It was not left to stand as a historical event with any lasting results of its own.

All of this is to say that history and the kerygma exist in a mutual but ambivalent relationship. They are joined and divorced simultaneously with respect to Jesus' death. That ambivalence has two implications that need emphasis here. One concerns the life of Jesus in general, the other his death in particular. The first bears on our study as a whole, while the second helps direct the movement of this chapter.

The significance of Jesus' life? Generally speaking, and cacophonous as first it may sound, the significance of the historical Jesus cannot be understood historically (even though, in this or that regard, he might be explained historically). As previous chapters have shown, we can discover various facts of his life – certain things he said and did, some indications of what he was like, reactions of people to him, and so on. But the historical significance of the historical Jesus himself, the man who lived and died, amounts flatly to zero. That is because his life, no less than his death, was robbed of its historical meaning by the Church's "Easter experience." Call it an act of God or muddled faith or anything else that may seem appropriate, *Easter happened.* Whether "on the third day" or whenever, Jesus was "seen" to be vitally present again among some of his followers. Whatever effects his life might otherwise have had were not permitted to exist for history to consider. Rather, the Easter experience dictated that Jesus of Nazareth, in his life and his death alike, be remembered and understood as one believed to have been raised by God from the dead. All the Gospel traditions about him were transmitted accordingly. From no other perspective, whether pro or con, is information provided for the historian to assess the importance of Jesus. Nor would it do to speculate about his role in history apart from that prevailing belief in the resurrection anymore than one could say what importance the former Soviet republics would have today had the Russian Revolution not occurred. Apples do not become oranges for the sampling.

True, New Testament scholars and others often speak of an achievable, historical understanding of Jesus the man. But, realistically, that can only mean historical knowledge about him – an understanding relative to his own moment in history, not an understanding relative to his place in history. Hence, the quest for the historical Jesus must not be mistaken as a search for his significance. If the man has any significance at all, it is that of the believed-in risen Christ, a significance intelligible only this side of Easter.

The nature and significance of Jesus' death? A similar observation may be made concerning Jesus' death in particular – that is, concerning its extent and meaning.

As we have noted in passing, the effect of death on the man Jesus can be considered only by faith, be it Christian faith or some other mixture. To contemplate the consequence of death for human personality at all is to confront a mystery. It is the Sacred Grove at Colonus, before which the historian and the scientist are professionally dumb. Doctors, for example, may pronounce a man medically dead; yet the question remains, not for them to address as doctors, "Quite so, but is *he* dead?" How anyone answers the query depends on what he or she believes personality is. The nature of human death, in other words, engages human nature. Is the individual mortal? Immortal? Partly both? Which part then is essential to one's existence? These questions summon from would-be speakers either a confession of faith or else unmitigated silence. Clearly, a vantage point is needed. Neither history nor science provides one. The kerygma, however, does – the resurrection of Jesus as the kerygma's first preachers understood it.

"As the kerygma's first preachers understood it"! No qualification is more crucial than this one as it spotlights the joined importance of Jesus' resurrection and of the early resurrection-believers. Critically, to speak of the one is to speak of the other. It is a kerygmatic circle that scholarship cannot pierce, divide into separate parts, and then analyze accordingly. The acts of God in history are not done for nothing, nor do they go unseen. Rather, by all reports, the risen Christ appeared to "the faithful," who believed in the resurrection because of that experience and, at very least, because of who they were – the faithful (e.g., 1 Cor. 15:3b–5).

Likewise, to reason from the kerygma, those people who first saw Jesus' death as a significant event did so because of their experiencing him as raised. They interpreted the former in light of the latter, not vice versa. Those followers of Jesus were not interested in his resurrection because they knew of his death. They were interested in his death because they believed in his resurrection. Not too long after that belief was born, but afterwards nevertheless, Jesus' death was newly viewed as a sacrifice.[3] Thus, for those early preachers of Christ crucified, resurrection-faith was the starting point. And in that beginning – the fact cannot be exaggerated – they understood Jesus of Nazareth (once crucified, dead, and buried) to be fully one with him who was raised and whom they saw.

From the kerygma's perspective, therefore, the resurrection of

Jesus finally offers the only focus for comprehending his death. That death, precisely as a historical event, has nothing to say of itself — nothing about its nature, nothing about its significance. Instead, to seek from the earliest Christians any word about the extent and meaning of Jesus' death is to meet with them, however strange the place, beside a conquered tomb.

The Fullness of Jesus' Death

When Jesus' death is viewed through early resurrection-faith, his divinity disappears in the wings as his humanity takes center stage. It was not divine beings for whom resurrection was hopefully expected, but human beings. So goes the movement in Paul's famous kenosis passage, a Christian hymn that has no New Testament match for its towering celebration of Christ's pre-existence (Phil. 2:5b–11). On his way to exaltation after death, Christ Jesus, who was in the form of God, first had to relinquish his equality with God by being born as a man (2:6–7). Although the majestic terms boggle the mind, the movement is clear when it gets to earth. Resurrection is for mortals.

One might argue that only the human side of Jesus Christ died, not his divine side or nature. Such was the contention of Nestorianism, a popular heresy which, though first appearing in the fifth century, had near to three hundred years of docetic tendencies for psychological building blocks.[4] But that kind of logic, full of Hellenistic mythmaking in its distinction between the Jesus who died and the Christ who did not, involves a christological ticket-splitting that Hellenistic Christianity itself was compelled to declare anathema.[5] More importantly, it removes christology about as far as possible from its origins — far away from the faithful of Jesus' followers, far away from their experience of his presence, and worlds away from their belief that he had been raised from the dead.

The "Jewishness" of earliest Christian belief. Who, then, were those first preachers of Jesus' death/resurrection? More exactly, *what* were they? The answer "Palestinian Jews" will not surprise any reader. But their belief about human personality might.

We have noted on occasion that Christian faith, whether that of first-century Palestine or of a different time and place, never exists in a vacuum. It never exists as a thing unto itself, magically isolated from its adherents' views of reality. At issue here is a particular view of reality which, though long recognized by biblical scholarship, may initially seem offensive. It conflicts with what has been, over the much longer haul, established non-Jewish church teaching. To put that early view rather bluntly, you can say "good-bye" to your soul.

Thanks mostly to the dualistic influences of Plato, popular Western thought divides personality into two essentially different "substances" that are only temporarily coexistent in the individual. The individual is matter and spirit, or body and soul, with the immortality of the latter eventually victorious over the demise and decay of the former. At death, the soul flees its erstwhile prison house and soars into the universe to live on eternally as a disembodied spirit. Once the Church became a predominantly Gentile institution, its small Jewish wing removed from significant view and weight, the idea of man's inherent immortality took hold. No less a comfort in life than in death, it has allowed the Church to busy itself with the eternal welfare of people's souls, often amidst a flagging concern for their immediate, bodily needs.

How different traditional Semitic thought! According to ancient Hebrew "psychology," which runs throughout the Old Testament and into the New, the individual was a totality of but one substance, flesh. What we call body and person were held to be one and the same.[6] In the Bible's depiction of man there are different Hebrew/Greek terms whose English translations might often seem to suggest otherwise. Those terms (translated) are *nephesh/psuchē* (soul), *rûach/pneuma* (spirit), and *bâsar/sarx* (flesh). To casual viewers the English translations may imply a Western psychology of parts, as if biblical man were part soul, part spirit, part flesh. But Western eyes are loaded with Western preconceptions. Consider, therefore, those ancient Hebrew terms to the contrary. When applied to the individual and read contextually, each of them clearly has the whole person in sight.[7]

As *nephesh* (soul), man is a conscious being whose life is received from and controlled by God (see note 7); at death, likewise, he is a dead *nephesh*, a corpse.[8] As *rûach* (spirit), man is what a living *nephesh* is, yet more; he is one who, under the force of God's *rûach*, can be moved to various accomplishments or conditions, from deeds of physical prowess, to acute insight or reverence, to mental incompetence.[9] As *bâsar* (flesh), he is again the whole man, but seen in his weak, external existence and thus contrasted with God, who is all-powerful *Rûach*.[10] The distinctions among these terms as they relate to human personality are relational rather than essential. Like our use of "daughter" and "wife" and "mother," they view the whole person merely from different angles, not in different essences. Contrary to Greek or Western thought, in the oft-quoted dictum of H. Wheeler Robinson, "The Hebrew idea of personality is an animated body, and not an incarnated soul."[11]

Small wonder, therefore, that the ancient Hebrews had no concept of conscious life after death or that late Jewish belief in it quickly took the form of belief in a resurrected body.[12] To the Hebrew mind that had not been Hellenized in this regard, conscious human existence without a body was simply unthinkable.[13]

That such was the mind-set of the earliest Christians seems beyond dispute in the New Testament's relentless concern with Jesus' being raised from the dead. The faith that began with their testimony saw his body and person as essentially one, whether first alive among them or dead in Jerusalem or later as resurrected. This assessment of the situation should not be disturbed by the fact that the resurrection body cannot be adequately described — not even by the apostle Paul. In his one extended, scriptural discussion of it (1 Cor. 15:35–55), he declared it to be the same body that died, but not exactly the same. The qualification would be unavoidable in any thoughtful distinction between a body/person that dies and the same body/person that will not.[14] Nor is the New Testament's "Hebrew psychology" diminished by continuing debate of Paul's teaching about the resurrection body, especially among critics trying to find a consistent logic that smoothes its difficult wording.[15] The fact could not be else, since language dulls from age to age, and all the more when it leaves home, venturing beyond this world. Straight to the point, nonetheless, are Paul's preceding remarks about the cruciality of the resurrection for the Church's faith. How cleanly they reflect the attitude of a Christian schooled in Hebraic thought. Taking the kerygma's proclamation of Jesus' death/resurrection as the model for all people, he writes,

> If Christ has not been raised, your faith is futile and you are still in your sins. Then those also who have fallen asleep in Christ have perished. (1 Cor. 15:17–18)

Which is to say that, apart from the resurrection, Jesus Christ, too, has perished!

New Testament texts to the contrary? Some may want to question claim of a Hebrew mind-set for the earliest preachers of Jesus' death.

After all, had Hellenism made no inroads among Palestinian Jews? And is it not true that certain New Testament texts seem to indicate that conscious individual existence continues beyond death, independent of resurrection? Granted, Palestinian Judaism was not devoid of Hellenistic and other influences. And, yes, four prominent New Testament texts do suggest to some readers that disembodied life after death had a share of "apostolic" thought.[16] When carefully considered, however, none of those texts has persuasive force. Rather than detracting from the New Testament's wholesale witness to the totality of Jesus' death, their combined failure to tell against it in the least only adds to that witness.

1. PAUL'S "DEATH WISH." Late in his career, while under Roman detention, Paul confided to his friends in the Philippian church that he would just as soon die on the spot, "depart and be with Christ" (Phil. 1:23). The apostle seems to be saying – and many a Christian wants to think it about a loved one gone – that at death the believer is ushered right into Christ's presence. But with that idea, implied or maybe only inferred, confusion often enters as a handmaid.

In truth, since it is part of a passage charged with emotion, Paul's word about departing and being with Christ may be more a cry of frustration mixed with longing for vindication than a precise statement of his beliefs. Imprisoned, made sport of by people who mock his preaching, older now and no doubt weary, Paul rehearses his tribulations and is fed up with it all – yet he is determined to rejoice in his ministry (1:12–26). Given the intensity of his ambivalent feelings, which needed to be purged or else put in order, he could be allowed a faithful exaggeration made to dear friends! That such was actually the case seems almost dictated by two related facts: (1) nowhere else does Paul plainly suggest consciousness for the dead;[17] on the contrary, (2) he often speaks of them, and in most cases with dead Christians in mind, as "asleep."[18]

However, if Paul ever thought, even for a moment, that he would be "with Christ" immediately upon his own death, he surely was not contemplating a bodiless existence. Rather, he believed that the Christian is actually united with Christ, is a member of Christ's own body, and with all its other members is sharing Christ's resurrected life (cf. Rom. 6:1–11; 1 Cor. 12:12–27).[19] Hence, in Paul's view, any existence for Christians during the interim between their earthly demise and a future resurrection of the dead would not be a disembodied existence. It would be, instead, existence in the body of Christ, already raised by God and alive.

2. CHRIST "PREACHING" TO THE SPIRITS IN PRISON. **Another text ostensibly to counter the Hebrew idea of body and person as one stands out in the epistle 1 Peter.** In a passage often seen to be rich with difficulties (3:18–22), the author says that Christ, having been killed in the flesh but made alive in the spirit, "went and preached to the spirits in prison" (3:18–19).[20] Likely quoting from a Christian hymn and employing well-known figures from Jewish apocalyptic literature, the writer thus encourages his readers to take heart. Although beset by abuse and threats in a hostile world, they need not fear; for Christ "proclaimed" to the evil, heathen spirits that habitually oppose faith and righteousness. In his death/resurrection he *spoke* to them.[21]

That, I admit, puts the matter tersely and pays no tribute to the wide variety of other interpretations this text has received.[22] Owing often to Hellenistic influences, not to mention the rather early Christian imagery of Jesus' descent into Hades, Christ's "preaching" to the spirits in prison has largely been taken to signify an occasion of Christ's own preaching some time between his death and his resurrection. Though murdered and buried, he actually went to those spirits and, what is more, had something to say to them. In other words, according to some, he wasn't fully dead.

To read this text along such lines is, I think, to slight its immediate terms and to disregard its larger context. On the one hand, it is not merely the crucified Christ that is said to have "preached" to the spirits in prison, but the crucified and resurrected Christ. The Greek participles speak of him as "*having been* killed" and "*having been* made alive" (= raised, as noted below). It was *that,* the facts of his death and of his resurrection taken together as one, "in which" Christ went and spoke to the disobedient spirits. Therefore, while pointing to a powerful reality, the allusion to an actual preaching seems figurative (and figurative language abounds in hymnody). This is further indicated by the conspicuous absence of any reference to either the time or the content of the preaching. What this text has in mind, then, is not a particular occasion when even the evil spirits were evangelized and given a chance to repent.[23] That, by the way, would suggest failure for Christ's own preaching(!) since those spirits were thought to be still at work, fostering the sundry ills and temptations that the epistle's readers had to endure (3:13–16). Rather, according to the imagery here, Christ, in simply the *fact* of his death/resurrection, has forcefully confronted the evil spirits as Christus Victor. Hence the author's rhetorical question to those who may very well suffer for righteousness' sake: "Now who is there to harm you...?" (3:13).

On the other hand, the resurrection as a life-giving act of God, without which the dead are thoroughly dead, is no less crucial in 1 Peter than in any other New Testament writing. Having been killed "in the flesh," mind you, the dead Christ was "made alive" (3:18). He had to be acted upon, as the passive voice tells. And in 1 Peter, as elsewhere in the New Testament, the dead being "made alive" is synonymous with their being raised.[24] Jesus' resurrection, moreover, is the avenue to an already realized new birth and hope and faith in God (1:3, 21). Indeed, resurrection is the only way to any life beyond death that the author of this epistle knows. To his Hebraic way of thinking, "all flesh" is like withering grass (1:24)!

The other New Testament texts (nos. 3 and 4 below) that may seem to bespeak early Christian belief in conscious, disembodied existence after death report two sayings assigned to Jesus. By his day several such ideas had found their way into Palestinian Judaism, particularly concerning Sheol.[25] Thanks to a blend of Yahwist concern for justice with Zoroastrian futuristic ideas from about the fifth century B.C. and subsequent Hellenistic influences, Sheol (= Hades) came to be regarded by many Jews as a holding place for the dead in an intermediate state. Scores needed to be settled, for the time being at least, and Sheol was just the place. There spirits or souls were variously thought to reside, in comfort or in pain, awaiting their final reward or punishment – given this or that qualification. With such thinking making the rounds, a kindred word from Jesus would not, in itself, be shocking. On careful examination, however, neither of these sayings appears to be that kind of word.

3. THE RICH MAN AND LAZARUS. Consistent with his disdain for the wealthy and his concern for the poor,[26] Luke singularly attributes to Jesus a tale about a rich man and a beggar named Lazarus, both of whose fortunes were, upon death, immediately and totally reversed (16:19–31). Whereas miserable Lazarus was whisked away to the comfort of Abraham's bosom, the rich man found himself in the fiery torment of Hades. Now he is the beggar: "Father Abraham, have mercy, . . . send Lazarus to dip the end of his finger in water and cool my tongue" (16:24). Once that request is said to be futile, the focus turns to an equally futile plea that Abraham send Lazarus back to earth to warn the rich man's five impenitent brothers.

From church fathers of the second century to the occupants of countless pulpits today, the parable of the rich man and Lazarus has been read to mean exactly what it suggests on the surface. Life does not cease at death but merely assumes a different form. It continues, in blessedness or in unrelieved pain, and we have this on the authority of Jesus. It is an interpretation that churchgoers can scarcely miss, so frequently is the story used to whip people into line or to assure the bereaved that all is well with the faithful dead (who are not dead after all).

But is this parable either Jesus' own teaching or a reflection of earliest Christian thinking about life after death? The former can be maintained, it seems, only by a criticism with traditional axes to grind,[27] and the latter not at all. In both of these regards the parable is remarkably awkward, if not ridiculous. Yet, especially in its awkwardness, the story makes for instructive discussion.

Against the traditional view that the parable of the rich man and Lazarus originated with Jesus, it does not look or sound like any other teaching that came from him. Besides the fact that no other parable alleged to be his contains a proper name, this parable has two parts that do not easily fit together. Its first part (16:19–26) teaches an amoral reversal of circumstances in the world to come: "Son," says Abraham matter-of-factly to the rich man in torment, "remember that you in your lifetime received your good things, and Lazarus in like manner evil things; but now he is comforted here, and you are in anguish" (16:25). The plot thins. Commentators wishing to erase this absurdity regularly appeal to the parable's subsequent focus involving the rich man's evil brothers (16:27–31), as if he too had been wicked – inconsiderate of the poor, perhaps. But that interpretation reads into the parable something that isn't there, in either of its parts. The only information provided about the lives of the two men is that one had it good, the other did not, with nothing said at all about their respective morality. And nowhere else in Jesus' parables must we make up for essentially important details that he did not himself supply. Nor is there much help in this matter from the Jewish folktale about a pious man and a rich tax collector whose fortunes were reversed in death from Piety's expectations – a tale often cited as background for this parable.[28] In that earlier story the reversals were only temporary, yet deserved and carefully explained as such. By comparison, how wanting are this parable's details.

And how clumsy its present structure. With reversed fortunes focused upon and arbitrarily settled, the parable's second part abruptly shifts to a quite different theme: the needless excess and, finally, the inability of a miracle to provoke impenitent Jews to faith and righteousness (16:27–31). If the rich man's brothers "do not hear Moses and the prophets, neither will they be convinced if some one should rise from the dead" (16:31). Defenders of this parable's authenticity see that to be its only point, since the drive of a parable normally climaxes in its final words. True. But to that point the first part of this story contributes nothing, save locating the rich man in painful Hades. How irrelevant, then, that he and Lazarus had their fortunes reversed. And, for Jesus, what an uncharacteristic waste of finely honed descriptions of their earthly conditions. In each of his other two-tiered parables,[29] the second part depends on the details and thrust of the first part. This parable, however, looks like something put together by a committee whose membership changed in the making. Not like a story from any one person, much less from Jesus of Nazareth.

To our other question, then. Does this parable, as popular opinion often has it, reflect primitive Christian thinking about life after death? Critics now generally agree it does not. Even those who still see the story as Jesus' own but customarily try to reduce its eschatological oddness, even they tend to regard its strange otherworldly details as simply part of the *mise en scène* — that is, a stage setting for the all-important, last words about someone rising from the dead. *Mise en scène* puts it gently. *Mise en désarroi* seems a better phrase for the parable's otherworldly details, so disarrayed is their arrangement against the backdrop of Jewish expectations. They are a potpourri of confusion, and so vividly so that it must have been intentional. Confronted with a patently fanciful tale, better would readers get the point (whatever) than take it as things one might expect the moment death arrives.

At that moment in this parable the unfamiliar enters with a rush: Lazarus is transported to "Abraham's bosom" (16:22). Found nowhere in pre-Christian Jewish literature and often ambiguous when it does appear in later Judaism,[30] the term here suggests full company with Abraham in Paradise. Lazarus, not just his soul, is "carried" away.[31] Also, he has a "finger" that can be dipped in "water" and, presumably, a hand, and so on, to go along with it. In Jewish thought, however, bodily existence after death awaited a *future* and *general* reality: an eschatological raising of the dead, either of all Israel, or of all righteous Jews, or of all humankind. Along this same incongruous line, the rich man in Hades, where only spirits or souls could come to the party, has "eyes" and a "tongue." By itself, any one of these terms depicting bodily existence — *carried, finger, water, eyes, tongue* — might be considered hyperbole. But strung together they add to the afterlife strangeness that pervades this parable from 16:22 onward (vs. 22b–23a alone void of it).

Especially strange is the fact that the rich man can *see* Lazarus and Abraham — an item sometimes noted, inappropriately, to cohere with expressions about life after death in two pieces of fairly contemporary Jewish pseudepigrapha.[32] According to 2 Baruch 51:5-6 (c. A.D. 100), the wicked dead shall see the righteous dead. But, as the context makes plain, the reference is to a time after they have all been *raised* (49:1-51:4). Only so *can* the dead be recognized (50:3-4). On the other hand, though 4 Ezra (c. A.D. 100) claims sight for both good and bad souls after death, none of them sees as the rich man does. Each group of souls sees the other group's locale or condition, but not them individually. The good ones see "the perplexity in which the souls of the ungodly wander, and the punishment that waits them" (7:93). Similarly, the ungodly souls see "how the habitations of the others are guarded by angels in profound quiet" (7:85).[33] That is a far cry from this parable's rich man, who not only recognizes Lazarus and Abraham but engages the latter in conversation.

The most widespread attempt to find a pre-Christian Jewish parallel for the afterlife situations of Lazarus and the rich man involves the imagery of 1 Enoch 22 (c. 250? B.C.), a picture of Sheol or Hades that has long attracted the attention of commentators. It shows the underworld (where all departed spirits reside prior to Judgment Day and the resurrection of some) to have three separating places. The first place, with a spring of water, is for the spirits of the righteous; the second is for the spirits of sinners who escaped judgment on earth and so who are in great pain, with the worst still to come; the third is for the spirits of sinners who were slain and so who (presumably) plead their case to God (22:9-13). That depiction of Hades does, to be sure, share with our parable a strict separation of those who have died. But in that similarity, particularly, they prove to be worlds apart. Though "a great chasm" divides Lazarus in Abraham's bosom and the rich man in Hades, a gulf permitting no travel from either place to the other (Lk. 16:26), at least they can talk about it. More importantly, while the separation in 1 Enoch 22 is within the confines of Hades, only the rich man is down there in the parable. Besides what we have already noted, the rich man in Hades looks *upward* to see Lazarus with Abraham afar off (16:23). They are not on the plane. Had the parable's author meant to locate Lazarus in Hades too, albeit in a more pleasant compartment than the rich man, he would have used different terms, whoever he was.

So much, then, for efforts to harmonize the parable with contemporary Jewish thought. Of all the parables ascribed to Jesus, this one stands alone. It is a story off the wall, furnished with items so strange and confused that they might in themselves make sense only to some other, unknown audience. Whatever the parable's original shape, neither Jews nor Christians in first-century Palestine could well have taken home from it a lesson about things that occur right after death.

4. ABILITY TO KILL THE BODY BUT NOT THE SOUL. Among New Testament texts supposed to imply continuing personal existence beyond death, the last one we have to consider likely lends the most to a popular confusion of early Christian faith with Hellenistic thought. In a saying that came to Matthew from Q, Jesus speaks of those who can kill the body but not the soul. A favorite homiletical launch for sailing in Platonic waters, it sends many a Christian toward finding the immortality of the soul as a heartening tenet of Jesus. "The body can be killed but not the soul." No interpretation could take the saying farther afield or miss more completely Matthew's kerygmatic use of it.

Since Matthew's and Luke's versions do not closely agree, the precise terms of the saying in Q are difficult to recover (and we need not try). Luke's version (12:4–5), which lacks the distinction between body and soul, is marked throughout by his editing. Relieved of most, if not all, of that editing, it reads:

> Do not fear those who kill the body and have no more that they can do. Fear him who, after he has killed, has power to cast into Gehenna.

If the Q-saying included the body/soul distinction, Luke omitted it probably to avoid confusion. His readers, being Gentiles, might mistake it as a Hellenism. In writing for an audience that included *Jewish* Christians, however, Matthew was spared that problem. His version reads:

> And do not fear those who kill the body but cannot kill the soul; rather fear him who can destroy both soul and body in Gehenna. (Mt. 10:28)

This saying confronts us then with *two* distinctions: one between "body" and "soul," the other between "kill" and "destroy." To understand its rich intent, one must see these distinctions not only in concert but also in view of the saying's eschatological framework within the life of the early Church. (And that will not be difficult here, whether the distinctions were originally found in Q or came from Matthew's own hand. We can easily allow for both possibilities.)

Consider first the distinction between "body" (*sōma*) and "soul" (*psuchē*). As is the case throughout the New Testament, neither elsewhere in Q nor in texts peculiar to Matthew do these terms stand for basically different parts of a person. On the one hand, "body" in Q signifies either the physical reality, whether alive or dead,[34] or else the person.[35] In Matthew's one peculiar text, it denotes the physical reality as raised from the dead (27:52). "Soul," on the other hand, connotes in Q one's life[36] and, in special Matthean appearances, either one's life (2:20) or one's self (12:18). Further — and this also reflects a Hebrew, not a Greek, mind-set — in the one Q-saying where these words appear together, "body" as one's physical reality is in parallel with "soul" as one's life (Lk. 12:22–23 = Mt. 6:25).

So how are we to read "body" and "soul" in this saying? Particularly since men can kill the one but not the other while God is able to destroy them both? Certainly not in any Hellenistic fashion. Rather than defining a part of the individual, each term bespeaks the whole person in view of the opportunity for end-time salvation. "Body" refers to the person that people can kill, while "soul" refers to the same person whose ultimate destiny is controlled by God alone. The saying belongs to a section of Q that treats Christian discipleship with contrasting, eschatological pledges.[37] Those who are faithful witnesses to Jesus will finally be vindicated. Those who are not — those who deny him to evade persecution — will finally be rejected. Hence, to Q's community of Christians in their struggles with the world, the saying brimmed with promise and warning: "Do not fear those who can kill you but cannot remove you from the victory of God's kingdom to come. Fear God alone, for only he has the power of Gehenna, the ability to destroy without hope of salvation."[38]

That intent of the saying seems confirmed beyond question in its juxtaposition of "kill" (*apokteinō*) and "destroy" (*apollumi*) — once again, a distinction not explicit in Luke's version.[39] Elsewhere in Q and in appearances peculiar to Matthew, these terms distinguish between death as merely a fact and death with no hope for the future. On the one hand, in Q and special Matthean texts alike, "kill" is associated exclusively with martyrdom: either the past killing of Israel's prophets[40] or the "predicted" killing of Jesus' emissaries.[41] What happened to the prophets is what faithful Christians could well expect for themselves. But only death as a fact in itself, not hopelessness or removal from God's salvation. For that, on the other hand, is rather conveyed by "destroy" when used in relation to death. Such usage in Q concerns the biblical flood that destroyed Noah's wicked neighbors and the rain of fire and brimstone that destroyed the people of Sodom.[42] Hence a merited destruction, reserved for those who flout God's will, as in the Matthean apologetic that those who take a sword will be destroyed by a sword (26:52). Much more to the point are Matthew's other peculiar texts, illuminating the difference between death as a fact and death as God-forsaken destruction. Especially pertinent is his version of Jesus' parable of the great supper (22:1–14), in which "kill" and "destroy" appear, significantly, with respect to the Church's mission. Editing and enlarging upon Q's form of the parable,[43] Matthew transformed the banquet into a marriage feast given by a king (= God) for his son (= Jesus) and inserted an item about servants (= Christians) commissioned to summon the invited guests. The servants were killed by men who, in turn, were to be destroyed at the king's direction (22:6–7). Again, men merely kill; God alone destroys. Consider also Matthew's two ironic uses of "destroy" with regard to the intention of misguided schemers: (1) the incompetent King Herod wants to destroy the holy infant (2:13); and (2) the chief priests and elders, lacking the insight even of Pilate's pagan wife that Jesus is a righteous man, persuade the people to ask that he be destroyed (27:19–20). Matthew's audience, however, knew the gospel, which labels all such designs absurd.[44]

That is precisely the case regarding Matthew's use of this saying, with its sharp distinction between men's limited ability and God's sovereign power. To first-century Jewish Christians armed with the gospel of Jesus' own death/resurrection, the saying was existentially kerygmatic as it almost never is today. Discipleship was dangerous then, but fear, nonetheless, is to be well-placed. Hence, whether recalled of Jesus or read from Matthew or in company with Q, the saying was not for early Christians that their souls would live on, come what may, but that the Eschaton is to come. And, as the next saying in Q aptly reminds, God will no more forget his martyrs than he forgets cheaply sold sparrows (Lk. 12:6–7 = Mt. 10:29–31).

Conclusion. Although Palestinian Judaism of the first century was fairly touched with speculation about consciousness immediately after death, early Jewish Christians seem to have been remarkably devoid of it. Why? Was it because Jesus himself had had no truck with such spiritual meanderings? While that may be attractive to self-styled realists, one ought not answer too quickly. Jesus' own teaching and example evidently failed to liberate at least some of his earliest followers from Jewish exclusiveness and legalistic thinking (Gal. 2). Could he nevertheless have swept from their minds all entertainment of conscious life on the heels of death? One person's guess about that is as good as another's.

On this side of Easter, however, the fact remains that early Christian faith understood Jesus' death as whole, not partial. And in that fact, or better to say, in that faith, must christology come to grips with Jesus' complete death *as a man* – if christology wants to keep a vital relationship with the kerygma. So taken were earliest Christians with the fullness of his resurrection that they could not, it seems, think otherwise of his death. Their experience of Jesus as raised was overpowering. If they had indeed entertained other Jewish expectations, Easter put the knife to those hopes. Instead, Jesus' death/resurrection, as his followers perceived it, would thereafter govern their faith, allowing no less a hope for themselves and the world. Surely in that lies the gospel's stark realism: its calm acceptance of what death actually appears to be – the full end of a man. For through a man, says the gospel without taking another breath, was death fully overcome.

When derived from earliest Christian faith, the answer to this chapter's leading question – Was Jesus of Nazareth immortal? – seems to be critically clear. The man was thoroughly mortal. Whatever later, Christian faith might affirm about his being divine, the first of Jesus' followers believed that every part of him died on the cross.

If those early Christians had put the matter so simply, we could easily understand their meaning. But, in effect, they said it another way: "Jesus of Nazareth – fully dead and fully raised." While that Easter word made sense to them, what are we to make of it? Rooted in their own experience, it was a brand-new word for them and carried immediate implications for victorious and confident faith. To us, however, the Easter word is old hat. The opportunity for experiencing its truth may not, perhaps, be radically different now from what it was at first. Who can certainly say? In any event, when the mysticism of formal worship is set aside (e.g., Christ's "presence" in the Eucharist), Christians today who claim experiences with the risen Jesus Christ are disproportionately few in number.

So we turn to a final consideration: the fullness of Jesus' resurrection, particularly its "credibility" and the meaning of that for Christian faith.

The Fullness of Jesus' Resurrection for Christian Faith

When Jesus' resurrection is commonly discussed by people who care about it, the question of credibility either tends to be the life of the party or else stands knocking at the door as an unwelcome guest. Is it believable? Dare one ask?

Extremes of theological debate. To ask the question critically, as scholar-theologians do, right off engages two other questions. (1) Of what event, if any, does the resurrection speak? (2) What were the earliest Christians essentially conveying in speaking of it themselves? Knowledgeable answers have ranged from a mythological interpretation of the continued meaning of Jesus' death, subjectively understood, to an actual resurrection that emptied Jesus' tomb.

How then is the gospel to be communicated? At one extreme, represented in the theology of Rudolph Bultmann,[45] stands the assumption that modern, scientific humankind cannot, without a sacrifice of intellect, accept the New Testament's worldview. Angels, Satan, demons, Judgment Day, miracles, raisings of the dead — these are obsolete myths that need to be removed, their underlying realities existentially recast, if the gospel is to make sense in today's world. The resurrection itself needs reworking for moderns to be confronted by the reality that preceded and gave rise to it. That reality is the saving event of the cross, which summons people now, as it first summoned the disciples of Jesus, to authentic existence in commitment to God. Those disciples, Bultmann recognizes, did come to believe that Jesus had actually been raised. But that was their mistaken interpretation of his continuing presence in the word of the cross, which is indeed *his* word. Accordingly, we are to see the resurrection word as reflecting an earlier and ongoing eschatological fact in the Church's preaching. Namely, Jesus is really present when the kerygma is spoken and heard, when people are faced with a decision about taking his cross as their own. In that sense of the spoken kerygma itself being an eschatological event, Bultmann is willing to say that "Jesus has risen in the kerygma" (not that the kerygma arose from his resurrection).[46]

At the other extreme, understandably, stands Tradition with a firm resolve. Although the New Testament may contain some mythological items that are no longer useful, the resurrection is not among them. Indeed, to remove *it* is not merely to demythologize the gospel but rather to desiccate it. Hence, the resurrection as an "objective" event, empty tomb and all, is to be accepted on authority, either that of the Scriptures or that of the Church. (Critics are loath to defer to such powers, but occasionally one detects a bottom line. More importantly here, the appeal to external authority is familiar enough to readers who have "been to church." So we will need to pay it some mind, particularly concerning the nature of Christian faith.)

To review the various shapes that critical debate has taken, together with the major issues involved in it, would too long sidetrack our primary concern.[47] Suffice to say that extreme positions are usually modified, often by their proponents' own students, as has often been the case with the positions just mentioned. Still, there are things to be said here for each of those extremes. On the one hand, Bultmann and others are no doubt correct in calling attention to both the "subjective" character of the early Church's resurrection word *and* its incredibility for modern humankind. Had it not been existentially meaningful to them, Jesus' followers would not have preached the resurrection at threat to life and limb. And were it a believable word nowadays, more people would surely believe it, including some theologians and regular churchgoers.

On the other hand, the traditional view has seemed increasingly on target in its insistence (against Bultmann) that belief in the resurrection derived from an "event" after and other than Jesus' death itself. Something happened to his followers which, evidence suggests, was not of the cross's own making. That occurrence, or series of occurrences, was not just existential confrontation with the meaning of his death. Rather, according to the oldest datable oral tradition, Jesus appeared to them (1 Cor. 15:3b–5). From that, if not from an empty tomb as well, they concluded that he had been raised. Although the nature of Jesus' appearances cannot be known, particularly since the Gospel accounts of them are most certainly later creations of Christian faith, literary-historical scholarship has largely agreed on the authenticity of those appearances.[48] After his death and burial, it seems, some of Jesus' followers saw him to be alive.

One so inclined may side even further with the traditional view in regarding the alleged empty tomb as "reasonably" authentic.[49] While the Gospel stories of it are also church creations with mythical items and unlikely details of their own, the tradition underlying them can be argued as basically factual. Were it, as many critics think, merely a later apologetic for the belief that Jesus had been raised, why was it made to depend largely (at first solely?) on women witnesses? In Jewish circles the testimony of women did not count as valid evidence. Also, if in fact the resurrection word began to be preached fairly soon after Jesus' death, one may wonder how it could have survived in the street *without* an empty tomb. Upon hearing that word, would not his opponents have rushed to the tomb, expecting to crush the crazy rumor? And then, with his remains still in place, are we to suppose that the resurrection word would not have been discredited beyond sane belief? Perhaps none of Jesus' opponents gave a whit about what his tomb contained. But would that have been so of his followers? The serious student, I think, must ask such questions (though many serious students think not). In no sense, however, does any conceivable argument for the tomb being empty verify the resurrection or even make belief in it compelling.

That brings us to one other observation here which, though settling nothing for historical scholarship, returns to the problem of viewing the kerygma through modern eyes – eyes that may or may not be attracted to early Christian eschatology. Should the tomb have been empty and assuming that no one removed the dead body of Jesus,[50] his resurrection could not rightly be associated with the revival of a corpse. Given the fact of decomposition – a decay that Jewish fancy postponed to the fourth day of death[51] – the resurrected body of Jesus would need be a new creation, anticipating the future resurrection of others. That Paul so regarded it is apparent from his discussion in 1 Corinthians 15, as did the author of Colossians in calling Christ "the first-born of all creation, ... the first-born from the dead" (1:15–18). In the case of such a new creation, those who affirm Jesus' "bodily resurrection" should certainly acknowledge that they don't know what the term means. Nor do those who take exception to it. Obviously, the nature of an immortal body/person raised from a mortal body/person is not for human comprehension.

Judgment of the powers and authorities. Having paid respects to the traditional view, we must now reconsider, with worldly and kerygmatic sympathy, two Bultmannian concerns: the resurrection's incredibility and the summons of Jesus' death to authentic existence. From the standpoint of early resurrection-faith itself, that may best be done initially in terms of judgment. To put it briefly, the self-contained powers and authorities that be, both outside and within the Church, are dead on their feet, though they seem to be as vigorous as ever.

From outside come the manifold powers of death itself. They are the forces at work in the world that sicken, rob, and destroy with abandon: the untimely cessation of life, putting the lie to innocence like a cat hit by a car; the emptiness that reigns in temporary survivors when adrenalin slows down to normal; the stench when putrefaction is not carted away or very soon disguised; the consumptive desire to beautify death while the poor go naked and hungry; invitations for the wounded and forlorn to thumb their bloodied noses at hope; the conglomerate forces that drive decent people to self-righteousness and war; the economic and political energies that corrupt privilege and lay poetry to waste; and so forth. All such powers to kill, according to resurrection-faith, are themselves condemned to death.

That's nice. It is also, let us admit, incredible. It is a word to which modern people, like many of their ancient forbears,[52] can in politeness only say, "Oh?" Imagine it all. Jesus of Nazareth, fully dead and fully raised, the first-born of a new creation – and in twenty Christian centuries the powers of death have shown no signs of sickness, much less of their promised demise. We have said much in behalf of the traditional view, but the question continues to nag. Were Jesus' disciples correct in their resurrection-interpretation of his experienced presence? As Bultmann and others have rightly observed, and as disbelief handily confirms, compelling evidence for that is wanting. Instead, the word of Jesus' resurrection remains what it was to early ears: a stumbling block and folly, beyond willy-nilly acceptance when faith is genuine and not self-deceptive (1 Cor. 1:23; 12:3). More about that in a moment.

Within the Church, on the other hand, are authorities grasping for power, themselves judged by the very word that they seek to support. They are the presumptuous forces that would minimize the incredibility of Jesus' resurrection or else manage belief in it. Either effort, when earliest belief in the resurrection serves as a model, must be deemed atheistic and foolish. In that model, resurrection-faith is created and controlled by God, not in the least by men, not even by the Church.

Most naive are the apologetic forces that try to facilitate belief in the resurrection, arguing, for example, that the divinity of Jesus meant that death could not contain him. *Voilà!* The resurrection then disappears as a relevant word of hope for beings merely human. Most confusing, however, is the counsel of would-be managers of Christian faith – those who make it a matter of bending the knee. Recognizing that the resurrection word may be hard to swallow, they advise (in fact, usually insist upon) submission to established Christian authorities – the teaching of the New Testament, the teaching of the Church as Christ's body in the world. Yet how removed is such advice from the initial reality and the saving presence of which the resurrection speaks. As if Christian faith basically derived from a collection of writings, not just the other way round. And as if the body of Christ were its own author and head. Better that Paul, missionary extraordinaire, be heard from: "No one can say 'Jesus is Lord' except by the Holy Spirit" (1 Cor. 12:3). Better too that resurrection-belief be now understood as it originally understood itself — the result of a surprising, creative act of God.

The fundamental error of the forces that would either facilitate or manage belief in the resurrection is, therefore, both historical and kerygmatic. Like ambitious amnesiacs, fuzzy on biography but holding high hopes, those forces forget their roots and try to usurp the role of God. And, often, they seem to succeed, the managers in particular. They stifle doubt with indoctrination, playing on unavoidable insecurity and guilt while evoking lip service to the resurrection through habit and with threats of purgatory or hell. Acquiescence, however, is not genuine belief, at least nowhere within the New Testament. Rather than a simple acceptance of ideas, whether or not they make sense, genuine belief about Jesus Christ is belief *in* Jesus Christ. It is a relationship *with* him, which brings profoundest joy and often disturbing pain — a recognition of his meaningful, demanding presence as Lord. Kerygmatically understood, therefore, authentic resurrection-belief is indeed a new, eschatological reality. It entails experience with Jesus of Nazareth, the man made victorious over death by God and, as ever, subject to no one else. Certainly, no force within the Church can effect or maintain *that.* Could it, Christian faith would need be reduced to autosuggestion, and the Church properly regarded as author of its own existence and life.

Creaturehood and authentic existence. How then is Christian faith to behave in a way that agrees with its historical self-understanding? Or more precisely to ask from the kerygma, in a way that keeps with Christian faith's own being in Jesus' death/resurrection? About this most difficult question, which has received from the Church's first days constant attention and always is in need of more, a few remarks may be appropriate here. An examination of Jesus' humanity, his mortality especially, would seem to call for them — even if they border on preaching.

What follows, by the way, focuses on the Church, though not to subtract from individual obligation. Jesus was not a team player. Still, discussion must have its limits; and genuine Christian faith is communal, not private. That holds even when individual Christians, for reasons perhaps justified by the gospel itself, often choose to "stay away from church," finding meaningful Christian fellowship elsewhere. They are members of the body. Moreover, to discuss Jesus' death/resurrection from the kerygma's perspective is to do so "in Christ," that is, in the fellowship of the Church. Hence the focus here.

To begin, as a Christian I am not unwilling to acknowledge the fact that the Church is under the judgment of history and, if the Scriptures are right, under God's judgment as well. Effusive about its own importance, rich in pomp and furnishings that would have made erstwhile kings salivate, self-indulgent in expenditures of money and time and energy (most apparent at the local level, where it lives out most of its life), the Church, so frequently removed from people's visible needs, incurs and deserves the wrath of compassionate atheists. Though its self-styled guardians feverishly engage in sandbagging — apologetic defenses here, there pennies and prayers for the poor — and though prophets preach repentance, the flood waters rise and fall and rise again, and the basement is never dry.

Amidst that judgment, nonetheless, stands the Church in its authentic being. That is the being of creaturehood. Christian belief and the Church are creatures, no more, no less. Historically, like all created things, they came into existence in the passive voice. After his death, Jesus "appeared" to his followers. Not that they sought him, but that he confronted them. They were caught up short, were acted upon, were made to believe in his resurrection. Ever since, the Church in main has understood itself as a community of the resurrection. And so it is. Not by choice, not by merit, not by anything its own. However the resurrection is to be interpreted, the Church's existence as a community of the resurrection is quite authentic, precisely because of its creatureliness. That seems a historical fact from which there is no escape, not even by the Church itself. Only God has the power of Gehenna.

At the same time, as we have observed, from their belief in the fullness of Jesus' resurrection those early Christians reviewed his death, seeing it both as full and as the outcome of his trusting obedience to God. The cross thus became not merely an ugly symbol of helpless death, which it already was anyway, but the preeminent symbol of Christian discipleship — a summons, to use Bultmann's term again, to "authentic existence." It signifies the kind of life intended for men and women as creatures. That is a life lived in trustful commitment to God, whose will takes precedence over all selfish interests, including the interest of staying alive.

This is to say — and so very generally that readers must supply particulars — that the Church, which *is* the community of the resurrection, must strive to *become* that. Same as someone who *is* a parent must learn what it means to *be* a parent. The Church should strive to authenticate its real existence by trustfully living and, if need be, dying as a creaturely community of the resurrection — preaching the gospel by all means, living not for itself but for God and the world, and let those who will have the carcass. Only God has the power of Gehenna.

But notice, I say *strive*. Whereas the Church has known and venerated its martyrs, it is not about to become one. It may well view the historical Jesus as self-denyingly mortal and properly so, but it can hardly see itself that way. The Church in this world, while part of the body of Christ, is also a worldly institution — in fact, numerous institutions — and institutions are notorious for promoting their own self-interests. Of such is their nature. Which is to say the End is not yet. The powers of death, though said to be condemned, are still alive and kicking. And what but the most arrogant congregation would deny its own contamination by them?

Admittedly then, the institutional Church may not realistically be expected to practice the way of the cross that it preaches. Even so, in any number of situations one is overwhelmed by the realization that the Church, like oneself as often, could make a nobler effort, a *much* nobler effort.

Is that disturbing awareness prompted by Jesus of Nazareth, in the fact of his mortality and now in his risen presence?

Postscript

Talk! About Jesus the man. On and on it goes, as well it should. Talk about his humanity. His divinity. His origin. His knowledge. His words and deeds. His fate. His significance for the world. His continuing presence among us. How very much we seem to know, even when we do not know.

Christian faith must talk about Jesus. Indeed, when speaking faithfully, his followers must say *more* about him than can be known — more than empirically gained facts verify. That is the nature of Christian confession, and the Church faces no sleepless nights in losing ability for it. Just the opposite condition might trouble us, though. I mean the inclination, when talking about Jesus of Nazareth, to say *less* than can be known.

Almost always, that's when his humanity is slighted.

Notes

Preface

1. For a recent survey of critical tools, see B. L. Mack, A *Myth of Innocence* (1988), 16–23 nn. 6–10.

2. For different images of Jesus from contemporary scholars, see J. D. Crossan, *The Historical Jesus* (1991), xxvii–xxviii. Somewhat similar to the image proposed by Crossan himself (Jesus as a Cynic-like sage) is the image offered by Mack in *A Myth.*

Introduction

1. A critical analysis and evaluation of Paul's formulaic report of "the kerygma," or early Christian beliefs, is beyond the constraints of this book. As indicated above (pp. 11–12), particularly regarding "resurrectional" appearances of Jesus, the trustworthiness of Paul's report is a working assumption here — critically viable and adopted to date by most critics, but an assumption nevertheless. Additionally, I am not bothered by the fact that the appearances cannot be evidentially explained — either what form they took or what verifiable factors caused some of Jesus' disciples to see him. Those are biographical questions, and the Jesus-tradition is notoriously wanting in routine concerns of biography.

2. Above, p. 160.

3. What follows here is a general summation of N.T. teachings noted above in chap. 3.

4. Above, pp. 109–115.

Chapter 1: Conceived of a Virgin?

1. R. E. Brown, *The Birth of the Messiah* (1977).

2. Brown, *The Birth,* 529.

3. R. E. Brown, *The Virginal Conception and Bodily Resurrection of Jesus* (1973), 66–67.

4. Cf. Jn. 1:14; Rev. 12:4–5.

5. Above, p. 31, I deal with Mk. 6:3 and Jn. 8:41, sometimes taken as hints of an unusual birth.

6. Cf. Rom. 1:3, describing Jesus as "descended from David according to the flesh"; Gal. 3:6, alluding to Jesus' descent from Abraham; Gal. 4:4, speaking of Jesus as "born of a woman, born under the law." Though not contradicting the virginal conception, these texts do indicate its unimportance to Paul and most certainly his ignorance of it.

7. Cf. above, p. 30, and n. 10 below.

8. E.g., the widely respected Catholic scholar J. A. Fitzmyer, "The Virginal Conception of Jesus in the New Testament" (1973), 567–72; he has since disavowed that position and finds the virginal conception in Luke: see his commentary *The Gospel according to Luke (I–IX)* (1981), 338–42.

9. Nor in Luke's story of the boy Jesus in Jerusalem (2:41–51) do Mary and Joseph seem to appreciate that God is Jesus' Father; see above, p. 38.

10. This possibility is even more attractive if, as some MSS attest, Luke's version of the heavenly voice at 3:22, quoting from Ps. 2:7, included the words "today I have begotten you." That would suggest Luke meant to depict Jesus' messiahship as commencing at his baptism, not at his conception – an intent, by the way, that would demolish the originality of the parenthetical remark in 3:23. This more inclusive quotation from Ps. 2:7 is given by Luke in Acts 13:33, where he relates it to Jesus' resurrection. If "today I have begotten you" was subsequently excised from the original text of Lk. 3:22, that was to align Luke's version of the baptismal voice with the growing belief that Jesus' messianic anointment involved a miraculous conception. That would also have been the reason for the parenthetical insertion in 3:23, which denies Joseph's role as Jesus' natural father and makes the virginal conception explicit in Luke's Gospel.

11. One may not argue that Matthew, a disciple of Jesus, was privy to the virginal conception and simply kept it to himself until writing the First Gospel. That Gospel was not composed by an eyewitness. When reporting items of Jesus' public life, instead of recalling them from memory, the author relies on Mark and other sources. The First Gospel makes no claim that an eyewitness wrote it (ditto for the Gospels of Mark and Luke, which also depend on previously formulated traditions of Jesus' ministry). While I will call him Matthew for convenience, we do not know the author's identity (ditto again for Mark and Luke). But whoever he was, he either invented the virginal conception or got it via tradition.

12. Most recently J. Schaberg, *The Illegitimacy of Jesus* (1987), who argues that Matthew and Luke, without wishing to refute "the tradition" of Jesus' illegitimacy, meant to direct attention *away* from it and *toward* the theological and christological points which they respectively made of that tradition. Though sharply arranged, her argument often seems strained. Her observations are mainly instructive and ever serving a compassionate theology; but she *wants* to find an authentic tradition of Jesus' illegitimacy and, in my judgment, occasionally bends reason and crucial texts accordingly (e.g., Mk. 6:3; Lk. 11:27–28; Jn. 8:41). While I remain unconvinced that such a tradition existed prior to the circulation of Matthew's

Gospel, her book deserves grateful attention, in its feminist concerns especially.

13. Initially the Gospels were to be read aloud in specific communities of Christian believers. Each such reading was a performance of sorts, likely with mixed reactions at points, particularly when not all listeners were adequately "in the know." One can imagine interruptions of the reading – questions, comments, etc. – and certainly discussions following it. A Gospel writer could thus expect that knowledgeable readers/listeners would help get his intended meaning across to others of the audience who were not as well informed. More generally, regarding the interpretation of N.T. texts as they were written to be heard, see P. J. Achtemeier, "*Omne Verbum Sonat:* The New Testament and the Oral Environment of Late Western Antiquity" (1990).

14. This intent of Matthew and Luke is my own contention; it does not reflect the opinion of most N.T. scholars, but I think a case can be made for it.

15. I.e., Lk. 1:5–7, 80; 2:1–7, 22–24, 39–40.

16. Both of these difficulties and attempts to solve them are too complex for discussion here; see Brown, *The Birth,* 547–55.

17. Additional support for Luke's nonhistorical intent appears above, p. 38, and nn. 21–22 below.

18. Cf. Isa. 7:3; 8:1–4. For such symbolism in general, see H. W. Robinson, "Prophetic Symbolism" (1927).

19. R. E. Brown, *The Gospel according to John (i–xii)* (1966), 103; Brown in this commentary nonetheless defends the story's authenticity; see below, chap. 4 n. 37.

20. Likely a variant of the tradition underlying Mk. 3:31–35, because of the similarity of the sayings reported. It is curious that Luke used the form that singled out Mary; see n. 21 below.

21. Note the inconsistency of Lk. 11:27–28 with Luke's birth narrative at 1:42, 48. Although Elizabeth calls Mary blessed, as will all generations according to the Magnificat, Jesus refuses to do so! Since it is impossible to think Luke was unaware of the inconsistency, this seems further evidence that he intended no part of his birth narrative to be taken historically.

22. Some critics observe that Matthew and Luke excluded the comment from Mk. 3:21 about Jesus' being mad in order to protect the virginal conception's credibility. In that case their inclusion of other items noted above – at Mt. 12:46–50; 13:57; Lk. 8:19–21; 11:27–28 – is strange, openly suggesting a tension between Jesus and his mother/siblings which those writers, supposedly, meant to keep from their readers. This would indicate that Matthew and Luke, each of them twice(!), lost control of their materials. The implicit weakness of such an argument seems self-defeating.

23. Cf. Brown, *The Birth,* 46–47; *The Virginal Conception,* 47.

24. E.g., see the prophecies in Isa. 9:2–7; 11:1–9.

25. Cf. Ex. 4:22–23; Hos. 11:1.

26. A rationale for such use of the term is given at 2 Sam. 7:8–17, God's promise to David. By Jesus' day God's "son" in Jewish usage was applied to

various persons (the coming Messiah included) who were seen to be in a special relationship with God; cf. J. H. Charlesworth, *Jesus within Judaism* (1988), 149-50.

27. E.g., Hag. 2:6-7, 20-23, expecting Zerubbabel, son of Shealtiel (or of Pedaiah), to be the Messiah.

28. E.g., Gen. 24:43. Experts have shown such was also the case with the Ugaritic *ǵlmt*, an ancient Semitic term corresponding exactly with the Hebrew *almah;* see H. M. Wolf, "A Solution to the Immanuel Prophecy in Isaiah 7:14-8:22" (1972).

29. The story's wording and style are recognized to be largely Matthew's. This fact, coupled with his obvious editorial creativity in the infancy story which follows, suggests to me that the virginal conception was Matthew's own invention, especially since no underlying tradition of that conception has been found for its appearance in Mt. 1:18-25. While I hold with the majority that Luke did not rely on Matthew, a possible (but I think doubtful) Lucan reference to the virginal conception can perhaps be traced indirectly to Matthew; see above, p. 44.

30. Ably shown by H. Boers, *Who Was Jesus?* (1989), 11-16.

31. Brown, *The Birth*, 145-49.

32. E.g., Mt. 2:15 and 2:18, "fulfilling" Hos. 11:1 and Jer. 31:15.

33. Gr. *Theotokos*, "God-bearing," a creedal title for Mary since A.D. 431, when it was established over *Christotokos* ("Christ-bearing") by the Third Ecumenical Council, meeting at Ephesus and in bitter conflict about which term was to be preferred.

34. What follows regarding this is speculative, of course; however, in assessing the reality of an alleged event, historians must often speculate about the effects such an event could reasonably be expected to have had, including its effects on the players. That kind of speculation, which I employ in this chapter, is not to be confused with psychologizing, which tries to analyze and explain a person's known behavior in terms of his or her innermost being.

Chapter 2: All-Knowing?

1. For early non-Christian materials substantiating the reality of Jesus' life and death, see H. C. Kee, *Jesus in History* (1970), 29-43.

2. E.g., the Roman soldiers' hostile mocking of Jesus, as if they had felt threatened by him; their casting lots for his garments "to see what each should receive," as though he were heavily attired; his being reviled by simply everyone, including the two felons crucified alongside him!

3. Arguing that Mark brackets his account of Jesus' ministry with (1) the *tearing* of the heavens as seen by Jesus at his baptism (1:10) and (2) the *tearing* of the curtain as seen by the centurion at Jesus' death (15:38-39), some scholars suggest that Mark had in mind the outer curtain of the Temple since the centurion could not have seen the inner one; see D. Ulansey, "The Heavenly Veil Torn: Mark's Cosmic *Inclusio*" (1991), supporting re-

cent works with evidence from Josephus. Aside from the fact that at Jesus' baptism the heavens are not "torn" (passive voice) but instead are "being open" (middle voice), the position of Ulansey and others, while correct in noting Marcan brackets, reads too much and too little concerning them. (1) Too much in that the centurion does not see the torn curtain; what he sees is Jesus breathing no more (15:39)! And (2) too little in that the climax of each bracket is the confession that Jesus is the Son of God, who, according to Mark's arrangement of materials between the brackets, *must die*. At the outset of Jesus' career, this necessity is hinted by the baptismal heavenly voice (1:11), which links his sonship as Messiah with the Isaianic Servant whose death was to be sacrificial. And at the end of Jesus' ministry, the centurion's confession, which is the only public confession of Jesus' messiahship that Mark allows to stand on its own, is explicitly and immediately in sight of Jesus' death as "the King of the Jews." These observations of Mark's narration are substantiated below in this chapter and in chapter 3. If my observations are correct, Mark intended to depict the inner Temple curtain, symbolizing the barrier of sin between God and humanity, as destroyed by God in the good man Jesus, himself the righteous Son of God (= Messiah) *and* the righteous Servant (= the One whose death would be a sacrifice).

4. Quoted by Paul in 1 Cor. 15:3b–5.

5. Heb. 10:19–20; cf. 2:17; 7:27–28.

6. Against the view that Mark relied on a pre-Gospel Passion narrative, cf. H. C. Kee, *Community of the New Age* (1977), 30–32; F. J. Matera, *The Kingship of Jesus* (1982), giving a detailed analysis of Mark 15.

7. While most scholars of this century have cited Mk. 9:1; 13:30; and Mt. 10:23 to indicate Jesus' expectation of a near Eschaton, many of late have denied the authenticity of those sayings; e.g., B. S. Crawford, "Near Expectation in the Sayings of Jesus" (1982), suggesting an origin in early Christian prophecy. Perhaps excepting Mk. 9:1 as an editorial spin-off from the tradition reported in Mk. 13:30, I think the sayings reflect Jesus' teaching, though none of them need be close to his actual words, much less spoken in the context provided; see n. 12 below.

8. 1 Cor. 7:25–35.

9. E.g., Rev. 13–14 in light of 1:1–3, 7.

10. Relying largely on a proposed earlier stage of the Synoptic sayings source Q (defined below, chap. 4 n. 20) and on the Gospel of Thomas (discovered in late 1945), many scholars have recently suggested that Jesus was not eschatologically oriented: so, e.g., J. D. Crossan and B. L. Mack as cited above, nn. 1–2 for the preface. In his presidential address to the Society of Biblical Literature (Nov. 23, 1991), Helmut Koester opposed the current image of a noneschatological Jesus on several grounds and, I think, convincingly: see his "Jesus the Victim" (1992). Both Q and the Gospel of Thomas are conveniently translated with introductions and notes in J. S. Kloppenborg et al., *Q Thomas Reader* (1990).

11. Among reasons for this conclusion, Jesus apparently did not regard himself as the Christ or the Son of God, as we will see later in this chapter.

12. Although it is possible that Mk. 13:30 was originally understood as a prophecy from the *risen* Christ, Mark certainly did not take it that way; see above, pp. 62–63. It is also possible that sayings about the End being near, while showing nothing of Jesus' own expectation, were attributed to him before the passing of time proved them to be wrong. I think that is unlikely, partly since three aspects of his ethical teaching seem best explained by the assumption of an imminent Eschaton: (1) the instruction to endure hostility (e.g., Lk. 6:29–30 = Mt. 5:39b–40); and (2) absence of any word that people work together toward the solution or alleviation of major social problems. In the event of a near Eschaton, short-term endurance of hostility would be preferable to additional disharmony, and all social ills would soon be righted by God. And (3) Jesus often intensified the Torah's ethics (e.g., see Mt. 5), calling for stricter moral obligations than the Torah stipulated, as did Jewish communities that expected an imminent Eschaton; see P. Fredriksen, *From Jesus to Christ* (1988), 98–101.

13. E.g., Mark's other uses at 8:12, 38; 9:19.

14. In a different form and context, the saying is reported by Matthew (5:18) and Luke (16:17), who received it from so-called Q, a source they commonly used in addition to using Mark; see chap. 4 n. 20.

15. So a major commentator, V. Taylor, *The Gospel according to St. Mark* (1957), 522–23, agreeing with many others.

16. See E. Haenchen, *The Acts of the Apostles* (1971), 260–68.

17. Cf. Mk. 14:22–24, based on a eucharistic formula, itself reflecting post-Easter belief in the saving significance of Jesus' obedience unto death.

18. Indicated by MS evidence and internal considerations; see Taylor, *St. Mark,* 610–15.

19. Mark's intent in presenting Jesus as if he did so think of himself is a concern of this chapter's next major section.

20. On Mark's description of each meeting, see, respectively, J. R. Donahue, *Are You the Christ?* (1973), 53–102; and Matera, *The Kingship,* passim.

21. If the response in Mk. 14:62a was later shortened for confessional reasons, those same reasons contributed to its popularity. Even Taylor, who wants to find evidence of Jesus' messianic self-awareness, prefers the longer reading (*St. Mark,* 568). Also, while accepting the shorter reading, most recent critics regard Mk. 14:62 as Mark's own creation, which would mean that it must be read in sync with the rest of his narration; cf. J. R. Donahue, "Temple, Trial, and Royal Christology" (1976), 71–72.

22. See J. H. Charlesworth, *Jesus within Judaism* (1988), 132–35, 139–49.

23. Jesus' response to a question from John the Baptist (Lk. 7:22–23 = Mt. 11:4–6) may suggest that he verbally *implied* that he was the Messiah. But both the context of John's question and Jesus' response itself appear to be Christian formulations; see above, pp. 140–144. This judgment holds also for the tradition of Jesus' triumphal entry into Jerusalem (first reported in Mk. 11:1–10), which *dramatically* implies messianic self-awareness for him; see above, pp. 84–85, and n. 45 below.

24. E.g., Taylor, *St. Mark,* 122–24.

25. For a review of scholarly opinions on the messianic secret as a Marcan invention, see J. D. Kingsbury, *The Christology of Mark's Gospel* (1983), 3–13.

26. E.g., Mk. 1:7–8; 2:18–22; 6:14–15; 9:2–8, 11–13.

27. The last decade or so has seen a notable increase of scholarly books offering a "holistic" interpretation of the historical Jesus — reconstructions of his ministry in its Jewish milieu and interweaving what may be said of Jesus' intention, his self-awareness, the reasons for his execution evidently as a messianic pretender, and his ongoing effects among his followers. For our present concern, these books fall into two categories. (1) One group promotes the basic historical reliability of the Gospels. Though numerous texts may not be trustworthy, the Jesus of the Gospels is, in all probability and with little variation, the Jesus who actually existed. He felt called to be or become the Messiah, shared that with his disciples as they were able to receive it, agreed with Peter's confession of him as the Christ, rode into Jerusalem as would the Messiah, etc. Among representatives of this approach are: B. F. Meyer, *The Aims of Jesus* (1979); A. E. Harvey, *Jesus and the Constraints of History* (1982); R. Lievestad, *Jesus in His Own Perspective* (1987; originally in Norwegian, 1982); and B. Witherington III, *The Christology of Jesus* (1990). Dissatisfied with the limited and often skeptical results coming from the use of generally accepted criteria of authenticity in Jesus-research (see above, pp. 132–133), these and kindred scholars have in effect changed the rules by adding "new" (and often overriding) criteria of their own — criteria favoring continuity between the historical Jesus and post-Easter views of him. When examining their assumptions and exegetical methods, one is hard pressed not to see christological interests at work. In any case, such studies have not to date turned scholarly consensus toward Jesus' actual messianic self-awareness (which, say all of these but Harvey's, included an expiatory death). Nor may that be expected of Witherington's study, which brings the Synoptic Jesus home in spades (he cursed and killed the fig tree, fed the five thousand, said to the high priest what Mark reports, etc.). (2) The other books grouped together here do not attribute to Jesus a self-awareness that includes distinctive ideas of early Christian faith. Among this group are: E. P. Sanders, *Jesus and Judaism* (1985); M. J. Borg, *Jesus, a New Vision* (1987); P. Fredriksen, *From Jesus to Christ* (1988); and H. Boers, *Who Was Jesus?* (1989). Of these four only Sanders and Boers find "strong" support for the speculation that Jesus implied himself to be a messiah of sorts: God's "viceroy" and, respectively, a leader of "armed resistance against Rome"(!). Yet these speculations of Sanders and Boers are guarded at that. While the evidence they marshal in this regard seems strained at times, I need not argue that. The point here is that the studies represented in this second group do not find for the historical Jesus a messianic or expiatory self-awareness that post-Easter traditions assigned to him. And by comparison, it is this group that better reflects ongoing scholarly consensus in this matter.

28. J. W. Bowman, *Which Jesus?* (1970); his view is fully developed in

The Intention of Jesus (1943). For more recent arguments favoring the traditional view, see the works of Meyer, Lievestad, and Witherington cited above in note 27.

29. Bowman, *The Intention,* 86.

30. Acts 2:14–36, 38–39; 3:12–26; 4:8–12; 5:29–32; 10:34–43.

31. See Acts (*a*) 2:38; 22:16; (*b*) 2:38; 3:19; 5:31; 26:18; (*c*) 10:43; 13:38–39; (*d*) 2:38; 10:43; (*e*) 5:31.

32. E.g., see Gal. 1–2.

33. Carefully treated by Haenchen, *The Acts,* 81–132. But cf. C. J. Hemer, *The Book of Acts in the Setting of Hellenistic History* (1989), saying Acts was written c. A.D. 62 by a companion of Paul and, essentially, is historically reliable; reworking old arguments, Hemer's book is not apt to have much effect on current scholarship.

34. See the explicit reference in Lk. 22:37 to Isa. 53:12, which clearly suggests atoning significance for Jesus' death in terms of the Suffering Servant. While that is not Luke's point, he could hardly have missed the suggestion. This holds also for the Lucan eucharistic words, including 22:19b–20 in the original text as shown by J. Jeremias, *The Eucharistic Words of Jesus* (1955), 87–106. Several recent critics have argued that Luke, without implying atonement, intended to present Jesus' death as a saving work; e.g., R. J. Karris, *Luke, Artist and Theologian* (1985).

35. Classically argued by C. H. Dodd, *The Apostolic Preaching and Its Developments* (1951), 7–35,

36. Cf. Kingsbury, *The Christology,* similarly relating the secret to Mark's overall narrative of Jesus as the royal Son of God (though not, as I do, within the framework of his also being the Suffering Servant).

37. For this division into three stages I am indebted to T. J. Weeden, "The Heresy That Necessitated Mark's Gospel" (1968).

38. That Mark intended his abrupt ending is shown from his storytelling technique by T. E. Boomershine and G. L. Bartholomew, "The Narrative Technique of Mark 16:8" (1981); cf. Boomershine's companion article, "Mark 16:8 and the Apostolic Commission," relating the ending to Mark's use of the messianic secret.

39. The centurion's words may also be read, "Truly, this man was *a* son of God." Unlike the English requirement of a definite article, the Greek text, while lacking the article, permits either translation. If my interpretation of the larger context is correct, what follows should indicate that Mark intended the centurion to confess Jesus as *the* Son of God, particularly with regard to the fact and significance of his death.

40. When such confessions are "silenced," it is either by Jesus' command (always Mark's creation) or, in the folksy ending to the demoniac story at 5:13, by Jesus sending away the confessing demons into a herd of pigs (through which demons *cannot* speak!). On the other hand, the messianic confessions of Bartimaeus (10:47–48) and of the people during the Triumphal Entry (11:9–10) are qualified (thus "corrected") by Mark in his back-to-back and peculiar treatment of those traditions, as explained above, pp. 84–85.

41. E.g., Kee, *Jesus,* 104–40. For a survey of current views of Mark's christology, see F. Matera, *What Are They Saying about Mark?* (1987), 18–37.

42. Except Mt. 20:28, following Mk. 10:45.

43. In his seminal study of the saying, "The Background of Mark 10:45" (1959), C. K. Barrett argued that Mk. 10:45 did not likely derive from the language of Isa. 53. His being correct in that would not disturb my contention about the appearance of the saying in Mark. That the saying is at least reminiscent of Isa. 53:11–12 seems attested by the fact that hordes of critical and other readers have found it so; and my contention is that Mark used the saying, not as a proof-text, but as part of his suggestive, dramatic depiction of Jesus as the Suffering Servant. This possibility is not considered in the erudite study of M. D. Hooker, *Jesus and the Suffering Servant* (1959), which denies Synoptic interest in the Suffering Servant and even questions Mk. 1:11b as a reference to Isa. 42:1; she would accept only slavish quotations from the Servant-poems, leaving nothing to imagination or art.

44. Cf. Mk. 12:35–37.

45. As tradition describes it, Jesus' entry into Jerusalem would most likely have provoked an *immediate* arrest of him, a roundup of his disciples, and executions of him *and* them without needless delays. At Passover time especially, when emotions ran high in the crowded city, the Romans would not tolerate a potential troublemaker, least of all one who seemed to be a messianic claimant with a following. Recognizing this, some critics tone down the "messianic" entry, to wit: the fanfare was minimal, and the incident was observed by only a few. Similar suggestions limiting the area and extent of Jesus' reported disruptive behavior in the Temple (Mk. 11:15–16) have circulated among critics to make that incident also plausible (cf. the works of Sanders, Borg, and Fredriksen cited above in n. 27). While such reconstructions serve historians' hypotheses, the suggestions indicated here seem strained. *In their every detail* these circumstantially difficult traditions dramatize post-Easter beliefs about Jesus' significance (see above, pp. 84–85, 89–90, and n. 52 below). So unrealistic and so thoroughly Christian, neither story, in my judgment, yields probably solid information about Jesus; but that makes them no less helpful to Christian faith as powerful dramatizations of the gospel. Further, I am not convinced by Bruce Chilton's *The Temple of Jesus* (1992), which builds a program of sacrificial purity for Jesus around his "occupation" of the Temple, focusing especially on Mk. 11:17 (which looks to me like Mark's addition in line with his presentation of Jesus as the Suffering Servant who redeems "all the nations").

46. Isa. 42:1–4; 49:1–6; 50:4–9; 52:13–53:12. This distinction of the Servant-poems has been opposed by T. N. D. Mettinger, *A Farewell to the Servant Songs* (1983); for a critical analysis of his too-easy thesis, see the review by F. J. Gaiser in *Interpretation* (1986), 310–12.

47. Cf. W. M. W. Roth, "The Anonymity of the Suffering Servant" (1964); L. E. Wilshire, "The Servant-City" (1975).

48. Especially regarding the fourth Servant-poem, Isa. 52:13–53:12. The "fluid" concept of the Servant's identity was classically advanced by the Christian O.T. scholar C. R. North, *The Suffering Servant in Deutero-Isaiah* (1948), 193–219. For detailed criticism of North's objections to a wholly corporate view of the Isaianic Servant, see Hooker, *Jesus,* 48–52.

49. Mk. 1:34; 3:11–12; 5:1–13.

50. Mk. 8:27–30; 9:7–9.

51. Mk. 1:44; 5:43; 7:36; 8:26.

52. The false accusation mentioned in Mk. 14:58 thus interprets the tradition of Jesus' Temple-disruptiveness reported earlier in 11:15–16; cf. Donahue, *Are You the Christ?* 103–15, showing that the accusatory saying in 14:58 is, in its present form, the result of Mark's editorial activity.

53. I.e., beginning with Bartimaeus's confession immediately before Jesus' messianic entry into Jerusalem *and* into the Temple house of sacrifice, as follows: Mk. 10:47, 48; 14:61; 15:2, 9, 12, 18, 26, 32 (previously, confused utterance of such titles appears only in 3:11; 5:7; 8:29).

54. Cf. H. L. Chronis, "The Torn Veil" (1982), 99, to which I am indebted.

55. Note also the barren fig tree's position in Mark: immediately following each of Jesus' first two visits to the Temple during Passion Week and just before his next visit there!

56. The basis for such a corporate view of the effects of Jesus' own righteousness is to be located in the old Semitic view of "corporate personality," discussed above, pp. 119–122. In a word, the individual and the group to which he/she belonged were held to be inseparably related, so much so that the actions of one person could be regarded as really involving all members of the group. The meaning of this for Mark's christology is further developed in chapter 4, where I suggest that the Marcan Christ is the righteous Messiah/Suffering Servant who has "repented" for the world and has thus made all people righteous.

57. Mk. 1:22, 27; 2:12; 4:41; 5:15, 33, 42; 6:49–52; 7:37; 9:32; 10:24, 26; 11:18; 12:17, 34. Cf. Boomershine, "Mark 16:8," 227–30.

58. Cf. Boomershine, "Mark 16:8," 237–39, to which I am indebted here.

Chapter 3: Without Sense of Being a Sinner?

1. Luke's report of the boy Jesus' visit to Jerusalem and subsequent maturation (2:41–52) is recognized as a Christian invention; e.g., J. A. Fitzmyer, *The Gospel according to Luke (I–IX)* (1981), 434–47.

2. See the variety of interpretations noted by V. Taylor, *The Gospel according to St. Mark* (1957), 426–27.

3. Taylor, *St. Mark,* 426–27, prefers the last of these explanations.

4. Above, pp. 69–79.

5. As in Matthew's account of the Great Commission at 28:18–20, the secondary nature of which is conceded by all respected critics.

6. Taylor, *St. Mark,* 617–19.

7. Ibid., 617–18.

8. Ibid., 618.

9. Ibid., 426–27.

10. Cf. Ps. 8; Gen. 1:1–2:4a.

11. Consistent with his view that Jesus neither broke the Law nor had any disagreement with it (except for burying the dead: Mk. 8:22), E. P. Sanders argues that Mk. 7:15, if authentic, would make the positions of "Peter and James" (as reflected in Gal. 2) "impossible to understand" (*Jesus and Judaism* [1985], 266). His reasoning is faulted, I think, by a combination of three factors. (1) The hypocritical "Cephas" of Gal. 2 perhaps wasn't Peter, but a Jewish Christian with the same nickname (see above, p. 149, and below, chap. 4 n. 42). More importantly, (2) James, "the Lord's brother" (Gal. 1:19), apparently had not been sympathetic with Jesus' public ministry (see above, pp. 37–40); as a leader in the Jerusalem church he would thus appreciate the common sense of giving "Judaizers" some breathing room. And (3) the practice of accommodation is characteristic of institutional growth. Should one assume that Jesus' followers, seeking additional church members among fellow Jews who valued Torah, would have disallowed any communal deviation from his teachings concerning it?

12. The reference in Gen. 1:26–27 to man's creation in "the image of God," while alluding to creaturely dominion, concerns man's intended vocation, not his nature. Confined in the O.T. to Genesis (cf. 5:1; 9:6), the "image" of God refers to man (Heb. *adam* = mankind) as a social being in relationship with others. Rather than saluting the special dignity or talents of man the individual, it points to the creaturely obligation of people to "image" God's social behavior. That function is to be served especially by the people Israel, who know what God is like from God's social dealings with them. Cf. G. von Rad, *Genesis* (1961), 55–57.

13. Except during a brief interlude of tumultuous independence, 165–63 B.C.

14. Sanders, *Jesus,* 266.

15. Cf. G. Bornkamm, *Jesus of Nazareth* (1960), 96–143, to whom I am indebted here and elsewhere in this chapter.

16. Ibid., 169–78, 226–31.

17. Ibid., 179–91.

18. E.g., see Isa. 9:5–7; 11:3b–9 for the Messiah; and Isa. 42:1–4; 49:6; 53:11b for the Servant.

19. The first, second, and fourth, according to current consensus; I would add the fifth as typical of Jesus.

20. This is not to their discredit; see above, p. 64.

21. Against the authenticity of this anti-Moses teaching in Mk. 10:2–9, some critics prefer the divorce saying that follows it: "Whoever divorces his wife and marries another, commits adultery against her" (Mk. 10:11). The latter is said to be more radical in making adultery a matter of a wife's honor, not just one of customary male honor and rights, whereas Mk. 10:2–9 is thought simply to forbid divorce by saying it is illegal: so, e.g., J. D. Crossan, *The Historical Jesus* (1991), 301–2. To the contrary, the teaching in Mk. 10:2–9 was both more radical and more pertinent to female honor

and welfare in Jesus' day. Mk. 10:11 allows a man to divorce his wife, which in Jewish society then brought her immediate shame (and often impoverishment!); only *if* he remarries does her honor come into play. Mk. 10:2-9, on the other hand, doesn't forbid divorce by making it illegal, which Jesus could not have effected anyway. Rather, his teaching there is that divorce is but a legal denial of a oneness effected by God. In fact, the saying in Mk. 10:11, like Q's version of it (Lk. 16:18 = Mt. 5:32), seems to be predicated on that teaching and assumes that the oneness in marriage continues beyond a decree of divorce – which is what makes any remarriage adulterous. "A man should not divorce his wife" or "A man should not divorce his wife and marry another." There can be no doubt which of these teachings in Jesus' society would have been most welcomed by women and most inconvenient for men. And, incidentally, that more difficult teaching keeps better with Jesus' expectation of an imminent Eschaton; see chap. 2 n. 12.

22. Mt. 5:38; cf. Ex. 21:23-25; Lev. 24:19-20; Deut. 19:21.

23. E.g., Ps. 41:9; Jn. 13:18; cf. Josh. 9:3-21; 1 Kgs. 13:8-9.

24. Mt. 9:10-11; 11:19; Lk. 5:29-30; 7:34; 15:1-2; 19:5-7.

25. Acts 11:2-3; Gal. 2:11-12; see above, p. 149, and below, chap. 4 n. 42.

26. Cf. J. B. Tyson, "The Blindness of the Disciples in Mark" (1961). While relating the disciples' poor showing to Mark's understanding of Jesus as a suffering Messiah whose death has redemptive meaning, Tyson does so without reference to Jesus as the Suffering Servant whose identity in life must remain hidden; thus he denies any connection between the disciples' poor showing and Mark's motif of the messianic secret.

27. Much of the following definition appeared in the author's book *The Lord's Supper* (1966), 42-46, and is used here by permission. For more thorough discussions of corporate personality, see H. W. Robinson, "The Hebrew Concept of Corporate Personality" (1936); A. R. Johnson, *The One and the Many in the Israelite Conception of God* (1961), 2-13.

28. Cf. Heb. 9:15ff.; Rom. 8:31-38.

29. Mk. 2:15-17; Isa. 53:11b-12.

Chapter 4: Able to Do Miracles at Will?

1. B. J. Friedman, *Steambath* (1971).

2. Regarding miracles attributed to Jesus, two helpful books for general readers are: R. H. Fuller, *Interpreting the Miracles* (1963), a study for laypersons, yet often cited by scholars; and *Miracles* (1966), ed. C. F. D. Moule, a collection of scholarly but readable essays dealing with issues more thoroughly than a study like Fuller's would allow – e.g., as it bears on this chapter's first section, the essay of G. W. H. Lampe, "Miracles and Early Christian Apologetic."

3. Lampe, "Miracles."

4. H. D. Betz, "Jesus as Divine Man" (1968), 116. First-century appli-

cation of "divine man" to Jesus has been strongly disputed; see J. D. Kingsbury, *The Christology of Mark's Gospel* (1983), 33–35.

5. Lampe, "Miracles," 208.

6. Ibid., 209–10.

7. Ibid., 214.

8. A. Richardson, *The Miracle-Stories of the Gospels* (1941), 36.

9. Translated by J. Klausner, *Jesus of Nazareth* (1925), 27, brackets his. Some scholars think the reference is not to Jesus of Nazareth.

10. Fuller, *Interpreting,* 23.

11. A useful introduction to form criticism for general readers is by E. V. McKnight, *What Is Form Criticism?* (1969).

12. The last stage in the traditions' development (apart from scribal changes in copying texts) was their being used and influenced by Gospel writers, each of whom functioned as a redactor (editor) as well as an author. Critical study focusing on this stage of form-history is called redaction criticism; see the popular introduction by N. Perrin, *What Is Redaction Criticism?* (1969).

13. Involving both the speaker's concerns and the social life and reaction of the audience, each oral transmission of Jesus-traditions was a live performance, not simply a memorized recitation that was always the same; see the seminal study of W. H. Kelber, *The Oral and the Written Gospel* (1983), 1–89, for such characteristics of "the oral gospel." His application of oral and media criticism to Mark's Gospel is governed by his contention that Mark was writing a polemic against Jesus' disciples and other conveyers of oral tradition. Though rejected by most critics, that application doesn't lessen the fundamental importance of Kelber's distinctions between oral and textual communication of Jesus-traditions.

14. E.g., our references in previous chapters to items that were embarrassing to early Christians, either faith-wise or personally.

15. The reasoning behind the second half of this criterion, which I have put in parentheses, involves the fact that the earliest Christians were Jews. An item reflecting Jewish thought or practice might simply be the product of their upbringing; *ergo,* many form critics maintained, it cannot be trusted for information about Jesus himself. Scholars have successfully objected that this aspect of the criterion leads to a non-Jewish Jesus, which of course would be absurd. I agree with current consensus that an item, not expressing Christian faith and interests, may likely be deemed reliable if it is dissimilar to Judaism in Jesus' time but that it should not be deemed unreliable merely because it reflects that Judaism.

16. This is part of the criterion of multiple attestation in general, which posits possible authenticity for an item that is found in independent sources and/or multiple literary types (including multiple forms of a Gospel item).

17. McKnight, *Form Criticism,* 65.

18. E.g., Mk. 1:23–27, Jesus cleansing the Capernaum demoniac, implying Jesus' messiahship in his victorious authority over the forces of Satan.

19. For similar examples, see Mk. 2:1–12; Lk. 13:10–17; 14:1–6. For rhe-

torical analysis of pronouncement stories, showing that the saying(s) *and* the setting in such a story are equally important to its point, see B. L. Mack and V. K. Robbins, *Patterns of Persuasion in the Gospels* (1989).

20. Matthew and Luke have many materials that are verbatim or nearly so, yet are not taken from Mark. Assuming that Matthew and Luke wrote independently of each other, the vast majority of critics conclude that they used another common source, designated "Q" (an abbreviation of the German *Quelle*, meaning source). See the facile discussion and analysis by H. C. Kee, *Jesus in History* (1970), 62–103. The leading critical analysis now is that of J. S. Kloppenborg, *The Formation of Q* (1987), positing that Q was formed of three distinct layers of sayings, the first of which was "nonapocalyptic." For the reconstructed text of Q, with introduction and critical notes, see Kloppenborg's *Q Parallels* (1988).

21. See (*a*) Mk. 3:23b; Lk. 11:19 = Mt. 12:27; (*b*) Lk. 11:20 = Mt. 12:28; Lk. 10:23b–24 = Mt. 13:16–17, the reference to miracles being implied in Q; (*c*) Lk. 10:13–15 = Mt. 11:21–24; (*d*) Lk. 4:23; and (*e*) Lk. 7:22–23 = Mt. 11:4–6; Lk. 13:31–32.

22. Fuller, *Interpreting,* 25.

23. See N. Perrin, *Rediscovering the Teaching of Jesus* (1967), 63–67.

24. R. Bultmann, *The History of the Synoptic Tradition* (1963), 162. All Synoptic form-critical efforts today, even by scholars who have important differences with Bultmann (as I do), are indebted to his seminal work. So influential have been his method and his observations, the debt could not be properly acknowledged without citing him page upon page. Like no other N.T. critic, Bultmann is common property – as occasionally in this study.

25. So Fuller, *Interpreting,* 26–27.

26. Above, pp. 111–113.

27. F. W. Beare, *The Earliest Records of Jesus* (1962), 175.

28. E.g., deeds assigned to Apollonius of Tyana (died c. A.D. 97); for a summary, see M. Hadas and M. Smith, *Heroes and Gods* (1965), 196–258.

29. For a detailed presentation, see Fuller, *Interpreting,* 47–68.

30. My translation, as follows: line 1 from Mt. 11:4b; lines 2–7 from Lk. 7:22; line 8 from Lk. 7:23 = Mt. 11:6.

31. See Mk. 1:2 for the same use of Mal. 3:1.

32. Fuller, *Interpreting,* 28, italics his.

33. I.e., six lines: three sets of doublets. Perhaps also influential at this point were the Elijah/Elisha cycles of miracles that, as noted above, played a part in the formulation of Gospel miracles; those cycles included raisings of the dead *and* the cleansing of a leper.

34. Excluding the addition of cleansing lepers, of all the words in this saying that refer to Jesus' mighty works, *only two* are changed from the Septuagint: a different verb for "see" and the use of "walk" instead of "leap." And each of those changes can be reasoned as necessary for poetic meter!

35. While some of the nature miracles seem to be variations of earlier traditions, eight such miracles are found in the Gospels themselves:

the stilling of the storm – Mk. 4:35-41 (Mt. 8:23-27; Lk. 8:22-25);

the feeding of five thousand – Mk. 6:30-44 (Mt. 14:13-21; Lk. 9:10-17); Jn. 6:1-13;

walking on water – Mk. 6:45-52 (Mt. 14:22-33); Jn. 6:16-21;

the feeding of four thousand – Mk. 8:1-10 (Mt. 15:32-39);

the cursing of the fig tree – Mk. 11:12-14, 20-24 (Mt. 21:18-22);

the shekel in the fish's mouth – Mt. 17:24-27;

the great netting of fish – Lk. 5:1-11; Jn. 21:1-14;

turning water into wine – Jn. 2:1-11.

According to leading Johannine critics, the three Synoptic nature miracles reported also in John came to John via a special signs-source, not from the Synoptic Gospels.

36. Following John's version of the feeding of the five thousand (6:1-13), some MSS read in 6:14 that the people saw "the sign" (singular) that Jesus did, as if all present were aware of the multiplication of loaves and fish. However, other MSS read "the signs" (plural) – i.e., alluding to Jesus' Galilean miracles in general, as in Jn. 6:2, where "the signs" refer to healings. On balance, principles of textual criticism favor the plural reading for 6:14. So even in John's Gospel, which makes much of public signs, the performance of nature miracles remains a private matter.

37. Cf. R. E. Brown, *The Gospel according to John (i–xii)* (1966), 101-10. Though not vigorously, Brown tries to explain how the story might have come from Jesus' ministry; but his suggestions require a Christian view for both Jesus and his disciples: seeing himself as the Messiah, Jesus performed the miracle as an adequate sign for his disciples to see him that way too!

38. From the Yahwist idea that God sustains his people, feasting on plenty was a natural symbol for Israel's end-time hope. While only three O.T. texts refer specifically to "messianic" feasting (Mic. 5:2-4; Ezek. 34:23-24; Zech. 9:17), unthwarted eating and drinking often signify future salvation: Amos 9:13-15; Jer. 31:12; Isa. 25:6; 51:14; 62:8-9; 65:21-22; Joel 2:26.

39. Cf. Jn. 12:31; 14:30; 16:11; 2 Cor. 4:4; Eph. 2:2.

40. Significantly, the verbs for Jesus' rebuking the wind (*epitimaō*) and commanding the sea to be silent (*phimoō*) occur in traditions where he rebukes demons (Mk. 1:25; 9:25) and silences one of them (Mk. 1:25).

41. Though most MSS at Mk. 1:40 read "moved with pity," the parallel accounts of Matthew (8:2-4) and Luke (5:12-16) include neither it nor "provoked to anger," likely indicating that the latter, offensive term had been excised (and not yet been replaced by the term of compassion) in their copies of Mark. Further, the unanimously attested, offensive appearances of "censure" and "cast out" at Mk. 1:43 are also absent in the Matthean and Lucan accounts, again indicating excision of Mark's original text. Conversely, had that text read "moved with pity," why would anyone replace it with "provoked to anger" and thereby compound the story's offensiveness?

42. See B. D. Ehrman, "Cephas and Peter" (1990), suggesting that "Cephas" in Paul's letters refers not to Peter but to a Jewish Christian who shared the nickname with Peter and who, while being a pillar of the Jerusalem church, was engaged in a mission to Gentiles. Though hardly a new position, Ehrman's formulation of it is intriguing; cf. the criticism of D. C. Allison, "Peter and Cephas: One and the Same" (1992).

43. Mk. 7:5–8 and 7:14b–15 represent two independent traditions concerning, respectively, handwashing in particular and impurity in general; cf. E. P. Sanders, *Jesus and Judaism* (1985), 264–66. Sanders interprets the saying in 7:15 (i.e., what goes *out* of a man defiles him, not what goes *into* him) from the perspective of 7:18–19a (referring to what passes *through* a man); he thereby limits 7:15 to the matter of food, thus removing it from the question of how Jesus valued ceremonial cleansing that was required by the Law. However, vss. 18–19a, as well as vss. 21–23, clearly seem to reflect later interpretation of the general saying reported in 7:15; cf. V. Taylor, *The Gospel according to St. Mark* (1957), 342–43. So the saying in Mk. 7:15 may reflect a negative attitude on Jesus' part toward nonpenitential, or all, ceremonial cleansing. I have already responded to Sanders's suggestion that Mk. 7:15 doesn't represent an actual saying of Jesus: above, chap. 3 n. 11.

44. I.e., "Rise and go your way; your faith had made you well." At 7:50 Luke adds the saying about faith to another tradition he received.

45. Bultmann, *The History*, 33.

46. Fuller, *Interpreting*, 95–96. R. Bultmann, *The Gospel of John* (1971), 396–401, offers a similar reconstruction in assigning to John's source vss. 1, 3, 5–6, 11–12, 14–15, 17–19, 33–39, 43–44.

47. E.g., J. N. Sanders and B. A. Mastin, *A Commentary on the Gospel according to St. John* (1968), 274.

48. Ibid., 276.

49. E.g., suggested by Brown, *John (i–xii)*, 428–29. Brown and others have shown that John's Gospel contains traditions that did not depend on a reworking of Synoptic details. But that surely does not lessen the probability, as Brown implies it does, that a *pre*-Lucan parable influenced the story of Lazarus's resurrection, however the latter story reached John.

50. Taylor, *St. Mark*, 295, cites many instances regarding 5:39.

51. See Bultmann, *The History*, 214–15.

52. Vss. 1a in part, 16 perhaps, and 17.

53. J. A. Fitzmyer, *The Gospel according to Luke (I–IX)* (1981), 656–57, treats in some detail three pagan stories often cited as parallels to this story.

54. In considering all of the Gospel miracles for their historical value and Christian meaning, Fuller, one of the more conservative of contemporary form critics, comes to virtually the same conclusion (*Interpreting*, 39).

55. Mk. 1:29–31, the healing of Peter's mother-in-law; see above, pp. 133–134.

Chapter 5: Immortal?

1. Not *what* died and was raised, as if resurrection were a resuscitation of the same old cells. That was Pharisaic materialism, not the teaching of Paul, the only N.T. writer who addressed the nature of the resurrection body; cf. M. E. Dahl, *The Resurrection of the Body* (1962).

2. E.g., on the exodus see J. Bright, *A History of Israel* (1981), 120-24.

3. See above, pp. 76-79.

4. Docetism, a denial of the real humanity of Christ, began to flourish in the first third of the second century.

5. Definitively at the Council of Chalcedon, A.D. 451.

6. The classical O.T. study of this is H. W. Robinson's "Hebrew Psychology" (1925).

7. The ancient Hebrew terms may also refer either to the life-principle or to what makes man what he is, yet without signifying basically different entities. Gen. 2:7, where *nephesh* appears twice, is instructive here: "The Lord God formed man of dust from the ground, and breathed into his nostrils the breath of life [*nephesh*]; and man became a living soul [*nephesh*]." In receiving life man became, not was given, a living soul; thus a soul *is* what man *is* — flesh, blood, bones, and all.

8. See Lev. 21:11; Num. 6:6; 19:11, 13.

9. See Judg. 14:6, 19; 1 Sam. 10:6, 10; 16:15; Isa. 11:2-3.

10. See Ps. 145:21, man in praise of God; Isa. 66:16; Jer. 25:31; 45:5 — man under judgment; Ps. 63:1, with *bâsar* and *nephesh* in parallel, the self that longs for God; 2 Chron. 32:8, ill-fated human weakness pitted against God; and Gen. 6:3; Ps. 78:39; Isa. 40:6-8 — the ultimate contrast, man who is sure to die and be no more.

11. Robinson, "Hebrew Psychology," 362.

12. All but absent in the O.T., belief in "eternal" life explicitly appears only in Dan. 12:2 (c. 165 B.C.), indicating resurrection, and twice(?) in the Isaianic Apocalypse (Isa. 24-27): perhaps at 26:19, foretelling resurrection (but this has been disputed), and at 25:6-8, where God's swallowing up death forever is linked with his providing food for all peoples, who still have to eat! Elsewhere the belief is scarcely even implied or anticipated: in Job 19:26 and some of the Psalms (49:15; 73:24; perhaps 16:10-11 and 17:15), yet never suggesting a disembodied life.

13. The Hebrew concept of Sheol (Gr. *Hadēs*), unfortunately translated "hell" in some versions of the Bible, originally bespoke a place of shadowy existence — the nether region where, upon one's death, the departed life-principle went — not a place where personalities continued to live. As a place, however, it was eventually subject to fanciful speculations, including conscious existence for the dead, as we shall see.

14. So Paul's distinction in 1 Cor. 15:42-44 between the perishable, "physical" (i.e., nature-controlled) body and the imperishable, "spiritual" (i.e., spirit-controlled) body.

15. See Dahl, *The Resurrection*, who admits that his own exegesis is surely more structured and systematic than Paul's conscious thinking.

16. Because of its historical irrelevance here, I have excluded from principal discussion Lk. 23:43, Jesus' alleged word to the penitent one of two felons shown to be crucified with him: "Truly, I say to you, today you will be with me in Paradise." Besides the fact that "today," especially when linked with the futuristic "Paradise," may denote the final Day of Salvation inaugurated by Jesus' death/resurrection, Luke's episode of the penitent versus the mocking criminal (23:39-43) is clearly legendary—a late revision and expansion of earlier tradition (cf. Mk. 15:32, followed in Mt. 27:44, where *both* criminals reviled Jesus). As such, it tells nothing of earliest Christian thought about life after death.

17. Many critics have found the idea also in 2 Cor. 5:1-10, some suggesting that Paul's thinking changed radically from belief in resurrection to a Hellenistic view of immortality; but that disregards 2 Cor. 4:14 in the passage next door. For detailed survey and criticism of such interpretation, see K. Hankart, "Paul's Hope in the Face of Death" (1969).

18. 1 Cor. 11:30; 15:6, 18, 20, 51; 1 Thess. 4:13, 14, 15; 5:10 (including himself among those who may fall asleep before the Parousia).

19. See above, pp. 121-122, regarding "corporate personality" and Paul's theology; cf. J. A. T. Robinson, *The Body* (1952).

20. A useful commentary on this text for general readers is B. Reicke, *The Epistles of James, Peter, and Jude* (1964), 109-15; neither he nor Barclay (cited below in n. 22) shares my interpretation of the text.

21. Though *kērussō* (to speak or proclaim as God's herald) most often in N.T. usage denotes a preaching of the gospel, for that meaning the author of 1 Peter uses *euangelizō* (to speak good news or evangelize): i.e., at 4:6, where he says (again figuratively, I think) that the gospel (or Christ) was preached to the dead (but not to the disobedient spirits). For other uses of *kērussō* that are not evangelistic or penitential, see Lk. 12:3; Rev. 5:2.

22. Conveniently summarized in the main by W. Barclay, *The Letters of James and Peter* (1976), 236-43.

23. Cf. n. 21 above.

24. So in vss. 18 and 21 of the passage at hand, regarding Christ himself; cf. Jn. 5:21; Rom. 4:17; 8:11; 1 Cor. 15:22, 36.

25. Tendencies to regard Palestinian Judaism as little affected by commerce with Hellenists have proved to be incorrect, even though the extent of Hellenism's ideological influences is difficult to gauge. For a positive statement of such influences, see J. Bonsirven, *Palestinian Judaism in the Time of Jesus Christ* (1964); but in making the point he claims too much regarding immortality of the soul (pp. 164-65). While Bonsirven notes that (1) Josephus attributes Hellenism's concept of the soul's immortality to the Essenes and (2) it is found in the Wisdom of Solomon, we may observe that (1) the language of Josephus, who wrongly attributed such belief also to the Pharisees, is suspect, even more so now since the Essenes' own writings from Qumran do not explicitly or clearly confirm any such belief; and (2) the Wisdom of Solomon came from *Alexandrian* Judaism. True, immortality for the soul (without anticipated resurrection of the body) occasionally appears in B.C. Jewish literature from Palestine: e.g., 1 Enoch

102:4–103:8; perhaps Jub. 23:31, itself ambiguous. Yet even those few appearances are in context of the rewards that *God* will effect for righteous and wicked souls. To my knowledge, solid evidence is wanting that Palestinian Jews of the first century or before believed in the natural immortality of the soul. Even so, it is clear that Palestinian Judaism of Jesus' day had been tickled by foreign hands.

26. For other expressions of this peculiar in Luke, see 1:53; 3:11; 6:20, 21, 24, 25, 34; 10:30–37; 12:13–15, 16–21, 33a; 14:12–14; 16:9, 10–12, 14–15; 19:2–9.

27. Most ably by J. Jeremias, *The Parables of Jesus* (1963), 182–87; cf. J. A. Fitzmyer, *The Gospel according to Luke (X–XXIV)* (1985), 1125–29. Major difficulties for the parable's authenticity are discussed by C. F. Evans, "Uncomfortable Words – V" (1970), to which I am much indebted.

28. The tale is reproduced in full in N. Perrin, *Rediscovering the Teaching of Jesus* (1967), 111–12.

29. I.e., the laborers in the vineyard (Mt. 20:1–8, 9–15) and the prodigal son (Lk. 15:11–24, 25–32). Matthew's two-tiered version of the great supper (22:1–10, 11–14) is now seen as a combination of originally distinct parables; regarding its first part, cf. Lk. 14:16–24; Gospel of Thomas 64, reproduced in Perrin, *Rediscovering*, 111, and in J. S. Kloppenborg et al., *Q Thomas Reader* (1990), 144–45.

30. Fitzmyer, *Luke (X–XXIV)*, 1132.

31. Cf. J. M. Creed, *The Gospel according to St. Luke* (1930), 212, noting that in old Jewish literature neither "Abraham's bosom" nor Paradise was associated with Sheol or Hades, where departed souls might exist.

32. So Jeremias, *The Parables*, 185; Fitzmyer, *Luke (X–XXIV)*, 1132.

33. Translations of 4 Ezra are from *The Old Testament Pseudepigrapha*, vol. 1 (1983), ed. J. H. Charlesworth.

34. Alive, Lk. 12:22–23 = Mt. 6:25; dead, Lk. 17:37 = Mt. 24:28 (reading "carcass").

35. Lk. 11:34, 36 = Mt. 6:22–23.

36. Lk. 12:22–23 = Mt. 6:25; Lk. 17:33 = Mt. 10:39; Lk. 14:26; perhaps also from Q is Lk. 12:19–20, where "soul" denotes one's self and life.

37. Lk. 12:2–12 = Mt. 10:19–20, 26–33.

38. While Gehenna (*geena*) in Jewish literature written or translated in Greek had a wide variety of meanings, including punishment of departed souls, it appears in the N.T. as a symbol of utter destruction, like that of a garbage dump (which it actually was outside Jerusalem); cf. Mt. 5:22; 23:15, 33; Mk. 9:43, 45 (Mt. 5:29; 18:9); Jas. 3:6. For Jewish meanings, see Bonsirven, *Palestinian Judaism*, 247–51.

39. Though the idea of utter destruction is clearly implied in Luke's reference to him who "can cast into Gehenna"; see n. 38 above.

40. In Q, Lk. 11:47–48 = Mt. 23:31; Lk. 13:34 = Mt. 23:37.

41. In Q, Lk. 11:49 = Mt. 23:34; in Matthew, 22:6; 24:9.

42. Lk. 17:27–29 = Mt. 24:39 (edited "took away").

43. Cf. Lk. 14:16–24; regarding Matthew's enlargement, see n. 29 above.

44. Matthew's other own use of "destroy" in relation to death also denotes hopelessness; see 18:14 in context of 18:5–10.

45. Most importantly for English readers in R. Bultmann, *Kerygma and Myth* (1961); for other translated works, see references in the collected essays edited by Moule, cited in n. 47 below.

46. R. Bultmann, "The Primitive Christian Kerygma and the Historical Jesus" (1964), 42.

47. Major approaches and key issues are presented in *The Significance of the Message of the Resurrection for Faith in Jesus Christ* (1968), ed. C. F. D. Moule; see especially Moule's introduction and the concluding survey by H. G. Geyer.

48. Cf. W. Marxsen, "The Resurrection of Jesus as a Historical and Theological Problem" (1968); G. Bornkamm, *Jesus of Nazareth* (1960), 180–86.

49. E.g., Moule, *The Significance,* 6–11.

50. Matthew's report (28:11–15; cf. 27:62–66) of the Jewish authorities arranging for Jesus' disciples to be accused of stealing his body is so obviously contrived that it has no historical value here.

51. Hence Jesus' resurrection "on the *third* day," which reflects *Jewish* Christian thinking and was designed to say that Jesus was actually raised, not simply vindicated by God in some other sense.

52. See R. M. Grant, *Miracle and Natural Law in Graeco-Roman and Early Christian Thought* (1952), esp. 41–60, 221ff., 235ff.

Bibliography

———— ✠ ————

Achtemeier, P. J. "*Omne Verbum Sonat:* The New Testament and the Oral Environment of Late Western Antiquity." *Journal of Biblical Literature* 109 (1990): 3–27.

Allison, D. C. "Peter and Cephas: One and the Same." *Journal of Biblical Literature* 111 (1992): 489–95.

Barclay, W. *The Letters of James and Peter.* Philadelphia: Westminster Press, 1976.

Barrett, C. K. "The Background of Mark 10:45." In *New Testament Essays: Studies in Memory of T. W. Manson, 1893–1958,* ed. A. J. B. Higgins, 1–18. Manchester: Manchester University Press, 1959.

Beare, F. W. *The Earliest Records of Jesus.* Nashville: Abingdon Press, 1962.

Betz, H. D. "Jesus as Divine Man." In *Jesus and the Historian: In Honor of Ernest Cadman Colwell,* ed. F. T. Trotter, 114–33. Philadelphia: Westminster Press, 1968.

Boers, H. *Who Was Jesus? The Historical Jesus and the Synoptic Gospels.* San Francisco: Harper and Row, 1989.

Bonsirven, J. *Palestinian Judaism in the Time of Jesus Christ.* Eng. trans. New York: Holt, Rinehart and Winston, 1964.

Boomershine, T. E. "Mark 16:8 and the Apostolic Commission." *Journal of Biblical Literature* 100 (1981): 225–39.

Boomershine, T. E., and G. L. Bartholomew. "The Narrative Technique of Mark 16:8." *Journal of Biblical Literature* 100 (1981): 213–23.

Borg, M. J. *Jesus, a New Vision: Spirit, Culture, and the Life of Discipleship.* San Francisco: Harper and Row, 1987.

Bornkamm, G. *Jesus of Nazareth.* Eng. trans. New York: Harper and Row, 1960.

Bowman, J. W. *The Intention of Jesus.* Philadelphia: Westminster Press, 1943.

———. *Which Jesus?* Philadelphia: Westminster Press, 1970.

Bright, J. *A History of Israel.* Philadelphia: Westminster Press, 1981.

Brown, R. E. *The Birth of the Messiah: A Commentary on the Infancy Narratives in Matthew and Luke.* Garden City, N.Y.: Doubleday, 1977.

———. *The Gospel according to John (i–xii).* Garden City, N.Y.: Doubleday, 1966.

———. *The Virginal Conception and Bodily Resurrection of Jesus.* New York: Paulist Press, 1973.

Bultmann, R. *The Gospel of John.* Eng. trans. Philadelphia: Westminster Press, 1971.

――――. *The History of the Synoptic Tradition.* Eng. trans. New York: Harper and Row, 1963.

――――. *Kerygma and Myth: A Theological Debate.* Eng. trans. New York: Harper and Row, 1961.

――――. "The Primitive Christian Kerygma and the Historical Jesus." In *The Historical Jesus and the Kerygmatic Christ: Essays on the New Quest of the Historical Jesus,* ed. and trans. C. E. Braaten and R. A. Harrisville, 15–42. Nashville: Abingdon Press, 1964.

Charlesworth, J. H. *Jesus within Judaism: New Light from Exciting Archaeological Discoveries.* New York: Doubleday, 1988.

――――, ed. *The Old Testament Pseudepigrapha.* Vol. 1. Garden City, N.Y.: Doubleday, 1983.

Chilton, B. *The Temple of Jesus: His Sacrificial Program within a Cultural History of Sacrifice.* University Park: Pennsylvania State University Press, 1992.

Chronis, H. L. "The Torn Veil: Cultus and Christology in Mark 15:37–39." *Journal of Biblical Literature* 101 (1982): 97–114.

Crawford, B. S. "Near Expectation in the Sayings of Jesus." *Journal of Biblical Literature* 101 (1982): 225–44.

Creed, J. M. *The Gospel according to St. Luke.* London: Macmillan, 1930.

Crossan, J. D. *The Historical Jesus: The Life of a Mediterranean Jewish Peasant.* San Francisco: Harper, 1991.

Dahl, M. E. *The Resurrection of the Body: A Study of 1 Corinthians 15.* Naperville, Ill.: Alec R. Allenson, 1962.

Dodd, C. H. *The Apostolic Preaching and Its Developments.* New York: Harper and Brothers, 1951.

Donahue, J. R. *Are You the Christ? The Trial Narrative in the Gospel of Mark.* Missoula, Mont.: Society of Biblical Literature, 1973.

――――. "Temple, Trial, and Royal Christology." In *The Passion in Mark: Studies on Mark 14–16,* ed. W. H. Kelber, 61–69. Philadelphia: Fortress Press, 1976.

Ehrman, B. D. "Cephas and Peter." *Journal of Biblical Literature* 109 (1990): 463–74.

Elkin, S. *The Living End.* New York: Dutton, 1979.

Evans, C. F. "Uncomfortable Words – V." *Expository Times* 81 (1970): 228–31.

Fitzmyer, J. A. *The Gospel according to Luke (I–IX).* Garden City, N.Y.: Doubleday, 1981.

――――. *The Gospel according to Luke (X–XXIV).* Garden City, N.Y.: Doubleday, 1985.

――――. "The Virginal Conception of Jesus in the New Testament." *Theological Studies* 34 (1973): 541–75.

Fredriksen, P. *From Jesus to Christ: The Origins of the New Testament Images of Jesus.* New Haven: Yale University Press, 1988.

Friedman, B. J. *Steambath.* New York: Alfred A. Knopf, 1971.

Frost, R. *A Masque of Reason.* New York: Henry Holt, 1945.

Fuller, R. H. *Interpreting the Miracles.* Naperville, Ill.: SCM Book Club, 1963.

Gaiser, F. J. Review of *A Farewell to the Servant Songs: A Critical Examination of an Exegetical Axiom,* by T. N. D. Mettinger. *Interpretation* 40 (1986): 310–12.

Geyer, H. G. "The Resurrection of Jesus Christ: A Survey of the Debate in Present Day Theology." In *The Significance of the Message of the Resurrection for Faith in Jesus Christ,* ed. C. F. D. Moule, 105–35. Naperville, Ill.: Alec R. Allenson, 1968.

Grant, R. M. *Miracle and Natural Law in Graeco-Roman and Early Christian Thought.* Amsterdam: North-Holland Publishing Co., 1952.

Hadas, M., and M. Smith. *Heroes and Gods: Spiritual Biographies in Antiquity.* New York: Harper and Row, 1965.

Haenchen, E. *The Acts of the Apostles.* Eng. trans. Oxford: Basil Blackwell, 1971.

Hankart, K. "Paul's Hope in the Face of Death." *Journal of Biblical Literature* 88 (1969): 445–57.

Harvey, A. E. *Jesus and the Constraints of History.* Philadelphia: Westminster Press, 1982.

Hemer, C. J. *The Book of Acts in the Setting of Hellenistic History.* Tübingen: Mohr-Siebeck, 1989.

Hoffer, E. *The True Believer: Thoughts on the Nature of Mass Movements.* New York: Harper and Row, 1951.

Hooker, M. D. *Jesus and the Suffering Servant: The Influence of the Servant Concept in Deutero-Isaiah in the New Testament.* London: SPCK, 1959.

Jeremias, J. *The Eucharistic Words of Jesus.* Eng. trans. New York: Macmillan, 1955.

————. *The Parables of Jesus.* Eng. trans. New York: Scribner's, 1963.

Johnson, A. R. *The One and the Many in the Israelite Conception of God.* Cardiff: University of Wales Press, 1961.

Karris, R. J. *Luke, Artist and Theologian: Luke's Passion Account as Literature.* New York: Paulist Press, 1985.

Kee, H. C. *Community of the New Age: Studies in Mark's Gospel.* Philadelphia: Westminster Press, 1977.

————. *Jesus in History: An Approach to the Study of the Gospels.* New York: Harcourt, Brace and World, 1970.

Kelber, W. H. *The Oral and the Written Gospel: The Hermeneutics of Speaking and Writing in the Synoptic Tradition, Mark, Paul, and Q.* Philadelphia: Fortress Press, 1983.

Kingsbury, J. D. *The Christology of Mark's Gospel.* Philadelphia: Fortress Press, 1983.

Klausner, J. *Jesus of Nazareth: His Life, Times, and Teaching.* Eng. trans. New York: Macmillan, 1925.

Kloppenborg, J. S. *The Formation of Q: Trajectories in Ancient Wisdom Collections.* Philadelphia: Fortress Press, 1987.

———. *Q Parallels.* Sonoma, Calif.: Polebridge Press, 1988.
———, et al. *Q Thomas Reader.* Sonoma, Calif.: Polebridge Press, 1990.
Koester, H. "Jesus the Victim." *Journal of Biblical Literature* 111 (1992): 3–15.
Lampe, G. W. H. "Miracles and Early Christian Apologetic." In *Miracles: Cambridge Studies in Their Philosophy and History,* ed. C. F. D. Moule, 203–18. London: A. R. Mowbray, 1966.
Lievestad, R. *Jesus in His Own Perspective: An Examination of His Sayings, Actions, and Eschatological Titles.* Eng. trans. Minneapolis: Augsburg Publishing House, 1987.
McCormick, S. *The Lord's Supper: A Biblical Interpretation.* Philadelphia: Westminster Press, 1966.
Mack, B. L. *A Myth of Innocence: Mark and Christian Origins.* Philadelphia: Fortress Press, 1988.
Mack, B. L., and V. K. Robbins. *Patterns of Persuasion in the Gospels.* Sonoma, Calif.: Polebridge Press, 1989.
McKnight, E. V. *What Is Form Criticism?* Philadelphia: Fortress Press, 1969.
Marxsen, W. "The Resurrection of Jesus as a Historical and Theological Problem." In *The Significance of the Message of the Resurrection for Faith in Jesus Christ,* ed. C. F. D. Moule, 15–50. Naperville, Ill.: Alec R. Allenson, 1968.
Matera, F. J. *The Kingship of Jesus: Composition and Theology in Mark 15.* Chico, Calif.: Scholars Press, 1982.
———. *What Are They Saying about Mark?* New York: Paulist Press, 1987.
Mettinger, T. N. D. *A Farewell to the Servant Songs: A Critical Examination of an Exegetical Axiom.* Lund: G. W. K. Gleerup, 1983.
Meyer, B. F. *The Aims of Jesus.* London: SCM Press, 1979.
Moule, C. F. D. Editor's introduction in *The Significance of the Message of the Resurrection for Faith in Jesus Christ,* 1–11. Naperville, Ill.: Alec R. Allenson, 1968.
———, ed. *Miracles: Cambridge Studies in Their Philosophy and History.* London: A. R. Mowbray, 1966.
North, C. R. *The Suffering Servant in Deutero-Isaiah.* London: Oxford University Press, 1948.
Perrin, N. *Rediscovering the Teaching of Jesus.* New York: Harper and Row, 1967.
———. *What Is Redaction Criticism?* Philadelphia: Fortress Press, 1969.
Reicke, B. *The Epistles of James, Peter, and Jude.* Garden City, N.Y.: Doubleday, 1964.
Richardson, A. *The Miracle-Stories of the Gospels.* New York: Harper Brothers, 1941.
Robinson, H. W. "The Hebrew Concept of Corporate Personality." In *Werden und Wesen des Alten Testaments,* ed. P. Volz et al., 49–62. Berlin: Alfred Töpplemann, 1936.
———. "Hebrew Psychology." In *The People and the Book,* ed. A. S. Peake, 353–82. Oxford: Clarendon Press, 1925.

————. "Prophetic Symbolism." In *Old Testament Essays,* 1–17. London: Charles Griffin, 1927.

Robinson, J. A. T. *The Body: A Study in Pauline Theology.* London: SCM Press, 1952.

Roth, W. M. W. "The Anonymity of the Suffering Servant." *Journal of Biblical Literature* 83 (1964): 171–79.

Sanders, E. P. *Jesus and Judaism.* Philadelphia: Fortress Press, 1985.

Sanders, J. N., and B. A. Mastin. *A Commentary on the Gospel according to St. John.* New York: Harper and Row, 1968.

Schaberg, J. *The Illegitimacy of Jesus: A Feminist Theological Interpretation of the Infancy Narratives.* San Francisco: Harper and Row, 1987.

Taylor, V. *The Gospel according to St. Mark.* London: Macmillan, 1957.

Tyson, J. B. "The Blindness of the Disciples in Mark." *Journal of Biblical Literature* 80 (1961): 261–68.

Ulansey, D. "The Heavenly Veil Torn: Mark's Cosmic *Inclusio.*" *Journal of Biblical Literature* 110 (1991): 123–25.

von Rad, G. *Genesis: A Commentary.* Eng. trans. Philadelphia: Westminster Press, 1961.

Weeden, T. J. "The Heresy That Necessitated Mark's Gospel." *Zeitschrift für neutestamentliche Wissenschaft* 59 (1968): 145–58.

Wilshire, L. E. "The Servant-City: A New Interpretation of the 'Servant of the Lord' in the Servant Songs of Deutero-Isaiah." *Journal of Biblical Literature* 94 (1975): 356–67.

Witherington, B., III. *The Christology of Jesus.* Minneapolis: Fortress Press, 1990.

Wolf, H. M. "A Solution to the Immanuel Prophecy in Isaiah 7:14–8:22." *Journal of Biblical Literature* 91 (1972): 449–56.

Index of Passages

OLD TESTAMENT

Genesis
1:1–2:4a	195n.10
1:26–27	103, 195n.12
1:27b	113
2:7	201n.7
2:24	113
5:1	195n.12
6:3	201n.10
9:6	195n.12
24:43	188n.28

Exodus
1:8–2:10	42–43
4:22–23	187n.25
21:23–25	196n.22

Leviticus
13–14	148
19:2	103
21:11	201n.8
24:19–20	196n.22

Numbers
6:6	201n.8
19:11	201n.8
19:13	201n.8

Deuteronomy
19:21	196n.22
24:1–4	107, 112

Joshua
9:3–21	196n.23

Judges
14:6	201n.9
14:19	201n.9

1 Samuel
10:6	201n.9
10:10	201n.9
16:15	201n.9

2 Samuel
7:8–17	187n.26

1 Kings
13:8–9	196n.23
17:8–24	153–54
17:23	154
17:24	154

2 Kings
4:42–44	147
5:1–14	148

2 Chronicles
32:8	201n.10

Job
19:26	201n.12

Psalms
1	102
2:7	42, 76, 186n.10
8	195n.10
14:3	102
16:10–11	201n.12
17:15	201n.12
22	55–56, 90
22:1	90
41:9	196n.23
49:15	201n.12
53:3	102
63:1	201n.10
73:24	201n.12
78:39	201n.10
89:26–27	42
145:21	201n.10

Isaiah
6:5	101
7:3	187n.18
7:10–17	35–36, 45–46
7:14	33, 35–36, 41, 43–46
7:14–8:22	188n.28
7:18	45
8:1–4	187n.18
9:2–7	187n.24
9:5–7	195n.18
10:20–23	45
11:1–9	187n.24
11:2–3	201n.9
11:3b–9	195n.18
24–27	201n.12
25:6	199n.38
25:6–8	201n.12
26:19	143–44, 201n.12
29:18	143–44
35:5–6a	143–44
40–55	76
40:6b–7	157

40:6-8	*201n.10*
42:1	76, 84, *193n.43*
42:1-4	76, 84, 86-88, 116-17, *193n.46, 195n.18*
42:4a	86, 117
49:1	87
49:1-6	86-88, *193n.46*
49:2	86
49:3	86-87
49:5	87
49:6	86, *195n.18*
50:4-9	86-88, *193n.46*
50:7b	86
51:14	*199n.38*
52:13-53:12	84, 86-88, 116, *193n.46, 194n.48*
52:14-15	86, 91
52:15	86
53	94
53:3a	86
53:3b	86
53:4	87-88
53:4ff.	86
53:6b	86
53:7	72
53:10a	86
53:10-11	86-87
53:11	88, *195n.18*
53:11-12	84, *193n.43, 196n.29*
53:12	86, 90, *192n.34*
55:8	96
61:1a	*143-44*
62:8-9	*199n.38*
65:21-22	*199n.38*
66:16	*201n.10*

Jeremiah

25:31	*201n.10*
31:2	*199n.38*
31:15	*188n.32*
31:33	103
45:5	*201n.10*

Ezekiel

34:23-24	*199n.38*

Daniel

7:13	62
12:2	*201n.12*

Hosea

11:1	*187n.25, 188n.32*

Joel

2:26	*199n.38*

Amos

9:13-15	*199n.38*

Micah

5:2	34
5:2-4	*199n.38*
6:8	103

Haggai

2:6-7	*188n.27*
2:20-23	*188n.27*

Zechariah

9:9	85
9:17	*199n.38*

Malachi

3:1	142, *198n.31*

NEW TESTAMENT

Matthew	10, 27-28, 44, *186n.11*
1:18-25	28, 33, 42-45, *188n.29*
1:18-2:23	29, 32-35, 41-48
1:21	46
1:22-23	35-36, 43-46
1:23-25	37
1:25	31-32
2:1-2	33
2:1-23	33-34, 36-37, 42-43
2:3-5	33
2:6	34
2:9-11	33
2:12	33
2:13	173
2:13-15	33
2:15	*188n.32*
2:16	36
2:18	*188n.32*
2:19-21	33
2:20	172
2:22	33
3:11-12	142
3:14-15	99
5	106, *190n.12*
5:3-12	111
5:18	*190n.14*
5:21-48	106, 111
5:22	*203n.38*
5:27-28	106-7
5:29	*203n.38*
5:32	*196n.21*
5:38	106, 113, *196n.22*
5:39b-40	*190n.12*
5:48	106
6:22-23	*203n.35*
6:24	105-6
6:25	172, *203nn.34, 36*
8:2-4	*199n.41*
8:23-27	*199n.35*
9:8	140
9:10-11	*196n.24*
9:18-19	152-53
9:23-26	152-53
10:1	154
10:5-23	61, 154
10:8	154
10:19-20	*203n.37*

Matthew (continued) _____
10:23	61–62, 189n.7
10:26-33	203n.37
10:28	171–73
10:29-31	173
10:39	105, 203n.36
11:2-4a	142
11:3	142
11:4-6	140–44, 190n.23, 198nn.21, 30, 33–34
11:10	142
11:19	196n.24
11:21-23	140
11:21-24	198n.21
11:27	72–73
12:18	172
12:24	127
12:27	135–37, 198n.21
12:28	135–37, 198n.21
12:39	139
12:46-50	40, 187n.22
13:16-17	140–41, 143, 198n.21
13:57	40, 187n.22
14:13-21	199n.35
14:22-33	199n.35
15:32-39	199n.35
17:24-27	145, 199n.35
18:5-10	204n.44
18:14	204n.44
18:19	203n.38
19:16b-17b	98
20:1-15	203n.29
20:28	193n.42
21:18-22	199n.35
22:1-14	173, 203n.29
22:6	203n.41
22:6-7	173
23:15	203n.38
23:23	104
23:31	203n.40
23:33	203n.38
23:34	203n.41
23:37	203n.40
24:9	203n.41
24:28	203n.34
24:39	203n.42
26:52	173
26:64	72
27:19-20	173
27:44	202n.16
27:52	172
27:62-66	204n.50
28:11-15	204n.50
28:17	68
28:18-20	194n.5

Mark _____ 10, 52, 57, 186n.11
1:1	76
1:1-8	69
1:1-15	81, 116
1-10	130
1:2	198n.31
1:2-8	115
1:4	99, 117
1:5	99, 119
1:9-11	69, 75, 98–100, 115–22
1:10	188n.3
1:11	76, 83–84, 88–89, 91, 189n.3, 193n.43
1:14-15	118
1:15	117, 123
1:16-20	118, 147
1:16-8:26	81–82
1:22	111, 194n.57
1:23-27	197n.18
1:24	81
1:25	199n.40
1:27	194n.57
1:27-28	140
1:29-31	133–34, 200n.55
1:32-34	145
1:40	199n.41
1:40-45	148–49
1:42b	148
1:43	199n.41
1:44a	148
1:44	70, 194n.51
1:45	148
2:1-12	81
2:12	194n.57, 197n.19
2:15-16	114
2:15-17	89–91, 196n.29
2:18-22	90, 147, 191n.26
2:20	89
2:23-24	104
2:27	104–5, 112
2:28	81
3:1-5	104, 133
3:2	89
3:4	112, 133
3:6	65, 89
3:7-12	145
3:11	81, 194n.53
3:11-12	70, 194n.49
3:13-19a	118
3:19b	38–39
3:19b-21	38–39
3:20	38
3:21	38–40, 187n.22
3:21-22	89
3:22	127–28, 131
3:22-30	38–39
3:23	134–37, 198n.21
3:31	39
3:31-35	38–40, 89, 187n.20
4:1-12	119
4:10-34	81
4:33-34	119
4:35-41	146–47, 199n.35
4:41	81, 194n.57
5:1-13	194n.49
5:7	108, 194n.53

5:13	88, 192n.40	9:30-32	89
5:15	194n.57	9:31	67
5:21-23	152-53	9:32	82, 194n.57
5:24-34	152-53	9:33-34	82, 119
5:34	149	9:35	89
5:35-43	152-53	9:38	82
5:36	153	9:43	203n.38
5:39	151, 153, 200n.50	9:45	203n.38
5:40	89	10:2	89
5:42	194n.57	10:2-9	107, 111-13, 195n.21
5:43	70, 194n.51	10:11	195n.21
6:1-6	89	10:13-15	82
6:3	31, 186nn.5, 12	10:17-18	120
6:4	40	10:17-22	97-98, 123
6:7-13	154	10:18	97-98, 100-101
6:12	117-19, 123	10:24	194n.57
6:14-15	191n.26	10:26	194n.57
6:30-44	146, 199n.35	10:32-34	89
6:45-52	146-47, 199n.35	10:33	64
6:49-52	194n.57	10:33-34	67-68
6:53-56	145	10:35-37	82
7:1-23	57, 81	10:38-39	89
7:5-8	149, 200n.43	10:45	84, 88-89, 193nn.42-43
7:14b-15	200n.43	10:46-48	84-85, 88
7:15	103, 149, 195n.11, 200n.43	10:47-48	192n.40, 194n.53
		10:52	149
7:18-19a	200n.43	11:1-10	190n.23, 193n.45
7:21-23	200n.43	11:1-11	84-85, 89
7:36	70, 194n.51	11:9-10	84-85, 192n.40
7:37	194n.57	11:11	84-85
8:1-10	146, 199n.35	11:12-14	90, 145, 147, 199n.35
8:11-12	139	11:15-16	89, 193n.45, 194n.52
8:11-13	89	11:17	89, 193n.45
8:12	190n.13	11:18	89, 194n.57
8:14-21	81-82, 88	11:20	90
8:17	82	11:20-24	145, 147, 199n.35
8:21	82	11:28-30	99
8:22	195n.11	12:6-8	89
8:26	70, 194n.51	12:10	89
8:27-29	67, 73-74, 82	12:12	89
8:27-30	73-74, 81, 194n.50	12:13-15	89
8:27-31	69	12:17	194n.57
8:27-32	84	12:29-31	105
8:27-10:45	84	12:34	194n.57
8:27-14:9	82	12:35-37	193n.44
8:29	194n.53	13	60-62, 89-90
8:30	67, 70, 73-74	13:1-2	60-61, 89
8:31	64-65, 67	13:6	60
8:32-33	65, 67	13:7b	61
8:33	82	13:9-11	83
8:34	67-68, 89, 119	13:9-13	60
8:38	190n.13	13:11	60
9:1	61, 189n.7	13:14	60-61
9:2-8	70, 82, 191n.26	13:21-22	60
9:7	82	13:29	62
9:7-9	70, 194n.50	13:30	59-62, 189n.7, 190n.12
9:9	67, 89	13:31	62
9:10	82	13:32	60, 62-63, 72-73
9:11-13	89, 191n.26	13:32-35	61
9:12	67	14:1-2	89
9:19	190n.13	14:7-8	89
9:25	199n.40		

Mark (continued)
14:10–12	89
14:10–72	82
14:18–21	89
14:22–24	85, 89, 190n.17
14:25	65
14:27	82, 89
14:27–31	67
14:28	91
14:30	63–64, 67, 89
14:31	118
14:32–36	89
14:32–41	66–67
14:41–42	89
14:50	82, 118
14:54	82
14:55–65	71
14:58	89, 194n.52
14:61	72, 194n.53
14:62a	71–73, 190n.21
14:62	190n.21
14:66–72	64, 67, 82
14:72	67
15:1–5	71
15:2	72, 194n.53
15:9	194n.53
15:12	194n.53
15:16–20	88
15:17–39	91
15:18	194n.53
15:26	194n.53
15:31	88
15:32	88, 194n.53, 202n.16
15:34	90
15:35–36	90
15:37b–38	56, 83
15:38	55–57
15:38–39	188n.3
15:39	83
16:1–8	83
16:6–8	91
16:8	91–92, 192n.38, 194nn.57–58
16:9–20	68
16:11	68

Luke — 10, 27–28, 44, 186n.11
1:5	34
1:5–7	187n.15
1:5–2:40	28–30, 32–33, 46–48
1:8–23	32–33
1:26–38	33
1:27	30
1:34	30
1:34–35	28, 38
1:35	30
1:39–45	33
1:42	187n.21
1:48	187n.21
1:53	203n.26
1:80	187n.15

2:1–5	30
2:1–7	34, 187n.15
2:2	34
2:8–12	33
2:13–14	33
2:22–24	187n.15
2:25–38	33
2:39–40	187n.15
2:41–51	38, 186n.9
2:41–52	194n.1
3:1	34
3:11	203n.26
3:16–17	142
3:22	186n.10
3:23	28, 30, 34, 186n.10
4:13	134
4:23	134, 139–40, 198n.21
5:1–11	145–47, 199n.35
5:12–16	199n.41
5:29–30	196n.24
6:20	203n.26
6:21	203n.26
6:24	203n.26
6:25	203n.26
6:27–36	113
6:29–30	190n.12
6:34	203n.26
7:11–17	153–54
7:18–19	142
7:19	142
7:22–23	140–44, 190n.23, 198nn.21, 30, 33–34
7:27	142
7:34	196n.24
7:50	200n.44
8:19–21	40, 187n.22
8:22–25	199n.35
8:40–42	152–53
8:49–56	152–53
9:1–6	154
9:10–17	199n.35
9:24	105
10:2–12	154
10:13–15	140, 198n.21
10:22	72–73
10:23b–24	140–41, 143, 198n.21
10:30–35	106
10:30–37	203n.26
10:38–42	152
11:15	127
11:19	135–37, 198n.21
11:20	135–37, 198n.21
11:27–28	40, 186n.12, 187nn.21–22
11:29	139
11:34	203n.35
11:36	203n.35
11:47–48	203n.40
11:49	203n.41
12:2–12	203n.37
12:3	203n.21

12:4–5	*171–73*
12:6–7	*173*
12:13–15	*203n.26*
12:16–21	*203n.26*
12:19–20	*203n.36*
12:22–23	*172, 203nn.34, 36*
12:33a	*203n.26*
13:6–9	*147*
13:10–17	*197n.19*
13:31–32	*198n.21*
13:31–33	*137*
13:32	*134, 137*
13:34	*203n.40*
14:1–6	*197n.19*
14:12–14	*203n.26*
14:16–24	*203nn.29, 43*
14:26	*203n.36*
15:1–2	*196n.24*
15:3–9	*113*
15:11–24	*113, 203n.29*
15:25–32	*203n.29*
16:9	*203n.26*
16:10–12	*203n.26*
16:13	*105–6*
16:14–15	*203n.26*
16:17	*190n.14*
16:18	*196n.21*
16:19–31	*152, 167–71*
16:22	*169*
16:22b–23a	*169*
16:23	*170*
16:24	*167*
16:25	*168*
16:26	*170*
16:31	*170*
17:12–19	*147–50*
17:19	*149*
17:27–29	*203n.42*
17:33	*203n.36*
17:37	*203n.34*
18:10–14	*105, 113*
18:13	*105, 107–8*
18:18–19	*97–98*
19:2–9	*203n.26*
19:5–7	*196n.24*
22:15–16	*65*
22:19b–20	*192n.34*
22:70	*72*
23:39–43	*202n.16*
23:43	*202n.16*
24:11	*68*

John ————— *10, 27–28*
1:11	*46*
1:14	*185n.4*
2:1–11	*38, 145–47, 199nn.35, 37*
2:5	*38*
5:21	*202n.24*
6:1–13	*146, 199nn.35–36*
6:2	*199n.36*
6:14	*199n.36*

6:16–21	*146–47, 199n.35*
7:5	*40*
8:31–47	*31*
8:41	*31, 186n.12, 200n.46*
11:1–44	*150–52*
11:45–53	*151*
12:31	*199n.39*
13:18	*196n.23*
14:30	*199n.39*
16:11	*199n.39*
18:34	*72*
21:1–14	*146, 199n.35*

Acts ————— *77–78, 192n.33*
1–12	*77*
2:14–36	*192n.30*
2:38	*91, 192n.31*
2:38–39	*192n.30*
3:12–26	*192n.30*
3:19	*91, 192n.31*
4:8–12	*192n.30*
5:29–32	*192n.30*
5:31	*192n.31*
6:1	*64*
10:34–43	*192n.30*
10:36–43	*27, 79*
10:43	*79*
11:2–3	*196n.25*
13:33	*186n.10*
13:38–39	*192n.31*
20:28	*77–78*
22:16	*192n.31*
26:18	*192n.31*

Romans —————
1:2–5	*27*
1:3	*186n.6*
1:3–4	*44*
4:17	*202n.24*
5:12–21	*122*
5:18–19	*122*
6:1–11	*165*
6:1–19	*123*
8:11	*202n.24*
8:31–38	*196n.28*

1 Corinthians —————
1:23	*178*
7:25–35	*189n.8*
11:30	*202n.18*
12:3	*178–79*
12:12–26	*121*
12:12–27	*165*
15	*177*
15:3–5	*11*
15:3b	*22, 57*
15:3b–5	*16, 27, 77, 161, 176, 185n.1 (intro.), 189n.4*
15:6	*202n.18*
15:17–18	*164*
15:18	*202n.18*
15:20	*202n.18*

1 Corinthians (continued)
15:20–57	154
15:22	202n.24
15:35–55	164
15:36	202n.24
15:42–44	201n.14
15:45–47	122
15:51	202n.18

2 Corinthians
4:4	199n.39
4:14	202n.17
5:1–10	202n.17
5:19	57
5:21	93, 115

Galatians
1–2	192n.32
1:18–2:10	154
1:19	195n.11
2	173–74, 195n.11
2:11–12	196n.25
3:6	186n.6
4:4	186n.6

Ephesians
| 2:2 | 199n.39 |

Philippians
1:12–26	165
1:23	165
2:5b–8	28
2:5b–11	162
2:6–7	162

Colossians
| 1:15–18 | 177 |

1 Thessalonians
4:13	202n.18
4:14	202n.18
4:15	202n.18
5:10	202n.18

Hebrews — 51
1:1ff.	92
2:17	189n.5
4:15	93, 107, 115
7:26–27	93
7:27–28	189n.5
9:15ff.	196n.28
9:22	77
10:19–20	189n.5

James
| 3:6 | 203n.38 |

1 Peter
1:3	167
1:4	121
1:21	167
1:23	121

1:24	167
2:22–24	94
3:13	166
3:13–16	166
3:18	167, 202n.24
3:18–19	166–67
3:18–22	166
3:21	202n.24
4:6	202n.21

1 John
| 3:5 | 94 |

Revelation — 27–28, 60
1:1–3	189n.9
1:7	189n.9
5:2	202n.21
12:4–5	185n.4
13–14	189n.9

APOCRYPHA AND PSEUDEPIGRAPHA

2 Baruch
49:1–51:4	170
50:3–4	170
51:5–6	170

1 Enoch
22	170
22:9–13	170
102:4–103:8	202–3n.25

4 Ezra
| 7:85 | 170 |
| 7:93 | 170 |

Jubilees
| 23:31 | 203n.25 |

Wisdom of Solomon — 216n.25

BABYLONIAN TALMUD

Sanhedrin
| 43a | 131 |

OTHER ANCIENT LITERATURE AND AUTHORS

Josephus — 202n.25
The Antiquities of the Jews
| 18.3.3 | 131 |

Gospel of Thomas — 189n.10
| 64 | 203n.29 |